Pilar Hernández Mesa

Design and analysis of a content-based image retrieval system

Forschungsberichte aus der Industriellen Informationstechnik
Band 16

Institut für Industrielle Informationstechnik
Karlsruher Institut für Technologie
Hrsg. Prof. Dr.-Ing. Fernando Puente León
Prof. Dr.-Ing. habil. Klaus Dostert

Eine Übersicht aller bisher in dieser Schriftenreihe erschienenen Bände finden Sie am Ende des Buchs.

Design and analysis of a content-based image retrieval system

by
Pilar Hernández Mesa

KIT Scientific Publishing

Karlsruher Institut für Technologie
Institut für Industrielle Informationstechnik

Design and analysis of a content-based image retrieval system

Zur Erlangung des akademischen Grades eines Doktor-Ingenieurs von der Fakultät für Elektrotechnik und Informationstechnik des Karlsruher Instituts für Technologie (KIT) genehmigte Dissertation

von Dipl.-Ing. Pilar Hernández Mesa geb. in Firgas, Spanien

Tag der mündlichen Prüfung: 02. Juni 2017
Referent: Prof. Dr.-Ing. Fernando Puente León, KIT
Korreferent: apl. Prof. Dr.-Ing. Ralf Mikut, KIT

Impressum

KIT Scientific Publishing

Karlsruher Institut für Technologie (KIT)
KIT Scientific Publishing
Straße am Forum 2
D-76131 Karlsruhe

KIT Scientific Publishing is a registered trademark
of Karlsruhe Institute of Technology.
Reprint using the book cover is not allowed.

www.ksp.kit.edu

Print on Demand 2017 – Gedruckt auf FSC-zertifiziertem Papier

ISSN 2190-6629
ISBN 978-3-7315-0692-8
DOI 10.5445/KSP/1000071866

Design and analysis of a content-based image retrieval system

Zur Erlangung des akademischen Grades eines

DOKTOR-INGENIEURS

von der Fakultät für

Elektrotechnik und Informationstechnik

des Karlsruher Instituts für Technologie (KIT)

genehmigte

DISSERTATION

von

Dipl.-Ing. Pilar Hernández Mesa

geb. in Firgas, Spanien

Tag der mündl. Prüfung:	02. Juni 2017
Hauptreferent:	Prof. Dr.-Ing. Fernando Puente León, KIT
Korreferent:	apl. Prof. Dr.-Ing. Ralf Mikut, KIT

Acknowledgements

This doctoral thesis would not have been possible without the support of many people.

To begin I would like to thank Prof. Dr.-Ing. Fernando Puente León for supporting the execution of this thesis as supervisor and for letting me be part of his team over the last years. I am also extremely grateful to apl. Prof. Dr.-Ing. Ralf Mikut for taking over the duty of second examiner. Special thanks go to Prof. Dr. rer. nat. Olaf Dössel, Prof. Dr. rer. nat. Uli Lemmer, and Prof. Dr.-Ing. Eric Sax who kindly accepted to join the board of examiners.

This work was performed during my time as a research associate at the *Institut für Industrielle Informationstechnik* (IIIT) which belongs to the Karlsruhe Institute of Technology (KIT). I am extremely grateful to Prof. Dr.-Ing. Michael Heizmann for his advice, time, and support at the completion of the doctoral process as well as for encouraging me since he joined the IIIT. I also want to thank all my colleagues at the IIIT for their contributions. Special thanks go to Mario Lietz and Dr.-Ing. Johannes Pallauf, as well as to Manuela Moritz for her great support. During my time at the IIIT I had the opportunity to work with many students and supervise Bachelor, Master, and Diploma theses. I want to express to all of them my warmest gratitude.

It is a pleasure for me to thank Prof. Dr.-Ing. Barbara Deml, Dipl.-Psych., and her research associates Dr.-Ing. Marc Schneider and Tobias Heine. Without their support the psychology experiment in my work would not have been possible.

Last but not least I want to thank my friends and family for their unconditional support and trust in me. I thank Christoph for his support and encouragement over the last years as well as for his carefully proofreading of this thesis. I am deeply indebted with my sister María, who has carefully proofread this thesis and moreover supported me over this project and all the other ones in my life. Finally, I want to thank my parents, Toñi and Roque, for supporting and believing in me always, as well as for the possibilities, education, and everything that they have given me through my whole life. Without them and my sister María none of this would have been possible.

Karlsruhe, June 2017 Pilar Hernández Mesa

Kurzfassung

Sehen ist einer der fünf Sinne des Menschen, der uns ermöglicht, unsere visuelle Umgebung wahrzunehmen. Ein Bild zu zeigen ist oft einfacher, schneller und genauer als eine Beschreibung des Inhalts mit Worten, was nicht immer möglich ist. Die Technologie zur Herstellung von digitalen Kameras und Speichern hat in den letzten Jahrzehnten enorme Fortschritte gemacht. Heutzutage sind digitale Kameras sogar in vielen Geräten, wie Mobiltelefonen und Laptops, integriert. Eine schnelle und einfache Aufnahme von Bildern ist somit möglich. Tatsache ist, dass an jedem Tag sehr viele digitale Bilder generiert werden. Diese Bilder enthalten Informationen, die leider verloren gehen können, wenn es keine geeigneten Methoden gibt, um die Bilder inhaltlich miteinander zu vergleichen. Diese Problematik wird in der inhaltsbasierten Bildsuche behandelt. Ziel dieser Arbeit ist die Untersuchung der Sortierung von Bildern aufgrund deren Ähnlichkeit mit einem Eingangsbild. Für das Ähnlichkeitsmaß wird von der menschlichen Wahrnehmung ausgegangen, welche spontan und ohne Anstrengung und Überlegung durchgeführt wird, wie bei Julesz in [73] beschrieben. Ähnlichkeiten aufgrund weiterer Verarbeitungen im Gehirn, wie zum Beispiel aufgrund einer Objekterkennung, liegen außerhalb des Umfangs dieser Arbeit.

Die unabhängige Extraktion von Farb-, Form- und Texturmerkmalen, die getrennte Sortierung dieser Merkmale nach Ähnlichkeit und die Detektion von Regionen in Bildern, aufgrund zusammenhängender Flächen mit ähnlicher Farbe oder aufgrund von Mustern basierend auf abwechselnden Farbkombinationen, werden als Vorgehensweise ausgewählt. Methoden werden für alle diese Aspekte vorgeschlagen, getestet und evaluiert. Zudem ist, um die menschliche Ähnlichkeitswahrnehmung anhand von Mustermerkmalen bewerten zu können, mit Hilfe von Psychologen ein Experiment mit Probanden durchgeführt worden. Ein Wahrnehmungsraum wird aus diesen Daten erstellt.

Anschließend wird die Fusion der unterschiedlichen extrahierten Informationen untersucht. Zuerst werden die extrahierten Regionen durch die Fusion mit den Musterinformationen verbessert. Anschließend wird aus der Fusion aller extrahierter Informationen ein inhaltsbasiertes Suchsystem vorgestellt. Diese ist in der Lage, automatisch die Gewichtung der einzelnen Merkmale beim Ähnlichkeitsvergleich je nach Eigenschaften der verglichenen Bilder anzupassen. Die Ergebnisse zeigen, dass diese Methodik immer sehr gute Sortierungsergebnisse erreicht und sogar in vielen Fällen die Sortierungsergebnisse nach den einzelnen Merkmalen übertrifft.

Contents

Nomenclature

Common abbreviations

Abbreviation	Description
CIE	Commission Internationale de l'Éclairage
Com.	combination
e.g.	*exempli gratia* (latin, for example)
Eq.	equation
et al.	*et alii* (latin, and others)
etc.	*et cetera* (latin, and other things)
Fig.	figure
i.a.	*inter alia* (latin, among other things)
MSER	Maximally Stable Extremal Regions
NAD	Normal Angular Descriptor
SCR	Stable Color Region
Sec.	section
SURF	Speeded Up Robust Features
vs.	versus

Conventions

Operator	Description
u	scalar variable, node
U	scalar variable
$\mathbf{u}$	vector
$\mathbf{U}$	matrix
$\mathcal{U}$	set, environment
U	tested combination
$\bullet(u)$	continuous in u
$\bullet_u$, $\bullet[u]$	discrete in u

Letters

Latin letters

Symbol	Description
$\mathbf{A}^{\mathrm{Aff}}$	parameters of the affine transformation that may imply scale, shear, and rotation
$\mathbf{a}$	displacement vector of a one-dimensional texture in space domain
$\tilde{\mathbf{a}}$	second vector used to span a parallelogram for the extraction of a texel of a one-dimensional texture
$\mathbf{a}_k$	displacement vectors of two-dimensional textures in space domain, $k \in \{1,2\}$
B	width of the image
$\mathbf{B}$	similarity of the components
$b(\bullet)$	degree of a node
$b^{+}(\bullet)$	outdegree of a node
$b^{-}(\bullet)$	indegree of a node
$\mathsf{C1}, \ldots, \mathsf{C10}$	tested combinations to detect and extract color regions
$c_k^{\mathrm{Color}}(\bullet)$	color represented by the color category k
$\mathbf{c}^{\mathrm{Color}}(\bullet)$	vector representation of the colors represented with color categories
c^{PCA}	principal component
$d(\bullet,\bullet)$	distance function
$d^{\mathrm{Bound}}(\bullet)$	distance function to detect clusters consisting merely of contour points
$d^{\mathrm{CC},1}(\bullet)$	color distance based on the correlation coefficient of the color categories
$d^{\mathrm{CC},2}(\bullet)$	color distance based on the ℓ_2-norm of the color categories
$d^{\mathrm{Fourier}}(\bullet,\bullet)$	similarity distance between Fourier descriptors
$d_1^{\mathrm{NAD}}(\bullet,\bullet)$	similarity distance between normal angular descriptors based on the correlation for circular data
$d_2^{\mathrm{NAD}}(\bullet,\bullet)$	similarity distance between warped normal angular descriptors based on the correlation for circular data
$d_3^{\mathrm{NAD}}(\bullet,\bullet)$	similarity distance between warped normal angular descriptors based on the Euclidean distance
$d_{\mathbf{u}}^{\mathrm{SCR}}$	image of the difference between neighboring pixels

Symbol	Description
$d_{\mathbf{u}}^{\mathrm{SCR},1}$	image of the difference between neighboring pixels of a smoothed image
$d_{\mathbf{u}}^{\mathrm{SCR},2}$	image of the difference between neighboring pixels of a smoothed image that preserves edges
$d^{\mathrm{T},1}(\bullet,\bullet)$	similarity distance for the detection of regular textures in space domain
$\mathcal{E}(\bullet)$	set of edges
e	edge
$e_{\mathbf{u}}^{\mathrm{PCA}}$	eigentexel
$\mathbf{F}_{\mathbf{u}}^{k}$	maximum over all color channels and stages of the back projection of the detail signals per orientation, $k \in \{\text{horizontal, vertical, diagonal}\}$
f	frequency
f^{Fourier}	Fourier descriptors
$f^{\mathrm{norm,hor}}$	normalized frequency for the highest stage of the wavelet transform in horizontal direction
$f^{\mathrm{norm,ver}}$	normalized frequency for the highest stage of the wavelet transform in vertical direction
$f^{\mathrm{NT},1}$	relashionship of the length of the displacement vectors
$G(\bullet)$	Fourier transform of $g(\bullet)$
$\mathcal{G}$	graph
$g(u)$	one-dimensional signal
$g(\mathbf{u})$	single-channel image
$\tilde{g}(\mathbf{u})$	reconstructed single-channel image
$g^{\mathrm{bin}}(\mathbf{u})$	binary image describing the pixels that belong to a color region
$g^{\mathrm{Mod}}(\mathbf{u})$	modified single-channel image
$g^{\mathrm{Synth}}(\mathbf{u})$	synthetic single-channel image
$g^{\mathrm{win}}(u)$	one-dimensional windowed signal
$\mathbf{g}(\mathbf{u})$	three-channel image
$\mathbf{g}^{\mathrm{R}}(\mathbf{u})$	reconstructed three-channel image
H	height of the image
$\mathbf{h}$	histogram
$\mathbf{h}^{\mathrm{Area}}$	histogram of the area of the regions in a texel
$\mathbf{h}^{\mathrm{Bright}}$	histogram of the brightness
I	input
$I_{\mathcal{G}}$	relations between the nodes and edges of a graph $\mathcal{G}$
k	running index with K as maximum

Symbol	Description
L	length of a line containing alternating structures
l	minimal length of an alternating structure
l^*, a^*, b^*	channels of the CIELAB color space
$\mathbf{l}$	displacement vector of a one-dimensional texture in frequency domain
$\tilde{\mathbf{l}}$	vector orthogonal to the displacement vector of a one-dimensional texture in frequency domain
$\mathbf{l}_k$	displacement vectors of a two-dimensional texture in frequency domain, $k \in \{1,2\}$
m	feature
$m(\varphi)$	addition of the magnitudes of the Fourier transform along the radial projection with angle φ
m^{T1}	feature for the detection of regular textures in frequency space
m^{T2}	feature for the detection of regular textures in frequency space
m^{T3}	feature to describe the unlikeliness of a point to belong to the lattice of a near-regular texture
$\mathcal{N}(\bullet)$	set of neighbors of a node
$\mathcal{N}^+(\bullet)$	set of outneighbors of a node
$\mathcal{N}^-(\bullet)$	set of inneighbors of a node
N1, ..., N13	tested combinations to detect and extract near-regular textures
$\mathbb{N}$	natural numbers
n^{C}	color name
$n^{\mathrm{C,1}}$	number of different color names used by a user
$n^{\mathrm{C,2}}$	number of colors named by a user
$n^{\mathrm{C,3}}$	number of different subjects that used a color name
$n^{\mathrm{C,4}}$	number of times a color name has been used
n^{Edge}	number of edges
n^{GM}	number of good matches in a database
n_k^{GM}	number of good matches under k retrievals
n^{Line}	number of edge orientations in a texel
n^{Region}	number of regions in a texel
$n^{\mathrm{T,1}}$	number of spatially closest points to be considered
$n^{\mathrm{T,2}}$	number of considered rows, columns, to prove the repeatability of the texels at the contour
$\mathbf{n}$	normal vector

Symbol	Description
O	output
P1,...,P11	tested combinations to detect and extract patterned regions
$p(\bullet\,\vert\,\bullet)$	likelihood, probability distribution
$\mathbf{p}^{\mathrm{cons}}$	considered point
$\mathbf{p}^{\mathrm{grid}}$	point of a cell
$\mathbf{p}^{\mathrm{grid,2}}$	point of a quadrangle where the texels are projected
$\mathbf{p}_k$	point k
$\mathbf{p}_k^{\mathrm{Bound}}$	point k of the compact boundary
$\mathbf{p}^{\mathrm{latt}}$	point of the lattice
$\mathbf{p}^{\mathrm{poss}}$	possible point
q_k	color category k
$q^{\mathrm{P1}}(\bullet)$	quality criterion: number of detected color regions
$q^{\mathrm{P2}}(\bullet)$	quality criterion: percentage of the image included in a color region
$q^{\mathrm{P3}}(\bullet)$	quality criterion: mean image representation error
$q^{\mathrm{P4}}(\bullet)$	quality criterion: common area normalized by the area of the surface
$q^{\mathrm{P5}}(\bullet)$	quality criterion: common area normalized by the area of the extracted pattern
$q^{\mathrm{P6}}(\bullet)$	quality criterion: trade-off between $q^{\mathrm{P4}}(\bullet)$ and $q^{\mathrm{P5}}(\bullet)$
$q_{\bullet}^{\mathrm{pre}}$	precision
$q_{\bullet}^{\mathrm{pre,ideal}}$	ideal precision
$q_{\bullet}^{\mathrm{rec}}$	recall
q^{retr}	quality value of the retrieved results
q^{S1}	unnormalized separability coefficient
$\tilde{q}^{\mathrm{sep}}$	normalized separability coefficient
$q^{\mathrm{T1}}(\bullet)$	quality criterion: percentage of the surface covered by the extracted lattice
$q^{\mathrm{T2}}(\bullet)$	quality criterion: error between the synthetic image and the modified input image
$q\left(v^{\mathrm{C}}\right)$	most probably color name of v^{C}
$r(\bullet,\bullet)$	correlation coefficient
$r^{\mathrm{CC}}(\bullet)$	average correlation coefficient between neighboring pixels
$\mathcal{S}$	structuring element
S1,...,S8	tested combinations to sort shapes by similarity
s	similarity degree

Symbol	Description
$\mathbf{T}$	color term matrix
$t_{k,\mathbf{f}}^{\text{temp}}$	template function
$t_{k,\mathbf{u}}^{\text{Thresh}}$	thresholded texel
$t_{\mathbf{u}}$	texel
$t_{\mathbf{u}}^{\text{Aff}}$	affinely transformed texel
$t_{\mathbf{u}}^{\text{Det}}$	texel at a determined position
$t_{\mathbf{u}}^{\text{ind}}$	normalized affinely transformed texel
$\hat{t}_{\mathbf{u}}^{\text{ind}}$	normalized affinely transformed texel approximated via principal component analysis
$\overline{t_{\mathbf{u}}^{\text{ind}}}$	average texel over all normalized affinely transformed texels
$t_{\mathbf{u}}^{\text{Mod}}$	texels from the modified input image $g_{\mathbf{u}}^{\text{Mod}}$
$t_{\mathbf{u}}^{\text{rep}}$	representative texel
U_1, U_2	width and height of the quadrangles where the texels are projected
$\mathcal{U}$	environment in frequency domain dependent on the displacement vectors
u	position in one-dimensional domain
$\mathbf{u}$	position in image domain
$\mathcal{V}(\bullet)$	set of nodes
$\mathcal{V}^{\text{C}}$	set of pixels that belong to a color region
$\mathcal{V}^{N}$	set of pixels that belong at least to one of the extracted texels
v	node of a graph
v^{C}	color value
v^{latt}	node of a graph describing a lattice
$\mathbf{v}^{\text{Aff}}$	translation of the affine transformation
w	strength
$w(u)$	one-dimensional window function
$w(\mathbf{u})$	two-dimensional window function
Z	Fourier coefficients
$\mathbb{Z}$	integer numbers

Greek letters

Symbol	Description
α	angle spanned between a displacement vector and the u_1-axis
β	absolute difference between the smallest angles of not anti-parallel vectors
$\Gamma(\lambda, \kappa)$	wavelet transformed signal
γ	angle of the Fourier coefficients
Δ	distance value
$\delta(\bullet)$, $\delta_\bullet$	Dirac delta function
η	normal angular descriptor
κ	shift parameter of the wavelet transform
λ	scaling parameter of the wavelet transform
λ^{PCA}	eigenvalue
μ, $\mu(\bullet)$	mean value, average value
$\rho(\bullet, \bullet)$	correlation coefficient for circular data
σ, $\sigma(\bullet)$	standard deviation
τ	threshold value
τ^{C1}	threshold value: maximal allowed length along each color dimension
τ^{C2}	threshold value: minimum number of times a color name has to be named
τ^{CC}	threshold value: used for the obtention of color regions
τ^{PCA}	threshold value: number of strongest eigenvalues to be considered
τ^{SP1}	threshold value: maximal spatial distance to incorporate a pixel to the mask of a significant patterned region
τ^{T1}	threshold value: minimal relationship of the lengths of the vectors
τ^{T2}	threshold value: maximal angle difference
τ^{T3}	threshold value: maximal normalized difference to detect regular textures
τ^{T4}	threshold value: overlap of the texels for the computation of $g^{\text{Synth}}(\mathbf{u})$
φ	orientation
$\varphi(f)$	phase of the spectrum
$\psi(\bullet)$	mother wavelet

Mathematical operators

Operator	Description
$\mathrm{DFT}\{\bullet\}$	discrete Fourier transform
$\mathrm{E}\{\bullet\}$	expected value
$\max(\bullet)$	maximum
$\min(\bullet)$	minimum
$\mathrm{med}\{\bullet\}$	median
$\bullet\mathrm{rem}(\bullet)$	remainder
$\Sigma_{\bullet}\bullet$	addition
$\lvert\bullet\rvert$	magnitude, number of members in a set
$\lVert\bullet\rVert_2$	ℓ_2−norm
$\emptyset$	empty set
$(\bullet,\bullet)$	undirected edge
$[\bullet,\bullet]$	directed edge
$\measuredangle\bullet$, $\measuredangle(\bullet)$	angle
$\angle(\bullet,\bullet)$	angle between two vectors
$\forall$	for all
$*$	one-dimensional convolution
$**$	two-dimensional convolution
$(\bullet)^{\mathrm{T}}$	transpose
$(\bullet)^*$	complex conjugate

1 Introduction

Starting with the motivation of the problem that led to the elaboration of this work (Sec. 1.1) and an overview of the content-based image retrieval problem (Sec. 1.2), the scope of this thesis (Sec. 1.3) is presented and its outline is discussed (Sec. 1.4). The most important constributions of this work according to the author's best knowledge are presented at the end of this chapter (Sec. 1.5).

1.1 Motivation

Sight, one of the five humans' senses, allows the visual perception of the environment. Showing a picture is often easier, faster, more detailed, and more informative than describing its content. What is more, a full description with words of what we perceive with our eyes is not always even possible.

The huge technology progress over the last decades regarding digital cameras and storage devices enables us to take pictures very fast and easily. Nowadays, we even find digital cameras integrated in many devices like cellular phones, notebooks, etc.

Whether digital images make it possible to record the visual perception of humans, or due to the progress of the technology, or a combination of both, the fact is that a gigantic amount of digital images is created every day. However, this huge amount of data will not be optimally used and may even become useless if no adequate methods exist to compare and sort images automatically by their content according to our similarity perception. This is one of the goals of the content-based image retrieval.

Many applications will profit from an adequate content-based image retrieval like, e.g., search engines and database management systems. Robots are also likely to profit from such a system. Whereas nowadays they either recognize objects or categorize them as unknown, more powerful tasks could be performed if they are able to recognize similar objects and scenes.

1.2 Content-based image retrieval

The retrieval of images according to the similarity of their content is a challenging task. The initial attempts to solve this problem at the 1970s transfer it to a text-based retrieval. This implies that the images must be manually annotated by humans first. This is a tedious job, which is human dependent and impracticable with a big number of images. To overcome these drawbacks, the content-based image retrieval was introduced [87, 123].

"Find similar images to my query" seems to be a clear description of the content-based image retrieval problem, but what does "similar images" mean? The answer to this question depends, i.a., on the aim of the search. Smeulders et al. point in [127] three broad categories: the target search, where the user searches either for a specific image or an image of the same object of which he has an image, the category search, where the user searches image representatives of a specific class, and the association search, where the user is interested in finding interesting things and does not even have a specific aim of what he is searching for. Chalom et al. give in [31] an overview of some applications to measure image similarity. They describe a pattern recognition approach, which implies training a system, and image stabilization, where corresponding points of images are mapped.

Two gaps existing at the content-based image retrieval problem are described by Smeulders et al. in [127]. The sensory gap, which is the gap between the scene in the real world and the image representation (e.g., the occlusions of objects), and the semantic gap, which is the gap between the visual information and the interpretation derived from the user.

Depending on the aim of the search, different types of queries and system specifications are necessary. The query may be a text, a sketch, an image, or a group of images. Training the system with previous knowledge of object classes or even by interacting with the user (relevance feedback) is also possible. Overviews of content-based image retrieval methods are given in [38, 39, 87, 123, 127].

No matter what the concrete aim of the search is, the proceedings mentioned at the overview of the content-based image retrieval methods in [38, 39, 87, 123, 127] always propose the extraction of features from the images. These features are compared to measure the similarity or dissimilarity between the images. Global or local features are possible that describe, i.a., the color, the shape, or the texture information. Many researchers have focused on features describing only one type of the information. They consider the retrieval of the images using, e.g., only color, shape, or texture features. Furthermore, when local features are used, an image segmentation may also be necessary or the detection of regions or salient features [39, 87, 123, 127]. An overview of region-based image retrieval can be found in [69]. They also follow the procedure of extracting features from the images describing, e.g., their color, shape, or texture property and compare them next.

SIMPLIcity [139] and the system described in [30], that uses the Blobworld representation presented in [30], are examples of content-based image retrieval systems. In both cases the image is segmented first and the regions are compared based on their color, texture, and eventually shape features next. The overall similarity between two images is then calculated from a linear combination of the different properties. In [30] these may even be independently weighted from each other.

If we move over to image web search systems we find, e.g., TinEye [132] and Google Images [57]. TinEye states that they are the first image search engine in the web that only uses image identification technology without keywords, metadata, or watermarks. However, they do not present their system as a method to find similar images, but just altered copies of the input image, as the system cannot recognize the content of the images. The search of different images containing the same, or similar, objects is therefore not possible [133]. On the other hand, no detailed official publication of the procedure followed by Google Images is known to the author except the broad statement that from the most distinctive points, lines, and textures found at the input image a mathematical model is built [55]. However, in [56] Google states that the system works best if the query image is likely to be on the web.

1.3 Scope of this work

As the content-based image retrieval is a challenging task with no detailed requirements (see Sec. 1.2), the following system specifications are expected in this thesis.

- The query can only be formulated as a single image. No metadata, watermarks, labels, or several images are allowed as a query.
- Only information extracted directly from the images is used. No metadata, watermarks, text, etc., can be used from the system to compare and retrieve the images.
- The system searches images with similar content. This implies that similar images are not limited to altered copies of the input image, nor to the recognition of the same objects of the input image.
- As similarity, the focus is set on pure perception of humans. This implies similarity that is spontaneously applied without effort or deliberation as described by Julesz in [73]. Similarity assumptions due to further processing in the brain, e.g., object categorization, is beyond the scope of this work. This implies, i.a., that two objects should not be considered similar because they have the same functionality or are biologically classified into the same group. For example, a car and a motorcycle should not be retrieved as similar because they are both modes of transport.
- No interaction with the user is desired. Relevance feedback is therefore beyond the scope of this work. On the one hand the user should not be bothered, on the other hand an interaction with the user is not always possible, e.g., in applications where a robot "sees" something new and unknown.

1.4 Outline of this work

This work is organized in nine chapters. A brief introduction to the most important mathematical background needed is given in the next chapter (chapter 2). The use of features is considered for the content-based image retrieval problem (see Fig. 1.1). The extraction of the color, the shape, and the texture information from images are independently considered from each other. For this purpose, the extraction of these features, as well as their comparisons, are addressed in chapter 3, chapter 4, and chapter 5, respectively. However, as most images consist of several meaningful regions that are independent of each other, the features should not be extracted from the whole image but from the different regions. The detection and extraction of connected regions in the images due to areas with a similar color or a pattern, which is considered in this work as a repetition of alternating colors, is therefore necessary. In chapter 6 the detection of such kind of regions is addressed. Both better extracted meaningful regions and better content-based image retrievals are expected from the fusion of the previously mentioned methods. Chapter 7 addresses the fusion of the methods and presents the proposed content-based image retrieval environment that works following the sketch of Fig. 1.1. Finally, the results of the presented methods are shown in chapter 8 followed by the conclusions of the work and an outlook in chapter 9.

1.5 Own contribution

The decomposition of the content-based image retrieval problem to the extraction of features describing the properties of the image is a common procedure that is likely to be combined with a segmentation or detection of salient features. Although several researchers have already investigated different possible features describing, i.a., color, shape, or texture properties, the author believes in the need for features and similarity comparisons strongly based on the human perception. Furthermore, the author also believes in the importance of a good fusion of features describing different properties together with an appropriate selection of significant regions of the image describing its content. This allows to create a prototype of a content-based image retrieval system.

The color, shape, and texture properties have been selected to describe the content of images. Particular focus has been set on the description and comparison of color and texture properties based on the human perception. The color representation with the help of human color categories is addressed in Sec. 3.3 and implemented in Secs. 6.3.2 and 6.4.2 for the detection and extraction of regions with a similar color and for the detection and extraction of patterns. The representation of the color information by the color categories is inspired by the psychological findings from Berlin and Kay [18], and Kay and Regier [75]. Among the texture properties of images, the author believes in the benefits of a prior identification of the textures into regular or irregular, as humans can easily perform this classification [20, 41, 107] apart from the difficulties that arise when they try to define what a texture is [19, 20, 41, 51, 54, 107]. This is presented in Sec. 5.2.2. The focus is then set on the extraction and comparison of features for regular textures (see Sec. 5.2.3), which consider, i.a., statistical properties up to a second order, which correlates with the statement of Julesz [73] that differences up to a second order can be perceived by humans in a perceptual way. However, as no perception map of regular textures is known to the author, an experiment has been performed with subjects to extract a human perception map in Sec. 5.2.4 of regular textures. With its help the extracted features and similarity comparisons from Sec. 5.2.3 are validated.

Furthermore, a compact color signature is proposed in Sec. 3.2 to compare the color information of images, the normal angular descriptors are presented in Sec. 4.2 as shape features, and a region detector for regions with a similar color or pattern are presented in Secs. 6.3.1 and 6.4.1. As perfectly regular textures are seldom found in digital images, the detection of near-regular textures and the extraction of their regular textures are considered in Sec. 5.3. Some methods indeed exist to detect near-regular textures, but the author proposes here, i.a., to detect an almost regular part of the texture first and to consider the color information. Although these last methods are not derived from psychological findings, they belong to blocks that are necessary to be able to fuse all of the methods and obtain the prototype presented in this thesis for the content-based image retrieval problem.

Finally, the fusion of all of the methods is considered in Sec. 7. On the one hand the detection of significant patterned regions is considered by fusing the extracted regions with the detected near-regular textures. On the other hand the content-based image retrieval method is presented with the singularity that the total similarity between the images is not measured as a linear combination of the similarities achieved by the different extracted features but as an adjustable comparison of the different features that is automatically determined.

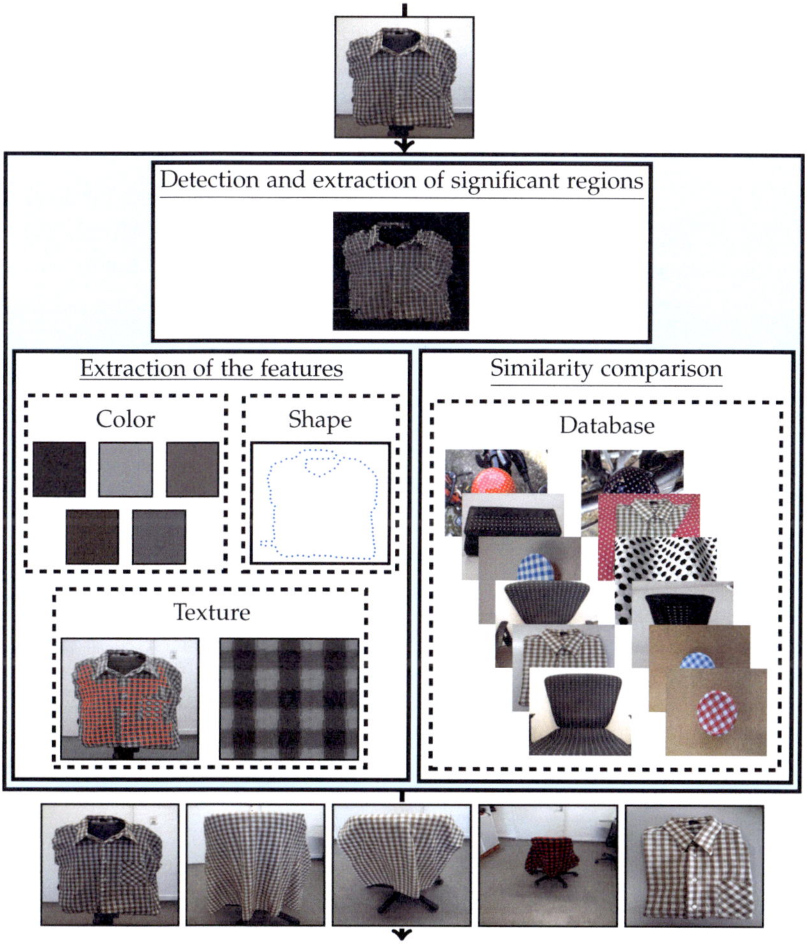

Figure 1.1 Overview of the proposed content-based image retrieval method (blue colored).

2 Mathematical background

Relevant distance functions and similarity comparisons used in this thesis are presented in Sec. 2.1. As graphs and space-frequency representations are necessary in several chapters of this thesis, a brief introduction to the most important topics needed for this work is respectively presented in Sec. 2.2 and Sec. 2.3.

2.1 Distance functions and similarity comparisons

The distance functions and similarity comparisons that are most relevant for this thesis are briefly introduced next.

The **Euclidean distance**, or also named ℓ_2-norm, between two vectors $\mathbf{y}^{\mathrm{A}}, \mathbf{y}^{\mathrm{B}}$ is calculated as [7, 45]

$$\left\| \mathbf{y}^{\mathrm{A}} - \mathbf{y}^{\mathrm{B}} \right\|_2, \tag{2.1}$$

where

$$\|\mathbf{x}\|_2 = \sqrt{\mathbf{x}^{\mathrm{T}}\mathbf{x}}. \tag{2.2}$$

In case of a function $g(u)$, the Euclidean distance is defined as [8]

$$\|g(u)\|_2 = \sqrt{\int |g(u)|^2}. \tag{2.3}$$

This distance can be found in this thesis in connection with shape (Sec. 4) and texture (Sec. 5) properties as well as with the detection of regions (Sec. 6).

The **quadratic-form distance** is a measure to compare two histograms $\mathbf{h}^{\mathrm{A}}, \mathbf{h}^{\mathrm{B}}$ taking into consideration the similarity between bins. It is defined as [108, 122]

$$d\left(\mathbf{h}^{\mathrm{A}}, \mathbf{h}^{\mathrm{B}}\right) = \sqrt{\left(\mathbf{h}^{\mathrm{A}} - \mathbf{h}^{\mathrm{B}}\right)^{\mathrm{T}} \mathbf{B} \left(\mathbf{h}^{\mathrm{A}} - \mathbf{h}^{\mathrm{B}}\right)}, \tag{2.4}$$

where $\mathbf{B}$ denotes a similarity matrix whose element $b_{k_1 k_2}$ expresses the cross-bin dependence between the bins k_1 and k_2. The quadratic-form distance is used in this work to compare regular textures (Sec. 5.2.3).

The **correlation coefficient** between $g^{\mathrm{A}}(u)$ and $g^{\mathrm{B}}(u)$ is calculated according to [45, 114, 119]

$$r\left(g^{\mathrm{A}}(u), g^{\mathrm{B}}(u)\right) = \frac{\mathrm{E}\left\{\left(g^{\mathrm{A}}(u) - \mathrm{E}\left\{g^{\mathrm{A}}(u)\right\}\right)\left(g^{\mathrm{B}}(u) - \mathrm{E}\left\{g^{\mathrm{B}}(u)\right\}\right)\right\}}{\sqrt{\mathrm{E}\left\{g^{\mathrm{A}}(u) - \mathrm{E}\left\{g^{\mathrm{A}}(u)\right\}\right\} \mathrm{E}\left\{g^{\mathrm{B}}(u) - \mathrm{E}\left\{g^{\mathrm{B}}(u)\right\}\right\}}}. \tag{2.5}$$

It is a normalized value between -1 and $+1$. In this thesis the correlation coefficient can be found at the detection and extraction of near-regular textures (Sec. 5.3) and at the detection of color regions (Sec. 6.3.2).

The **correlation for circular data** presented by Fisher and Lee in [49] is used to compare circular data $\varphi_k^{\mathrm{A}}, \varphi_k^{\mathrm{B}}$, $1 \leq k \leq N$, via the following "correlation":

$$\rho\left(\varphi^{\mathrm{A}}, \varphi^{\mathrm{B}}\right) = \frac{\sum\limits_{k_1=0}^{N-2} \sum\limits_{k_2=k_1+1}^{N-1} \sin\left(\theta_{k_1,k_2}^{\mathrm{A}}\right) \cdot \sin\left(\theta_{k_1,k_2}^{\mathrm{B}}\right)}{\sqrt{\left(\sum\limits_{k_1=0}^{N-2} \sum\limits_{k_2=k_1+1}^{N-1} \sin^2\left(\theta_{k_1,k_2}^{\mathrm{A}}\right)\right)\left(\sum\limits_{k_1=0}^{N-2} \sum\limits_{k_2=k_1+1}^{N-1} \sin^2\left(\theta_{k_1,k_2}^{\mathrm{B}}\right)\right)}}, \tag{2.6}$$

where $\theta_{k_1,k_2}^{\mathrm{s}} = \varphi_{k_1}^{\mathrm{s}} - \varphi_{k_2}^{\mathrm{s}}$, $s \in \{\mathrm{A}, \mathrm{B}\}$. In this thesis this correlation for circular data is used to compare shape features (Sec. 4.2.2).

The **earth mover's distance** as a metric for image retrieval is investigated by Rubner et al. in [122]. It represents the difference between two distributions as a transportation problem. The overall dissimilarity is obtained from the total cost, deduced from the conversion of one of the distributions into the other one. In order to calculate the costs of the transportation, the distributions must be represented as a set of cluster representatives and their corresponding weights. The dissimilarity between the cluster representatives and the weights of the cluster representatives are taken into consideration to obtain the total dissimilarity between the two inputs. The earth mover's distance is used in this work to evaluate the proposed compact color signature from Sec. 3.2 (Sec. 8.2.1).

2.2 Graph theory

Graphs are a powerful mathematical model to analyze many problems and to describe the relationship between objects. In this thesis graphs are used to obtain a compact color signature for images (Sec. 3.2), to detect near-regular textures (Sec. 5.3), to extract non-overlapping stable color regions (Sec. 6.3.1), and to extract patterns in images (Sec. 6.4). Because of their frequent application, a brief introduction to graph theory is given in the next sections. The focus is set on basics needed to understand the proposed methods. This introduction is mostly based on [12, 121, 141], where more detailed information about graph theory can be found.

2.2.1 Basic concepts of graph theory

A graph is a triple $\mathcal{G} = \left(\mathcal{V}(\mathcal{G}), \mathcal{E}(\mathcal{G}), I_{\mathcal{G}}\right)$ [12, 141]. $\mathcal{V}(\mathcal{G})$ is the set formed by the nodes v, also called vertices. Edges e are the elements of the set $\mathcal{E}(\mathcal{G})$, whereas

$$\mathcal{V}(\mathcal{G}) \cap \mathcal{E}(\mathcal{G}) = \emptyset \tag{2.7}$$

must apply [121]. $I_{\mathcal{G}}$ describes relations by associating each edge from $\mathcal{E}(\mathcal{G})$ a pair of nodes from $\mathcal{V}(\mathcal{G})$, which may be twice the same node in case of a loop:

$$I_{\mathcal{G}}(e) = \left(v_{k_1}, v_{k_2}\right), \tag{2.8}$$

where $e \in \mathcal{E}(\mathcal{G})$ and $v_{k_1}, v_{k_2} \in \mathcal{V}(\mathcal{G})$.

For simplification purposes, edges e will be denoted in this work as (v_{k_1}, v_{k_2}). This notation already contains the information of the nodes that are being connected by the corresponding edge. Some graph examples are shown in Fig. 2.1. If an edge (v_{k_1}, v_{k_2}) exists between two different nodes ($k_1 \neq k_2$), then the nodes are neighbors and adjacent [12, 141].

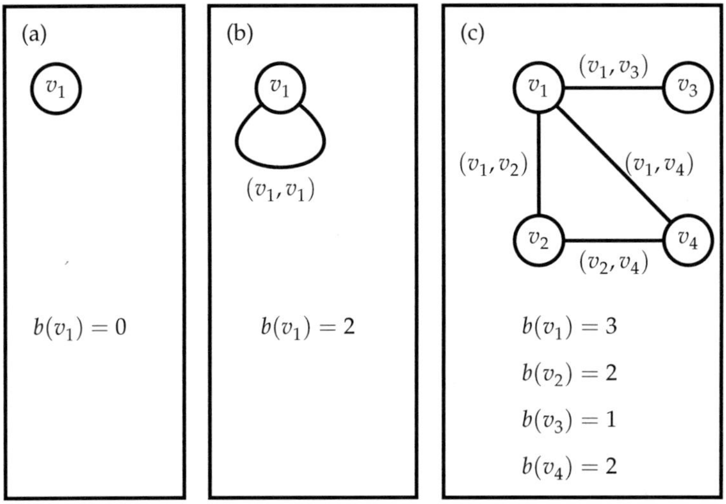

Figure 2.1 Degree of nodes. The graph at the left consists of an isolated node. A loop is shown in (b).

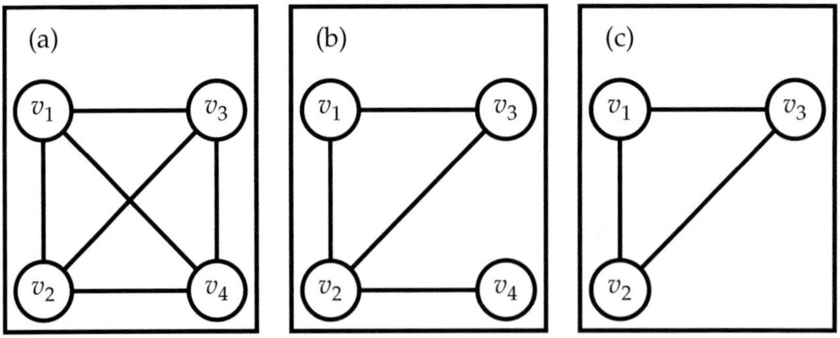

Figure 2.2 Some examples of graphs. (a) shows a connected, complete graph. (b) displays a connected graph that is not complete. (c) shows a clique from b).

$\mathcal{N}(v)$, $v \in \mathcal{V}(\mathcal{G})$, is the set of all neighbors of v and is called the neighbor set of v. The degree of a node $b(v)$ is its number of incident edges. Some examples are shown in Fig. 2.1. Loops are counted plus two when the degree of a node is calculated (see Fig. 2.1(b)). If a node has a degree of zero, no edge in $\mathcal{E}(\mathcal{G})$ exists that associates the node with another one in the graph. Such nodes are called isolated (see Fig. 2.1(a)) [12, 141].

A subgraph of $\mathcal{G}$ is any graph $\mathcal{G}_k$ with $\mathcal{V}(\mathcal{G}_k) \subseteq \mathcal{V}(\mathcal{G})$ and $\mathcal{E}(\mathcal{G}_k) \subseteq \mathcal{E}(\mathcal{G})$. A graph $\mathcal{G}$ is called complete if for every pair of nodes in $\mathcal{V}(\mathcal{G})$ an edge exists that associates them (see Fig. 2.2(a)). Complete subgraphs of a graph $\mathcal{G}$ are known as cliques (see Fig. 2.2(c)) [12, 141].

A walk is an alternating sequence of nodes and edges along the graph. If the edges that appear in the walk are not repeated, then the walk is called a trail, and if the nodes are not repeated, a path. As a consequence, every path is a valid trail, but every trail is not necessarily a valid path [12, 141].

Two nodes are connected if a path exists along them. Moreover, a graph $\mathcal{G}$ is called connected if paths exist between every pair of nodes. Every not connected graph can be divided into connected subgraphs called components of $\mathcal{G}$ [12, 141].

2.2.2 Directed graphs

A directed graph, also called digraph, is a triple $\mathcal{G} = \left(\mathcal{V}(\mathcal{G}), \mathcal{E}(\mathcal{G}), I_{\mathcal{G}}\right)$, where $\mathcal{V}(\mathcal{G})$ is the set of nodes in the graph and $\mathcal{E}(\mathcal{G})$ the set of arcs, which are called edges in this work [12, 141]. Equation 2.7 must also apply between $\mathcal{V}(\mathcal{G})$ and $\mathcal{E}(\mathcal{G})$ at digraphs. $I_{\mathcal{G}}$ associates each edge of the graph two nodes, however, the edges become a direction at digraphs (see Fig. 2.3(a),(b)). For simplification purposes, edges from digraphs are represented in this work as $[v_{k_1}, v_{k_2}]$, $v_{k_1}, v_{k_2} \in \mathcal{V}(\mathcal{G})$, with v_{k_1} defining the tail of the edge and v_{k_2} the head of the edge. v_{k_1}, v_{k_2} are also known as the ends of the edge $[v_{k_1}, v_{k_2}]$ [12, 121, 141]. Furthermore, the edge $[v_{k_1}, v_{k_2}]$ is incident out of v_{k_1} and incident into v_{k_2} (see Fig. 2.3(a)) [12].

If two nodes v_{k_1} and v_{k_2} are connected by an edge $[v_{k_1}, v_{k_2}]$, then v_{k_1} is an inneighbor of v_{k_2}, and v_{k_2} is an outneighbor of v_{k_1}. $\mathcal{N}^+(v_{k_1})$ is the set of outneighbors of v_{k_1} and $\mathcal{N}^-(v_{k_1})$ its set of inneighbors [12].

As the edges have a direction at digraphs, different kinds of degrees can be obtained per node. The outdegree $b^+(v_k)$ of v_k, $v_k \in \mathcal{V}(\mathcal{G})$, is the number of edges that are incident out of v_k, and the indegree $b^-(v_k)$ is the number of edges that are incident into v_k [141]. For digraphs the degree $b(v_k)$ of v_k is defined as

$$b(v_k) = b^+(v_k) + b^-(v_k) . \tag{2.9}$$

An isolated node at a directed graph is a node with a degree of zero [12].

An underlaying graph is obtained from a directed graph if the orientations are removed from the edges (see Fig. 2.3(b),(c)) [12]. If the underlaying graph is a connected one, then the directed graph is called weakly connected. If for every pair of nodes in a directed graph a sequence of edges exists connecting them, then the graph is strongly connected. The direction of the edges is taken into consideration to determine if a graph is strongly connected [141].

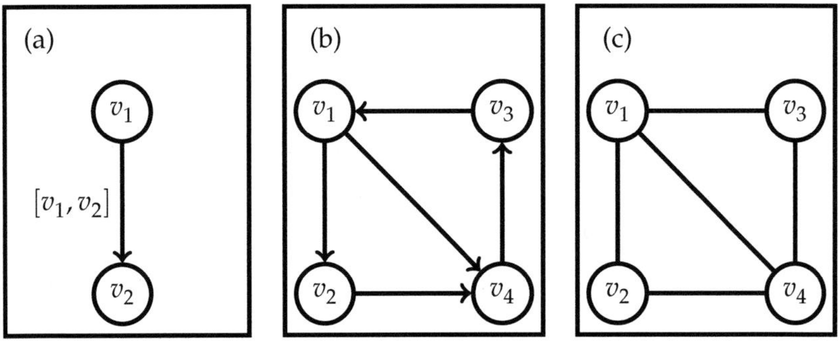

Figure 2.3 Examples of directed graphs. (a) shows a directed edge. (b) is a directed graph and (c) its corresponding underlaying graph.

2.2.3 Trees

Every graph and digraph that does not contain cycles is called a forest. A forest can be formed from trees, which are connected graphs without cycles (the underlaying graph is considered in case of a directed graph to determine the connectedness), and from isolated nodes. Therefore, every pair of vertices of a tree is connected by a unique path (its corresponding underlaying graph in case of a digraph) [12, 121]. An example is shown in Fig. 2.4. The forest there is composed of two trees and the isolated node v_8. At digraphs the root of a tree is the node, from which all nodes can be reached alternating nodes and edges (v_1 and v_9 in Fig. 2.4). The inneighbor of a node is also called its parent and its outneighbors its children [121, 141]. For example, in Fig. 2.4 the parent of v_{11} is v_9 and its children are v_{12} and v_{13}. Furthermore, nodes that do not have children are called the leaves of the tree (e.g., v_4 and v_5 in Fig. 2.4).

The last concept introduced in this section is the binary tree. A tree is of binary kind if every node has a maximum of two children. The right tree in Fig. 2.4 represents a binary tree [121, 141].

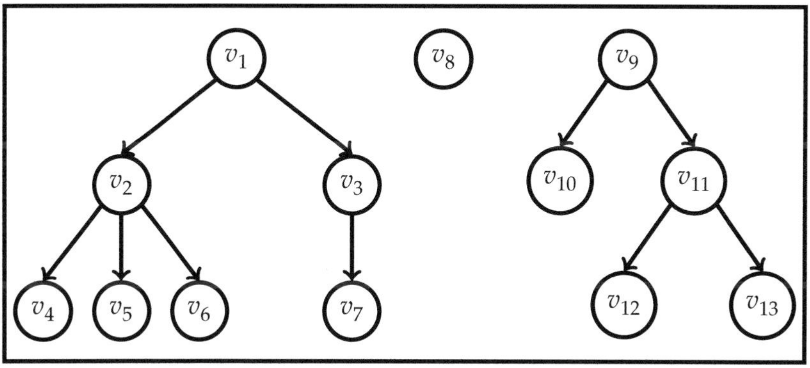

Figure 2.4 Example of a forest.

2.2.3.1 k-d tree

The *k*-d tree, which is a binary tree to structure *k*-dimensional data, was proposed by Bentley [17]. Every node in the tree represents a record of the data and each level in the tree corresponds to a dimension of the data, whereas the dimension changes cyclically along the depth of the tree. The nodes in the tree that are not leafs always point into two nodes, whereas according to the depth of the tree one node is always bigger along the considered dimension than the other one.

To obtain an optimal *k*-d tree, Bentley proposed an algorithm to assure that the number of nodes from the left branch of the tree, starting from the root, differ at most by one from the right branch [17]. For this purpose, the data set is divided along the tree alternating the dimension into two sets by their respective median value. Figure 2.5 shows an example for two-dimensional data.

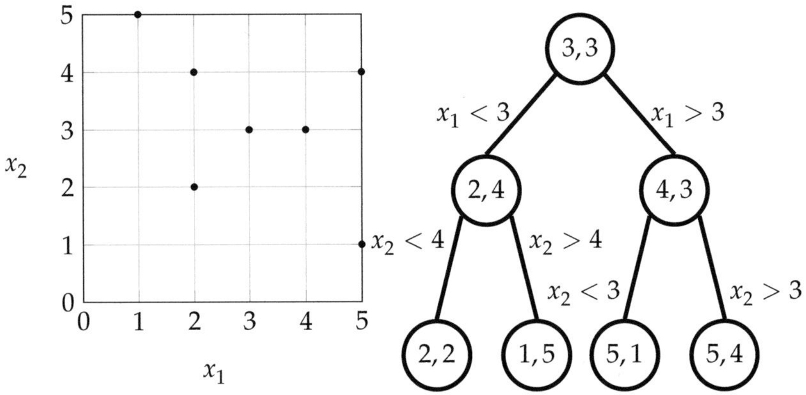

Figure 2.5 Example of a k-d tree for two-dimensional data.

2.3 Space-frequency representations

Depending on the available characteristics of signals and the processing intended with them, the space, the frequency, or the space-frequency domain may be favorable. Along this thesis all of the three mentioned domains are used. The one-dimensional frequency domain is used, e.g., in Sec. 4.3 to compare shapes, the two-dimensional frequency domain in Sec. 5.2 to detect regular textures and extract features from them, and the space-frequency domain in Sec. 6.4 to detect patterns in images. A brief overview of the corresponding transforms used in this thesis is given in the next sections.

2.3.1 One-dimensional Fourier transform

The Fourier transform of a signal $g(u)$ is an integral transformation calculated as [20, 76, 120]

$$G(f) = \int_{-\infty}^{\infty} g(u) \cdot \exp\left(-\mathrm{j}2\pi f u\right) \mathrm{d}u, \tag{2.10}$$

whereas $G(f)$ is also called the spectrum of $g(u)$ and it can be separated into its magnitude $|G(f)|$ and phase $\varphi(f)$:

$$G(f) = |G(f)| \cdot \exp\left(\mathrm{j}\,\varphi(f)\right). \tag{2.11}$$

Fine details (fast changes) in the space function $g(u)$ imply higher frequency components in the spectrum. Rough details imply lower frequency components [20].

According to Eq. 2.10 to obtain the spectrum of a space signal, the signal must be continuous and infinitely long to be integrated over the whole space domain. However, these two properties are not present in real environments and are therefore briefly discussed next.

Spectral leakage appears due to the limitation of $g(u)$ along the space domain when the Fourier transform is calculated. Mathematically, the Fourier transform is calculated from the windowed signal $g^{\mathrm{win}}(u)$:

$$g^{\mathrm{win}}(u) = w^{\mathrm{rect}}(u) \cdot g(u)\,, \tag{2.12}$$

where $w^{\mathrm{rect}}(u)$ denotes a rectangular window function of length l_{rect} defined as [63, 112, 113]

$$w^{\mathrm{rect}}(u) = \begin{cases} 1 & \text{if } -\frac{l_{\mathrm{rect}}}{2} \leq u \leq \frac{l_{\mathrm{rect}}}{2} \\ 0 & \text{otherwise.} \end{cases} \tag{2.13}$$

The product of the window function with the analyzing signal implies a convolution in frequency domain and may therefore distort the spectrum. An appropriate selection of the window function may smooth spectral leakage [20, 120].

The **discretization** of the space and frequency domains is necessary to handle images in computers, as they cannot process continuous signals. The discretization in space domain is mathematically described as the product of the continuous signal with an impulse train. This implies the convolution of the spectrum of the input image with an impulse train in frequency domain and therefore its repetition. A discretization of the frequency domain is also necessary. It can also be described as the multiplication of the spectrum with a new impulse train, whose consequence is the convolution of the discrete signal in space domain with the Fourier transform of the impulse train. Consequently, this implies its repetition over the space domain [20, 120]. The discretization in space domain and the discretization in frequency domain distort therefore the analysis of the signals.

2.3.2 Two-dimensional Fourier transform

The Fourier transform of two-dimensional signals $g(\mathbf{u})$, like, e.g., gray-level images $g(\mathbf{u})$, is calculated by the following relation [20]:

$$G(\mathbf{f}) = \int_{-\infty}^{\infty}\int_{-\infty}^{\infty} g(\mathbf{u}) \cdot \exp\left(-\mathrm{j}2\pi\mathbf{f}^{\mathrm{T}}\mathbf{u}\right)\mathrm{d}\mathbf{u}. \tag{2.14}$$

Due to the separability property it can be interpreted as two one-dimensional Fourier transforms of the input signal. The Fourier transform along the u_2 direction is calculated from the Fourier transformed signal along the u_1 direction [20]:

$$G(\mathbf{f}) = \int_{-\infty}^{\infty}\int_{-\infty}^{\infty} g(\mathbf{u}) \cdot \exp(-\mathrm{j}2\pi\,(f_1u_1 + f_2u_2))\mathrm{d}u_1\mathrm{d}u_2 \tag{2.15}$$

$$= \int_{-\infty}^{\infty}\left(\int_{-\infty}^{\infty} g(\mathbf{u})\cdot\exp(-\mathrm{j}2\pi f_1u_1)\mathrm{d}u_1\right)\exp(-\mathrm{j}2\pi f_2u_2)\mathrm{d}u_2. \tag{2.16}$$

As in the one-dimensional case, spectral leakage and discretization issues must be considered in the Fourier transform of two-dimensional signals.

2.3.3 One-dimensional wavelet transform

The wavelet transform of a one-dimensional signal $g(u)$ is obtained from the comparison with a mother wavelet $\psi(u)$ which is scaled and shifted:

$$\Gamma(\lambda,\kappa) = \int\limits_{-\infty}^{\infty} g(u)\,\frac{1}{\sqrt{\lambda}}\psi^*\left(\frac{u-\kappa}{\lambda}\right)\,\mathrm{d}u. \tag{2.17}$$

In contrast to the Fourier transform (see Sec. 2.3.1), the wavelet transform delivers a space-frequency description of the input signal. This allows the localization of signal components in space and frequency domain up to a certain resolution. Lower frequencies can be localized very good in frequency and therefore rougher in space, whereas higher frequencies can be localized very good in space and therefore rougher in frequency [20, 40, 76, 120].

2.3.3.1 Fast implementation of the wavelet transform for the discrete case

A discrete and fast wavelet transform is necessary to assure a reasonable signal processing with computers. Besides the discretization of the input signal g_u, the mother wavelet and its scaling and shifting parameters must also be quantized [20, 40, 76].

The fast wavelet transform is the consecutive projection of the input signal onto subspaces, whereas subspaces at a same stage are orthogonal to each other. The input signal is represented in a coarser manner with increasing stages. At every stage the coarse representation of g_u is divided into a detailed and a coarser representation, yielding the coarser approximation and detail coefficients of g_u at the following stage. This decomposition of the signal can be done very fast with the application of low-pass and band-pass filters with subsequent downsampling to the coarser approximation coefficients of the previous stage. Usually the quantized input signal is used as the coarser approximation coefficients at the initial stage. The projection of the input signal to the different subspaces can be calculated from the coarser approximation and detail coefficients. The original input signal can be reconstructed from the detail coefficients over all stages and the coarser approximation coefficients at the last stage via projection onto the higher spaces. This can also be implemented very fast by upsampling and subsequently using low-pass and band-pass filters [20, 40, 76].

2.3.4 Two-dimensional wavelet transform

As in the case of the two-dimensional Fourier transform (see Sec. 2.3.2), the two-dimensional wavelet transform is obtained applying the one-dimensional wavelet transform along one of the directions (e.g., u_1) and then along the other direction (e.g., u_2). Two dimensions and two filter types (low-pass and band-pass) must be considered, so four signals result from every stage of the two-dimensional wavelet transform: a coarser approximation of the input image and three detail signals, containing information about horizontal, vertical and diagonal structures. Like in the one-dimensional case, the approximation of the input image is further divided along the stages, and the input image can be totally reconstructed from the detail signals and the approximation of the image at the last stage (see Fig. 2.6) [20].

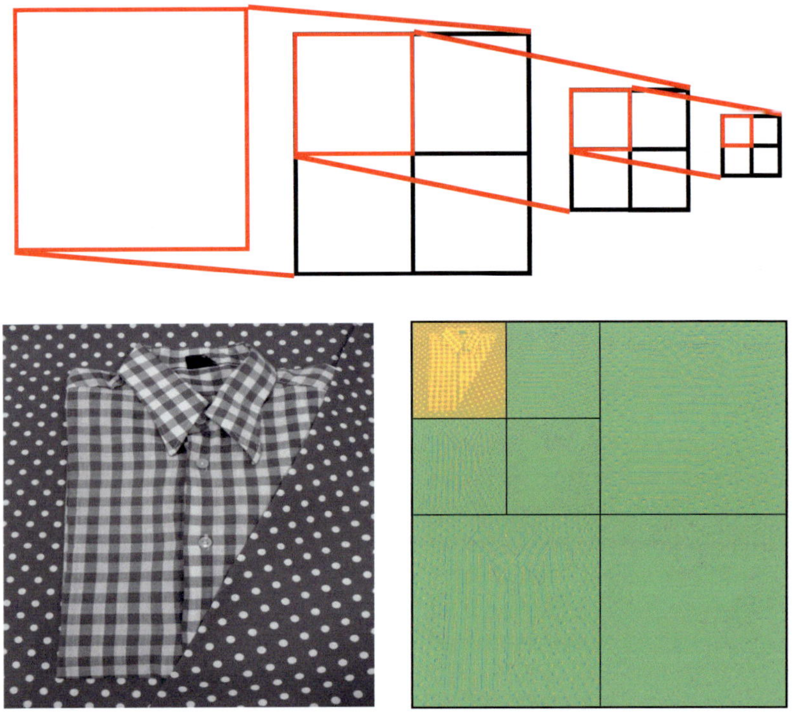

Figure 2.6 Sketch of a fast two-dimensional wavelet transform with three stages (up) and example of a fast two-dimensional wavelet transform, represented with pseudo-colors, for an input image with two stages (bottom).

3 Color

Many objects and materials in our environment only exist with certain colors. The grass is mostly green, the ocean blue, clouds white or gray, etc. The perception of color is therefore a powerful tool for classification and optical inspection of objects and materials. Due to this fact, the processing of the color information and its use as a feature for the content-based image retrieval is considered in this chapter.

First, an introduction to color considering what color is, how it can be represented, and an overview of the state of the art is given in Sec. 3.1. A compact color signature in CIELAB color space for content-based image retrieval purposes is then presented in Sec. 3.2. The representation of the color information using humans' color categories is considered in Sec. 3.3 together with the procedure followed in this thesis to determine representative humans' color categories. The result of the presented methods are shown in Sec. 8.2.

3.1 Introduction to color

Color is a perceptual property that derives from the spectrum of light interacting with the eye [20]. Visible light consists of frequencies in the electromagnetic spectrum. Depending on the electromagnetic spectrum that is emitted by or reflected from the surfaces of the objects, a color is perceived by humans. If the incident spectra consists of all frequencies belonging to visible light, then surfaces that reflect all of the frequencies of the electromagnetic spectrum appear white to humans [54]. However, the colors perceived by humans depend on many facts like the surfaces of the objects, the environment, and the human itself. It is therefore not a property of an object or material [20].

Berlin and Kay studied the universality of color naming across different languages and societies [18]. Although different basic color terms may exist depending on the language, they found that the evolution of the basic color terms is highly correlated between the languages. They concluded with eleven basic color terms in English language: *white, black, gray, yellow, brown, green, blue, purple, pink, orange, red*. Later Kay and Regier [75] studied the color naming from languages in industrialized and non-industrialized societies. Although the number of basic color terms and their boundaries may vary between different languages, they found that the eleven basic color terms of the English language seem to be anchored across the different languages as points in color space.

3.1.1 Color representation

When representing color information digitally, color spaces are used. Different color spaces exist depending on the final task. They can be roughly classified into device inspired color spaces or perception oriented inspired color spaces [20]. The widely spread RGB color space is an example of the first group, whereas the CIELAB color space is an example of the second group. An overview of these color spaces is given next, as they are used along this thesis. A more exhaustive consideration about color spaces can be found in [20, 54].

The **RGB color space** is based on the three primary colors red, green and blue [20, 54]. In this color space a color is represented as a three dimensional vector $\mathbf{g} \in [0, 1]^3$, whereas every dimension represents one of the three primary colors. A color is then the addition of their proportion of red, green, and blue colors. The RGB color space is widely spread, as the three primary colors are often the basic colors of cameras, displays, and projectors. However, not every perceivable color can be represented in this color space. Furthermore, the RGB color space is device dependent, as it depends on the exact red, green, and blue colors that are added to create new colors [20].

To overcome the drawbacks of a device dependent color space, the sRGB color space has been defined. For this purpose, the three primary colors are normalized [20].

The **CIELAB color space** also represents a color as a three dimensional vector $\mathbf{g}$. One dimension represents the brightness of the color, whereas the other two dimensions respectively represent the difference between green and red colors, and blue and yellow [20]. This color space is a so called uniform color space, where the distance between points in color space is a reference of their perceivable color difference for humans. However, the comparison is rather reasonable for smaller color differences than for bigger ones [20, 51].

3.1.2 State of the art

Many researchers have focused on the research of content-based image retrieval systems using the color information. For this purpose, appropriate features must be extracted from the images.

Swain and Ballard propose the use of color histograms to index images in a large database and the histogram intersection as a metric for image retrieval in [131]. To this end, the intersection between both histograms is regarded by a bin-by-bin comparison. Several metrics have been proposed to compare histograms bin-by-bin [122]. Their main drawback is that the result depends on the selected bin size and that no cross similarity between bins is considered. To overcome these problems, Niblack et al. also compare cross-bins taking into consideration the similarity between bins in [108].

While color histograms yield a global statement of the colors in an image and their amount, the information about the spatial relationship between the different colors gets lost. Pass et al. propose therefore the color coherence vectors in [117]. The pixels in the input image are classified into two groups, coherent or incoherent. A pixel is coherent if it forms a sufficiently big connected area with other pixels of the same color. For this purpose, the color space is quantized and every quantized unit is considered a color. The feature proposed by Pass et al. consists of a vector per input image formed out of pairs. Every pair represents one color of the image and it contains the amount of coherent pixels in the image with the considered color and the amount of incoherent pixels [117]. Huang et al. propose color correlograms to overcome the loss of the spatial relationship between the colors in [68]. It consists of a table indexed by color pairs that contains the probability of finding a pixel of a certain color at a given distance of a pixel with another considered color. Stehling et al. propose in [128] the cell/color histograms to consider the spatial displacement of the appearing colors and also to reduce the storage place needed, compared to the basic color histograms. The image is divided into cells but instead of computing one color histogram per cell, one histogram is computed per appearing color in the image. Each histogram contains the number of pixels of the considered color per cell. Consequently, only as many histograms are needed as colors appearing in the image [128]. This method is extended in [138] to enable cross-bins comparisons, which allows to consider rotations and translations of the images. Konstantinidis et al. propose in [77] a color histogram with only 10 bins to reduce storage. The histograms are obtained after considering the color space as a fuzzy set [145].

Several features have also been proposed without using histograms. Deng et al. propose in [43] to use only the dominant colors in an image. They searched for clusters in the colors of the pixels first and concluded that three to four colors are typically enough to represent the color information of the image [43]. Yoo et al. propose to sort images in three steps in [144]. First, the four major colors appearing in the query image are extracted. All images in the database that do not contain the major colors of the query are discarded. In a second step, images in the database whose major colors are not similarly distributed to the query image are discarded. Finally, the remaining images in the database are sorted [144]. Other systems use color moments like, e.g., the average of the appearing color [139].

Rubner et al. evaluate in [122], i.a., the earth mover's distance as a metric for content-based image retrieval using only color information. To this end, a color signature per image is extracted by partitioning the color space into regions in depedence of the considered image. Two *k*-d trees are used (see Sec. 2.2.3.1). First, one *k*-d tree is performed with all color pixels of the image. The data is divided into nodes until the length of the color regions along the dimensions is smaller or equal to a given threshold. In a second step a second *k*-d tree is performed over the centroids of the final color regions of the first *k*-d tree. In this case only the half of the previous threshold is the maximum allowed length per dimension. The color signature of an image is obtained from the centroids of the regions. What is specially interesting about this metric is that the number of color representatives describing the color distribution of the image may vary. The similarity is the total costs obtained if the distribution of one of the images is converted into the other one [122].

The eleven basic color terms from the English language have been an inspiration for many researchers dealing with image processing. Van den Broek et al. use the eleven basic color terms to create a user color selection interface for content-based image retrieval purposes in [24]. Furthermore, van den Broek et al. experimentally prove the eleven basic color terms in [23]. They also use them in [23] as a feature for the content-based image retrieval. The assignment of color values to the eleven basic color terms is a challenging task. In [140] van de Weijer et al. study how to learn the color values of the eleven basic color terms from real images. Heer and Stone propose in [65] a procedure to construct a probabilistic model for color naming. They obtain 153 color names associated to color regions in color subspaces and use this information to create, i.a., a color dictionary and a wand selector in images.

3.2 A compact color signature in CIELAB color space for images

Inspired by the work in [122], a color signature for the content-based image retrieval is proposed. The usage of k-d trees (see Sec. 2.2.3.1) enables a compact representation of the color information in an image. However, the compression of the color information may also lead to a loss of information. The second k-d tree in [122] may be specially critical as it reduces the representation of the color information from an already compressed representation. With these concerns the following method is proposed. Comparison results to the usage of the two k-d trees are shown in Sec. 8.2.1.

Color regions with a similar color are obtained first in CIELAB color space by grouping the data using a k-d tree as in [122]. For this purpose, the pixels are divided into groups along the k-d tree according to their color until the length spanned by the color of the pixels in each group over each color dimension is smaller than a given threshold value τ^{C1}. Some final nodes of the k-d tree may be merged without exceeding the maximum allowed length of the color regions along the different dimensions, due to the fact that the k-d tree divides the database alternating the dimensions. To detect and merge such color regions, a graph representation of the color information is used in Sec. 3.2.1. Characteristic nodes are defined in Sec. 3.2.2. The number of nodes is reduced in Sec. 3.2.3, and a compact color signature is obtained in Sec. 3.2.4.

3.2.1 Graph representation of the color information

Every leaf of the k-d tree is represented by a node v_k in the graph and it represents a subspace in CIELAB color space. The subspace of each node is characterized by the maximum and minimum value per channel from all pixels that have been assigned to it:

$$v_k = \left\{ \mathbf{u} \,\middle|\, \begin{pmatrix} l_k^{*\min} \\ a_k^{*\min} \\ b_k^{*\min} \end{pmatrix} \le \mathbf{g}(\mathbf{u}) \le \begin{pmatrix} l_k^{*\max} \\ a_k^{*\max} \\ b_k^{*\max} \end{pmatrix} \right\}. \tag{3.1}$$

Consequently, every node represents a set of points. Nodes spanning a similar color subspace are connected by an edge. The dissimilarity between two nodes v_{k_1}, v_{k_2} is measured via the following distance function:

$$\begin{aligned} d\left(v_{k_1}, v_{k_2}\right) = \max\Big[&\max\left(l_{k_1}^{*\max}, l_{k_2}^{*\max}\right) - \min\left(l_{k_1}^{*\min}, l_{k_2}^{*\min}\right), \\ &\max\left(a_{k_1}^{*\max}, a_{k_2}^{*\max}\right) - \min\left(a_{k_1}^{*\min}, a_{k_2}^{*\min}\right), \\ &\max\left(b_{k_1}^{*\max}, b_{k_2}^{*\max}\right) - \min\left(b_{k_1}^{*\min}, b_{k_2}^{*\min}\right)\Big]. \end{aligned} \tag{3.2}$$

Nodes with a distance smaller than τ^{C1} could be merged without exceeding the maximum allowed length per channel. Such nodes are considered similar and therefore connected by an edge in the graph. However, this is not a transitive relation. The node v_{k_2} may be similar to v_{k_1} and v_{k_3}, but this does no imply that v_{k_1} and v_{k_3} must be similar. An example is shown in Fig. 3.1(a), where v_2 is similar to v_1, v_3, and v_4. However, v_1 is only similar to v_2.

3.2.2 Types of nodes

Neighboring nodes are classified as identical or relative first, to obtain the compact color signature next.

Identical nodes are two nodes v_{k_1}, v_{k_2} if they are connected by edges to the same nodes and also between each other:

1. $d\left(v_{k_1}, v_{k_2}\right) \leq \tau^{\mathrm{C1}}$

2. $\left\{v_k | d\left(v_k, v_{k_1}\right) \leq \tau^{\mathrm{C1}}\right\} \cup \left\{v_{k_1}\right\} = \left\{v_k | d\left(v_k, v_{k_2}\right) \leq \tau^{\mathrm{C1}}\right\} \cup \left\{v_{k_2}\right\}$.

Such nodes could be merged without exceeding the maximum allowed length per channel and without changing the similarity, and therefore edges, between the remaining nodes (see, e.g., v_3 and v_4 in Fig. 3.1(a)).

Relative nodes in the graph are nodes that are directly connected by an edge and are not of identical type (see, e.g., v_1 and v_2 in Fig. 3.1(a)).

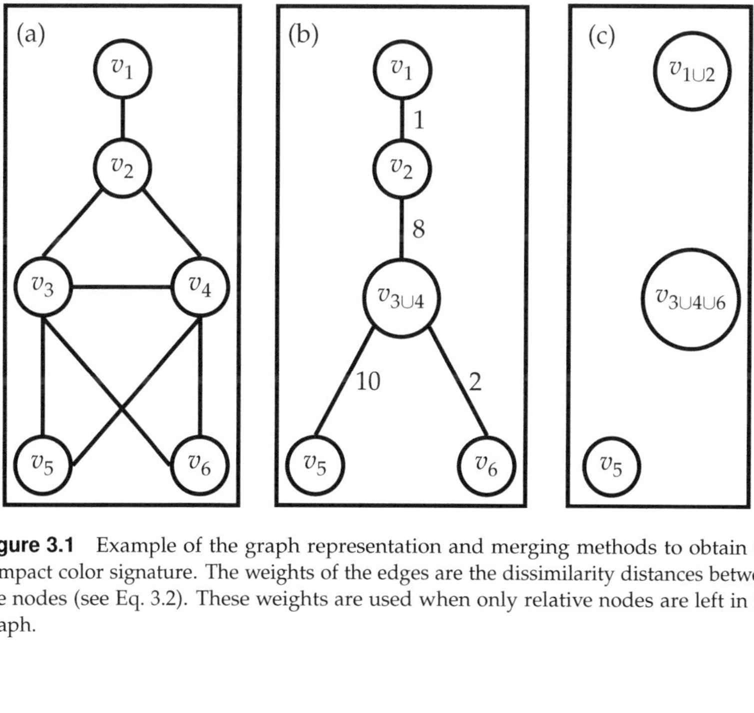

Figure 3.1 Example of the graph representation and merging methods to obtain the compact color signature. The weights of the edges are the dissimilarity distances between the nodes (see Eq. 3.2). These weights are used when only relative nodes are left in the graph.

3.2.3 Compact representation of the graph

As long as there are edges in the graph, nodes may be merged without violating the maximum size allowed per color subspace. Because of this, the graph is processed until it consists of isolated nodes.

Pairs of identical nodes v_{k_1}, v_{k_2} are merged first until no more identical nodes are left in the graph. Per pair of identical nodes merged, a new node $v_{k_1 \cup k_2}$ is created whose limits in color space are the extrema of the merged pairs:

$$\begin{aligned} l^{*min}_{k_1 \cup k_2} &= \min\left(l^{*min}_{k_1}, l^{*min}_{k_2}\right) & l^{*max}_{k_1 \cup k_2} &= \max\left(l^{*min}_{k_1}, l^{*max}_{k_2}\right) \\ a^{*min}_{k_1 \cup k_2} &= \min\left(a^{*min}_{k_1}, a^{*min}_{k_2}\right) & a^{*max}_{k_1 \cup k_2} &= \max\left(a^{*min}_{k_1}, a^{*max}_{k_2}\right) \\ b^{*min}_{k_1 \cup k_2} &= \min\left(b^{*min}_{k_1}, b^{*min}_{k_2}\right) & b^{*max}_{k_1 \cup k_2} &= \max\left(b^{*min}_{k_1}, b^{*max}_{k_2}\right). \end{aligned} \quad (3.3)$$

This step is exemplified in Fig. 3.1(a)-(b) (the weights of the edges are explained next).

Once all identical nodes have been merged, the relative nodes are processed and merged. An adequate selection of the relative nodes that are going to be merged is very important, as it will change the similarity relations of the spanned color subspaces. For example, in Fig. 3.1(b) if v_1 is merged with v_2, then the new node will not be similar with $v_{3 \cup 4}$ anymore. To select adequate merging pairs, the graph is extended to a weighted one (see Fig. 3.1(b)). The weights of the edges are obtained from the dissimilarity distance between the nodes (see Eq. 3.2). The number of nodes that can be reached directly via an edge is calculated for every pair of nodes. Iteratively the pair with the highest number of common nodes is merged. The boundaries in color space from the new node are calculated as in Eq. 3.3 and the edges in the graph are updated according to the similarity condition. In the case of the existence of many relative pairs with the highest number of relative nodes in common, then the pair with the smallest distance will be merged (see Fig. 3.1(c)).

3.2.4 Color signature of the image

The color signature of the image obtained via the *k*-d tree and the graph operations is formed from a color representative per node and its weight in the image. The color representative of each node is the mean color (calculated over the three color channels in CIELAB color space) from all pixels whose color values are in the spanned color subspace. However, the subspaces in color space spanned by the nodes may overlap. This is exemplified in Fig. 3.2 for two-dimensional subspaces. Points in the gray area are in the subspaces spanned by v_1 and $v_{2 \cup 3}$. Such points have been considered at the mean color calculation of all nodes to which they could belong.

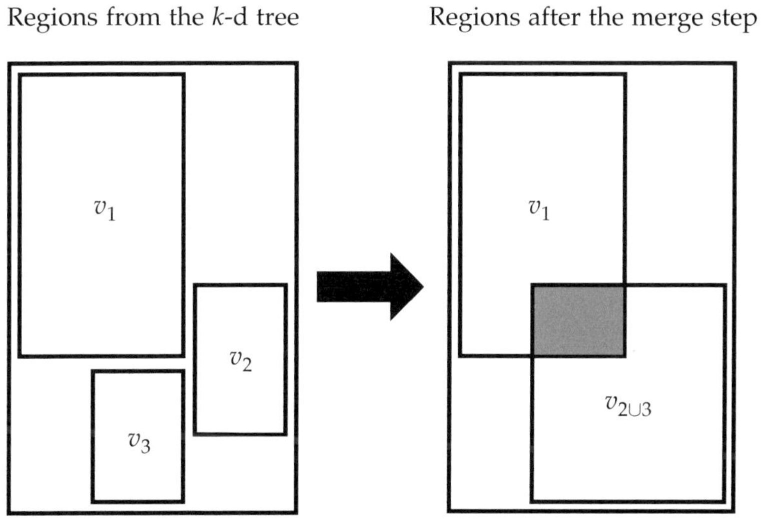

Figure 3.2 After merging two nodes the represented subspaces may overlap. Points in the gray area belong to v_1 and $v_{2\cup3}$.

Finally, the weight of each node is the percentage of pixels whose color values are closest to the mean color assigned to the node.

3.3 Humans' color categories

Due to the fact that the comparison of colors in the CIELAB color space is more reasonable for smaller color differences than for bigger ones [51], the representation of the color information via humans' color categories is considered in this section inspired by the psychological studies from Berlin and Kay [18], and Kay and Regier [75]. However, as the eleven basic color terms from the English language are insufficient to distinguish between shades, the extraction of representative humans' color categories is needed.

Here, the same database is processed as by Heer and Stone in [65] to extract the color categories. The database is online available [142] and consists of more than 3.4 million colors that have been named in an online survey by more than 145,000 subjects. Although it is not possible to assume that every monitor used for the survey was calibrated, the database is due to the high number of available answers important. In Sec. 3.3.1 the processing, followed in this thesis, of this database is presented, which differs from the one in [65]. Next, the method used to extract the representative humans' color categories from the processed database is explained in Sec. 3.3.2 followed by the presentation of the features used to represent color information via the extracted humans' color categories in Sec. 3.3.3. A preliminary version of this work has been presented in [160]. The extracted humans' color categories are shown in Sec. 8.2.2 and conclusions from the representation of the color using the humans' color categories can be drawn from the results from Sec. 8.5.

3.3.1 Processing the recorded database

The database [142] consists of more than 3.4 million colors sampled from the full RGB cube that were named by more than 145,000 subjects in an online survey. The subjects were asked to name a color displayed on their screens in a text input field. Any text answer was accepted and a subject could name as many colors as desired. However, the permission of all possible text answers also lead to misspellings (see Sec. 3.3.1.1) and spam answers (see Sec. 3.3.1.2) that should be handled first.

3.3.1.1 Editing of the color names

Consecutive space characters in the color names are merged into one first. Responses containing only special characters, less than three characters, or more than three words are removed from the database. Next, misspellings are corrected at some color names like *yyellow* or *gren*. The correction of all misspellings is not possible due to the big amount of responses and the ambiguity of some answers. For example, is *graen* green or gray?

3.3.1.2 Suppression of spam answers

After editing the color names, spam answers are suppressed. Swear-words, insults, and words with no color information as *not* or *asdf* are removed from the database. Like at the correction of misspellings, all disturbing answers cannot be removed due to the huge amount of data. However, 37.73 % of the color names in the database are removed by the editing and the suppression of disturbing words.

The responses from subjects that named almost all colors with the same color name are considered as spam and removed from the database. To detect such subjects, the number of different color names $n^{C,1}$ they used is compared to the total number of colors $n^{C,2}$ that they named. If

$$n^{C,1} < \left(n^{C,2}\right)^{\frac{1}{3}} \quad (3.4)$$

applies, then all responses from the subject are removed from the database as they are considered spam answers. This relationship has been obtained empirically.

Furthermore, color names in the database that are named by a low number of different subjects are also considered as spam answers. Such color names are detected by comparing the number of times a color name has been used $n^{C,4}$ to the number of different subjects that used the color name $n^{C,3}$. If

$$n^{C,3} < \left(n^{C,4}\right)^{\frac{1}{3}} \quad (3.5)$$

applies, then the analyzed color name is considered as a spam answer and removed from the database. This relationship has also been obtained empirically.

As representative color names from the full RGB cube are searched, color names named less than τ^{C2} times are excluded from the database.

3.3.2 Extraction of the color categories

Humans' color categories are extracted from the valid remaining answers of the database. For this purpose, the color values are transformed into the CIELAB color space, as it is based on human color perception in contrast to the RGB color space (see Sec. 3.1.1). The quantization of the l^*- , a^*- and b^*-channels divides the color values into subspaces of the CIELAB color space. From the color names n^{C} and the color values v^{C} a color term matrix **T** is obtained as in [65]. The rows of **T** represent the different subspaces in CIELAB color space v^{C}, and the columns represent the remaining color names n^{C} in the database. Each element in $\mathbf{T}$ contains the number of color values in the database that belong to the color subspace v^{C} and that have been named with the color name n^{C}.

From $\mathbf{T}$ the probability distribution $p(n^{\mathrm{C}} | v^{\mathrm{C}})$ of a color name n^{C} given a color value from a zone in color space v^{C} is calculated as

$$p\left(n^{\mathrm{C}} \middle| v^{\mathrm{C}}\right) = \frac{t\left[v^{\mathrm{C}} n^{\mathrm{C}}\right]}{\sum_{n^{\mathrm{C}}} t\left[v^{\mathrm{C}} n^{\mathrm{C}}\right]}, \tag{3.6}$$

where $t\left[v^{\mathrm{C}} n^{\mathrm{C}}\right]$ is the element of $\mathbf{T}$ at the row v^{C} and at the column n^{C}. The most probable color names over the color subspaces considered in $\mathbf{T}$ are

$$q\left(v^{\mathrm{C}}\right) = \arg\max_{n^{\mathrm{C}}} p\left(n^{\mathrm{C}} \middle| v^{\mathrm{C}}\right). \tag{3.7}$$

The extracted humans' color categories $Q = \{q_1, \ldots, q_K\}$ are the unique color names from $q(v^{\mathrm{C}})$ over all color subspaces v^{C}.

3.3.3 Representation of color using the extracted color categories

Every color value of a pixel can be represented by the extracted humans' color categories q_k, $1 \leq k \leq K$. For this purpose, the color categories are represented via their mean colors $\boldsymbol{\mu}_k$ and covariance matrices $\boldsymbol{\Sigma}_k$. The values are calculated in CIELAB color space from all color values whose assigned names in the database coincide with the respective color category q_k. The likelihood of the color of a pixel to belong to a color category q_k is approximated here as

$$p(\mathbf{g_u} | q_k) = \frac{1}{\sqrt{(2\pi)^3 |\boldsymbol{\Sigma}_k|}} \cdot \exp\left[-\frac{1}{2}(\mathbf{g_u} - \boldsymbol{\mu}_k)^{\mathrm{T}} \boldsymbol{\Sigma}_k^{-1} (\mathbf{g_u} - \boldsymbol{\mu}_k)\right]. \tag{3.8}$$

The color value of a pixel in an image $\mathbf{g_u}$ using humans' color categories is represented by the normalized likelihoods

$$c_k^{\text{Color}}(\mathbf{g_u}) = \frac{p(\mathbf{g_u} | q_k)}{\sum_k p(\mathbf{g_u} | q_k)} \tag{3.9}$$

over the color categories. In some applications a vector representation may be preferable. It is easily obtained by considering each color category as a dimension:

$$\mathbf{c}^{\text{Color}}(\mathbf{g_u}) = \left(c_1^{\text{Color}} \quad , \ldots , \quad c_K^{\text{Color}}\right)^{\mathrm{T}} . \tag{3.10}$$

4 Shape

Disregarding objects and materials that do not have a defined shape (like liquids and gases), many objects and living beings exist that have a defined shape: books, cars, trees, planes, and the like. The objects of all of these classes have a roughly basic shape in common. Although the concrete shape in-between a class may vary, they are coarsely similar. The shape information is therefore an interesting feature for content-based image retrieval, which is the reason for considering it in this chapter.

An overall introduction to shape is given first in Sec. 4.1. For this purpose, the basic concepts of shape representation needed in this thesis are presented followed by an impression of the state of the art. Normal angular descriptors and Fourier descriptors are considered next in Secs. 4.2 and 4.3 for shape retrieval. Retrieval results achieved by the normal angular descriptors and the Fourier descriptors are presented in Sec. 8.3.

4.1 Introduction to shape

Although many objects and living beings in our environment have a defined shape, their corresponding shapes in images may vary slightly. There are many reasons for this. On the one hand we find reasons related to the nature of the objects and living beings, like articulated limbs, the adaptation to the environment, and the individualism inside the classes. On the other hand we find reasons related to the acquisition of the image. The projection of the three-dimensional world to a two-dimensional one involves, i.a., affine transformations [54, 107]. An appropriate representation of the shape information, appropriate features, and an appropriate similarity comparison of the features are necessary for a successful retrieval of shapes.

4.1.1 Shape representation

The contour of an object in an image is represented by the pixel coordinates that span the boundary. The order of the points in the sequence is given after sampling the contour at a starting point in a given direction $\mathbf{u}_1, \ldots, \mathbf{u}_K$ (see Fig. 4.1). Many methods exist to represent and encode shape information [41, 54, 107]. As the Fourier coefficients play an important role in this thesis, they are explained next.

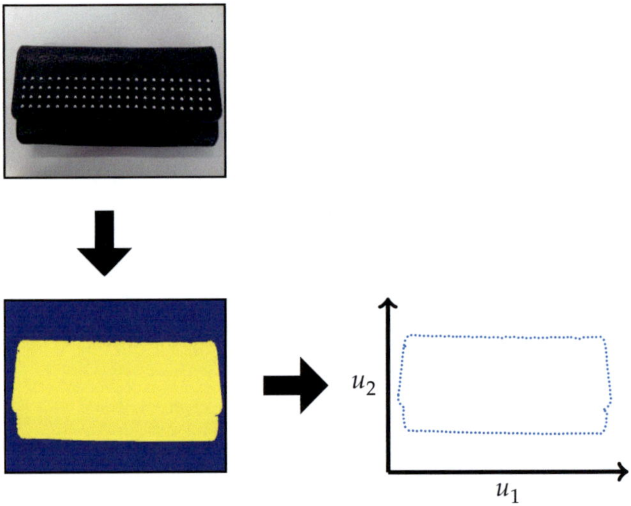

Figure 4.1 Shape representation in space domain.

A common way to represent shapes is using Fourier coefficients, which are obtained from a transformation of the pixel's coordinates [54]. Starting from the representation along the u_1, u_2 coordinates, every point $\mathbf{u}_k$ can be combined to a complex value z:

$$z_k = u_{1,k} + \mathrm{j}\, u_{2,k}, \tag{4.1}$$

where $\mathbf{u}_k = \begin{pmatrix} u_{1,k} & u_{2,k} \end{pmatrix}^{\mathrm{T}}$. The Fourier coefficients of the shape are obtained from the discrete Fourier transform of z (see upper row of Fig. 4.2):

$$
\begin{aligned}
Z_f &= \mathrm{DFT}\{z_k\} \\
&= \left|Z_f\right| \cdot \exp\left(\mathrm{j}\,\gamma_f\right),
\end{aligned}
\tag{4.2}
$$

where $-\frac{K}{2} \leq f < \frac{K}{2}$.

The Fourier coefficients possess important characteristics towards some shape transformations. If the size of an object changes, the space coordinates will change too. In the case of the Fourier coefficients their magnitude will be scaled over all frequencies by the same factor. However, the phase of the Fourier coefficients will be equal to the phase of the unscaled object (see the second row in Fig. 4.2). A rotation of an object implies a proportional change of the phase of the Fourier coefficients, but the magnitude will not change compared to the unrotated shape (see the third row in Fig. 4.2). Finally, if the starting point used to represent the coordinates of the shape is changed, the phase of the Fourier descriptors will change linearly compared to the representation with the original starting point. However, as in the case of the rotated shape, the magnitude of the Fourier descriptors will remain equal to the magnitude of the descriptors with the original starting point (see the bottom row in Fig. 4.2).

4.1.2 State of the art

The sorting of shapes has been studied by many researchers over the last years. Overviews can be found in [143, 149]. The proposed methods can be roughly classified into two groups depending on the way that the describing features of the shapes are extracted. These ones can be region-based, where the features are extracted from the object's area, or contour-based, which are extracted from the object's boundary [149].

Gupta and Srinath propose in [60] the classification of closed planar shapes using moments. The shapes are represented by the distances from their points along the contour to the centroids of the respective shape. From this shape representation moments are extracted which are used to classify shapes into groups. A method for shape retrieval based on grids is proposed by Sajjanhar and Lu in [124].

The use of histograms to obtain appropriate features has also been studied, e.g., in [16, 90]. Belongie et al. propose shape contexts in [16].

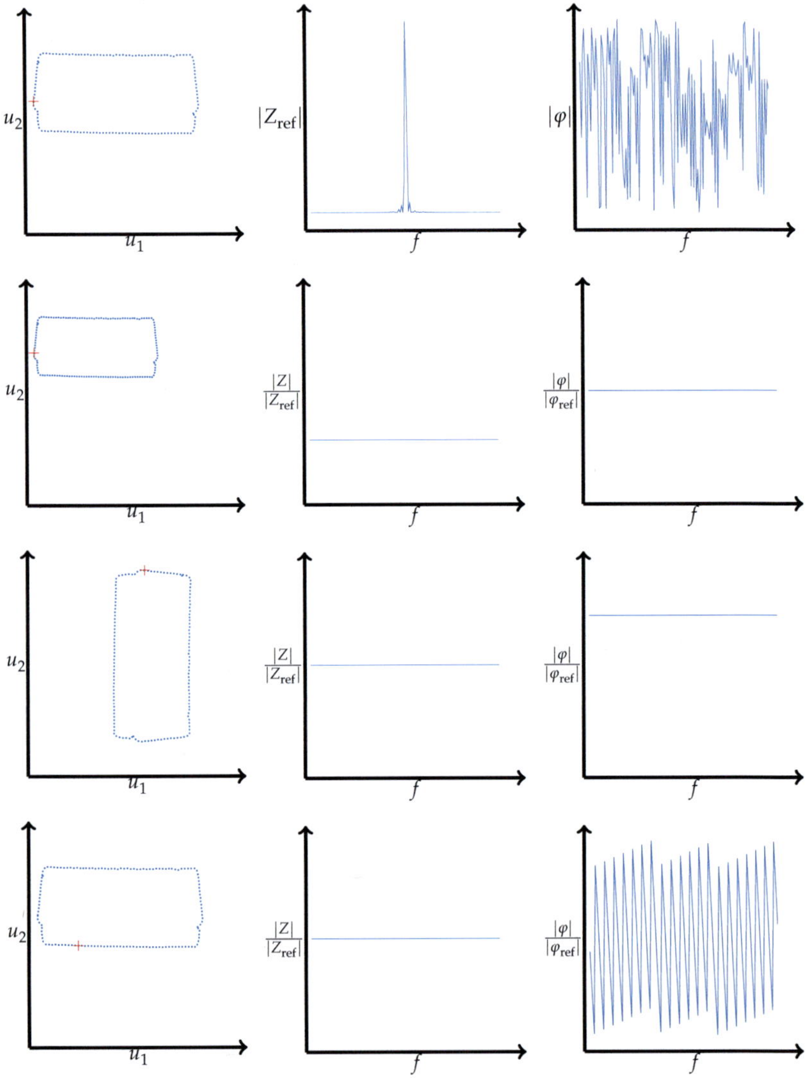

Figure 4.2 Fourier coefficients underlying affine transformations. The reference contour with its magnitude of its Fourier coefficients and phase are displayed in the first row. The starting point is marked in red.

The shape context of a point is a histogram of the boundary points in its neighborhood that depends on their proximity and angle. Mahmoudi et al. propose the edge orientation autocorrelogram, which is a histogram obtained from the most prominent edges in an image, in [90]. This histogram contains the number of edges with a similar orientation depending on their distances.

From a description of the boundary with some of its points, Latecki and Lakämper use the relative angle between the points and their distances as a feature in [81]. Petrakis et al. propose in [118] an approach that enables the comparison of open and closed shapes. Via dynamic programming two shapes are compared, which are divided first into concave and convex segments. Angular patterns and binary angular patterns are proposed by Hu et al. in [67]. For this purpose, the angles spanned by adjacent points along the boundary are calculated. Higher scales are considered by calculating the angles between adjacent points placed farther away. From the comparison of the magnitudes of the angles, a sort of local binary pattern for angles is built, which is used for shape retrieval.

Mokhtarian et al. consider a curvature scale space representation of shapes [105] to obtain information for shape retrieval in [103, 104]. The curvature scale space enables the description of the shape with different levels of detail.

Several researchers have studied the potential of the Fourier transform of shapes' signatures for retrieval purposes. Zhang and Lu consider different signatures for shape representation in [146], from which they calculate the Fourier transform. With the help of the Euclidean distance function the transformed signatures of the shapes are compared and sorted in a second step. In [150] Zhang and Lu give a more exhaustive evaluation about Fourier description methods. Fourier descriptors invariant to scale, rotation, and translation are proposed by Burkhardt in [25]. Affine-invariant Fourier descriptors, which are also shear-invariant, are proposed by Burkhardt et al. in [26]. Bartolini et al. also use Fourier descriptors for shape retrieval in [13]. However, in their work the features are transformed back into space domain for comparison purposes. A distance is used which considers that corresponding segments of different objects may vary on their length. Zhang and Lu propose and use the generic Fourier descriptor in [147, 148], which is a region-based Fourier descriptor.

4.2 Normal angular descriptors

The angles from the normal vectors along the contour of the shape are considered in this thesis for shape retrieval. For this purpose, the normal angular descriptor is extracted first from the analyzed shape (Sec. 4.2.1) and compared to the normal angular descriptors of other shapes next (Sec. 4.2.2). To this end, three different comparisons for the normal angular descriptors are presented. A preliminary version of this work has been presented in [157, 158].

4.2.1 Normal angular descriptor

The normal vectors $\mathbf{n}$ of a shape are calculated via the following relation:

$$\mathbf{n}_k = \begin{pmatrix} -\left(u_{2,k+1} - u_{2,k}\right) \\ u_{1,k+1} - u_{1,k} \end{pmatrix}. \tag{4.3}$$

The normal angular descriptor of a shape is obtained from the angles of the normal vectors along the shape:

$$\eta_k = \measuredangle \mathbf{n}_k. \tag{4.4}$$

These descriptors possess interesting characteristics towards some image transformations. The descriptors are invariant to a change of the shape's size (compare the diagrams in the first and second row of Fig. 4.3). Rotations of the object imply an offset over the angles compared to the descriptors of the unrotated shape (compare the diagrams in the first and third row of Fig. 4.3). If the starting point is changed when the shape is sampled, then the descriptor is circular shifted along the k axis in comparison with the descriptor of the originally sampled shape (compare the diagrams in the first and fourth row of Fig. 4.3).

4.2.2 Similarity comparisons

Three different distances, presented in [157] and [158], are explained in the following Secs. 4.2.2.1 and 4.2.2.2 to measure the similarity between shapes using normal angular descriptors. In Sec. 4.2.2.2 the descriptors compared are aligned first into each other before their similarity distance is calculated, and two different distances are presented.

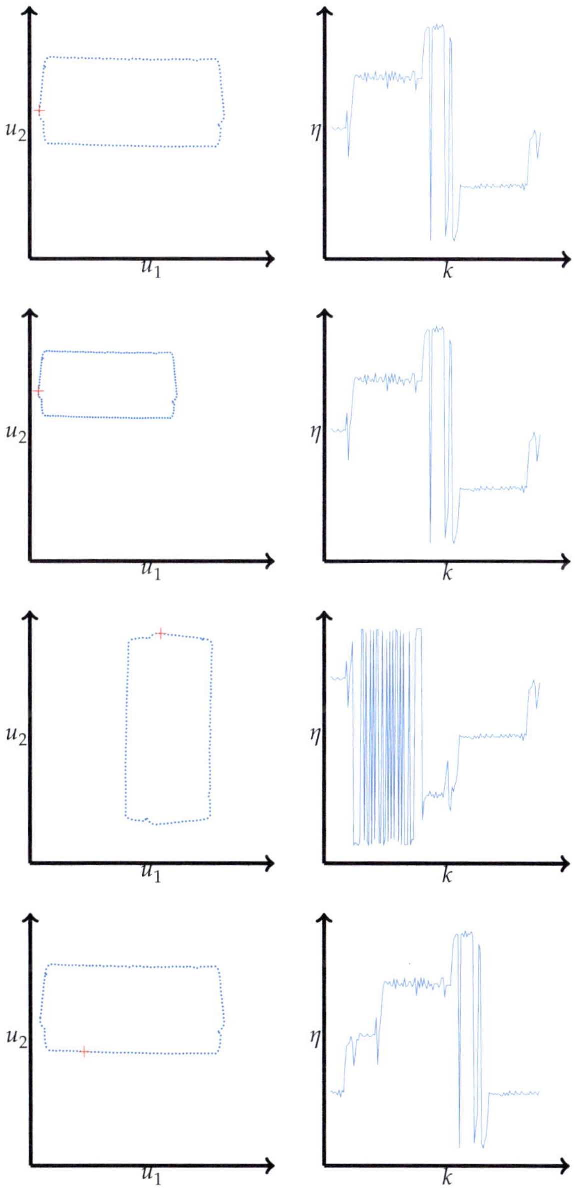

Figure 4.3 Normal angular descriptors underlying affine transformations.

4.2.2.1 Similarity distance based on the correlation for circular data for unwarped normal angular descriptors

Due to the fact that the rotation of the shape implies an offset over the normal angular descriptor values, the comparison via a correlation function should be invariant to rotations. As the normal angular descriptor values are circular data (from 0 to 2π), the correlation for circular data proposed by Fisher and Lee [49] and explained in Sec. 2.1 is used here.

The similarity value of the correlation will vary depending on the starting points of the compared normal angular descriptors $\eta^{\mathrm{I}}, \eta^{\mathrm{O}}$. To overcome this issue, the circular correlation is computed K times, comparing each time the angular descriptors of the input shape η^{I} with the angular descriptors of the compared shape η^{O} shifted by one along the k axis. The similarity value is the maximum over all shifted comparisons:

$$\rho\left(\eta_k^{\mathrm{I}}, \eta_{k+\Delta k}^{\mathrm{O}}\right) = \max_h \rho\left(\eta_k^{\mathrm{I}}, \eta_{(k+h)}^{\mathrm{O}}\right), \; 0 \leq h \leq K-1. \tag{4.5}$$

The similarity distance between the compared shapes is finally given as

$$d_1^{\mathrm{NAD}} = 1 - \rho\left(\eta_k^{\mathrm{I}}, \eta_{k+\Delta k}^{\mathrm{O}}\right). \tag{4.6}$$

4.2.2.2 Similarity distances for warped normal angular descriptors

If normal angular descriptors of similar objects are compared, similar segments will be recognized at the descriptors (see the diagrams in the two upper rows of Fig. 4.4). The length of such segments is object dependent and may be different between the descriptors. This fact may involve huge differences when the similarity between the descriptors is compared, so that the objects may not be appreciated as similar anymore by the comparing system.

The comparison of signals with similar segments of different lengths is a well known problem in speech processing [58], solved by aligning the segments of the signals to each other, adapting hereby the lengths of the segments. Such warping can be solved using dynamic programming [125].

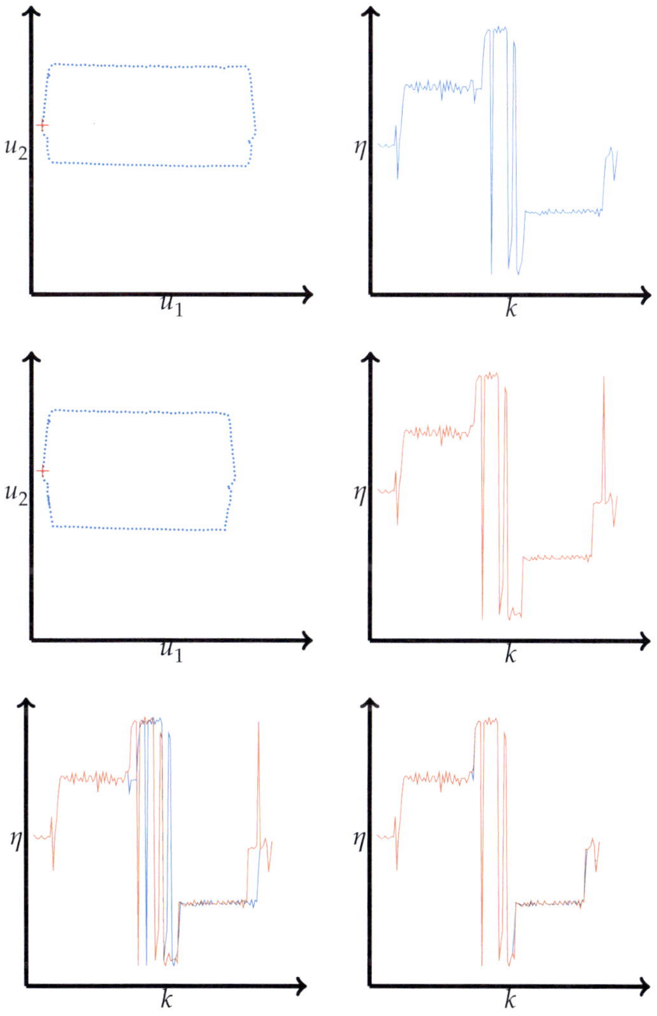

Figure 4.4 Alignment of normal angular descriptors.

Equivalent to speech processing, the normal angular descriptors are treated as non-circular features first and the values that can be projected into each other are calculated using dynamic programming. However, as a cyclic displacement along the k axis may occur due to a different starting point, the circular shift between the angular descriptors of the compared features must be calculated before aligning the features into each other (bottom left diagram in Fig. 4.4). For this purpose, the cyclic shift Δk along the k axis between the compared features is calculated first using the correlation for circular data proposed by Fisher and Lee [49] and explained in Sec. 2.1:

$$\rho\left(\eta_k^{\mathrm{I}}, \eta_{k+\Delta k}^{\mathrm{O}}\right) = \max_h \rho\left(\eta_k^{\mathrm{I}}, \eta_{k+h}^{\mathrm{O}}\right). \tag{4.7}$$

The aligned descriptors $\tilde{\eta}_{k_1}^{\mathrm{I}}$ and $\tilde{\eta}_{k_1}^{\mathrm{O}}, 1 \le k_1 \le K_1, 1 \le K_1 \le K$, are finally calculated from η_k^{I} and $\eta_{k+\Delta k}^{\mathrm{O}}$ and are ready to be compared (bottom right diagram of Fig. 4.4).

The **comparison via the correlation for circular data** is considered first. The similarity distance between $\tilde{\eta}_{k_1}^{\mathrm{I}}$ and $\tilde{\eta}_{k_1}^{\mathrm{O}}$ can be obtained as in Sec. 4.2.2.1 using the correlation for circular data:

$$d_2^{\mathrm{NAD}} = 1 - \rho\left(\tilde{\eta}_{k_1}^{\mathrm{I}}, \tilde{\eta}_{k_1}^{\mathrm{O}}\right). \tag{4.8}$$

The **comparison based on the Euclidean distance** (see Sec. 2.1) is also considered as a similarity distance. This was presented in [158] to compare $\tilde{\eta}_{k_1}^{\mathrm{I}}$ and $\tilde{\eta}_{k_1}^{\mathrm{O}}$, and it is inspired by [9]:

$$d_3^{\mathrm{NAD}} = \frac{\sum\limits_{k_1} \left(\tilde{\eta}_{k_1}^{\mathrm{I}} - \tilde{\eta}_{k_1}^{\mathrm{O}} + \theta\right)^2}{K_1}, \tag{4.9}$$

where θ is calculated as

$$\theta = \frac{\sum\limits_{k_1} \tilde{\eta}_{k_1}^{\mathrm{O}} - \tilde{\eta}_{k_1}^{\mathrm{I}}}{K_1}. \tag{4.10}$$

4.3 Fourier descriptors

The Fourier descriptors presented in the following Sections 4.3.1 – 4.3.3 are based on the extracted Fourier coefficients of the contour and were used in [157] and [158]. They are used to compare the normal angular descriptors with descriptors extracted from the established Fourier coefficients (see Sec. 4.1.1).

The similarity distance between the Fourier descriptors f_f^{Fourier} of two objects is calculated using the ℓ_2-norm (see Sec. 2.1):

$$d^{\text{Fourier}} = \left\| f_f^{\text{Fourier,I}} - f_f^{\text{Fourier,O}} \right\|_2 . \tag{4.11}$$

4.3.1 Scaling-invariant descriptor

If the magnitudes of the Fourier coefficients of the input object are divided by the magnitude at any determined position p, then a scaling-invariant Fourier descriptor is obtained, as the proportional factor implied by the scale is suppressed (see Sec. 4.1.1):

$$f_{1,f}^{\text{Fourier}} = \frac{\left|Z_f\right|}{\left|Z_p\right|} \cdot \exp\left(\mathrm{j}\,\gamma_f\right) . \tag{4.12}$$

4.3.2 Descriptor with normalized energy

Fourier descriptors with normalized energy are obtained here from the original Fourier coefficients, by dividing its magnitudes by their energy:

$$f_{2,f}^{\text{Fourier}} = \frac{\left|Z_f\right|}{\sum_f \left|Z_f\right|} \cdot \exp\left(\mathrm{j}\,\gamma_f\right) . \tag{4.13}$$

4.3.3 Scaling- and rotation-invariant descriptor

Scaling- and rotation-invariant descriptors are extracted here as in [25]:

$$f_{3,f}^{\text{Fourier}} = \frac{\left|Z_f\right|}{\left|Z_q\right|} \cdot \exp\left(\mathrm{j}\left[\gamma_f + \alpha\gamma_r - \beta\gamma_q\right]\right) , \tag{4.14}$$

where α, β, and r are defined as

$$\alpha = \frac{q-f}{r-q},\ \beta = \frac{r-f}{r-q},$$
$$r = q + s,\ q \in \mathbb{N}_+ . \tag{4.15}$$

s is the desired rotation symmetry of the object. To define the parameter q, three options are tested:

1. $q = 1$,
2. $q = p,\ \left|Z_p\right| = \max_f \left|Z_f\right|,\ p \in \mathbb{N}_+$,
3. $q = p,\ \left|Z_p\right| = \max_f \left|Z_f\right|,\ p \in \mathbb{Z}$.

Please note that although $q \in \mathbb{N}_+$ is expected in [25], $q \in \mathbb{Z}$ is allowed in the third option.

5 Texture

If we take a look at our environment, we will see that we are surrounded by textures everywhere. We find textures, e.g., at textiles, buildings, tilings, and the surfaces of skins and objects. Because textures are so common in our lives and they also describe many specific information (e.g., at surfaces), its use as a feature for the content-based image retrieval is considered in this chapter.

A brief introduction to textures including its types and an overview of the state of the art is given in Sec. 5.1. The analysis, detection, and sorting of regular textures is then considered in Sec. 5.2 together with the procedure followed to extract a perception map of regular textures from an experiment executed with subjects. As near-regular textures are more common in digital images than perfectly regular textures, the extraction of regular textures from near-regular ones is considered in Sec. 5.3. The results of the methods presented along this chapter are shown in Sec. 8.4.

5.1 Introduction to texture

Although we can easily recognize textures in a visual way, it is really hard to define them using words [19, 20, 41, 51, 54, 107]. In the next section 5.1.1 a classification of types of texture is given. Section 5.1.2 gives an overview of methods proposed in the literature to describe textures' information and to classify and sort them.

5.1.1 Texture representation

Textures can easily be classified into two groups: regular and irregular ones [20, 41, 107]. However, there is not a clear boundary between both groups (see Fig. 5.1) [20, 41].

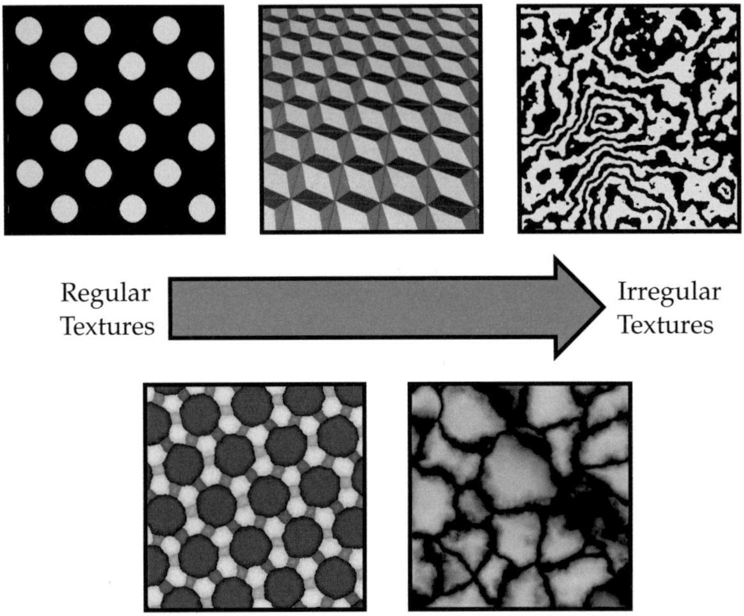

Figure 5.1 Types of textures.

Regular textures are also called structural textures [20]. They have an element called texel, which is placed all over the image at equal distances. The positions where the texels appear form a grid or also called lattice. The lattice is completely described by the displacement vectors, as the texels appear at multiple combinations of the displacement vectors.

Mathematically, each regular texture is described by a texel $t(\mathbf{x})$ and its displacement vectors $\mathbf{a}$ (in case of one-dimensional textures), $\mathbf{a}_k$, $k = 1, 2$ (for two-dimensional textures) [20]:

$$g(\mathbf{u}) = \begin{cases} t(\mathbf{u}) * \sum\limits_{k \in \mathbb{Z}} \delta(\mathbf{u} - k\mathbf{a}) & \text{for 1-D textures} \\ t(\mathbf{u}) ** \sum\limits_{(k_1, k_2) \in \mathbb{Z}^2} \delta(\mathbf{u} - k_1\mathbf{a}_1 - k_2\mathbf{a}_2) & \text{for 2-D textures.} \end{cases} \tag{5.1}$$

However, there is not a unique valid texel per regular texture. In the case of two dimensional textures, different pairs of displacement vectors may describe a valid lattice (see Fig. 5.2).

Structural-statistical textures also possess a texel and displacement vectors, but both characteristics may vary along the image bringing some irregularities [20]. The texel may vary due to, e.g., different brightening conditions along the image. The displacement vectors may also vary along the lattice due to, e.g., the projection of the three-dimensional space onto the two-dimensional image plain. However, no physical explanation may always be possible for the irregularities at structural-statistical textures.

Near-regular textures form a subgroup of the structural-statistical textures. Near-regular textures are textures with small variations of the displacement vectors and/or the texels [86], e.g., when a regular texture is placed over the three dimensional surface of an object. Although in the three-dimensional world every texel has the same distance to each other, in the image domain, due to the loss of the third dimension and different lighting conditions, the texture doesn't appear perfectly regular anymore. These kinds of textures are specially considered in Sec. 5.3.

Irregular textures, or also named statistical textures, are obtained when the irregularities of the texels and the displacement vectors along the image get bigger. In this case the textures will become more irregular until we arrive at completely irregular textures where not even the texels and the displacement vectors can be recognized [20].

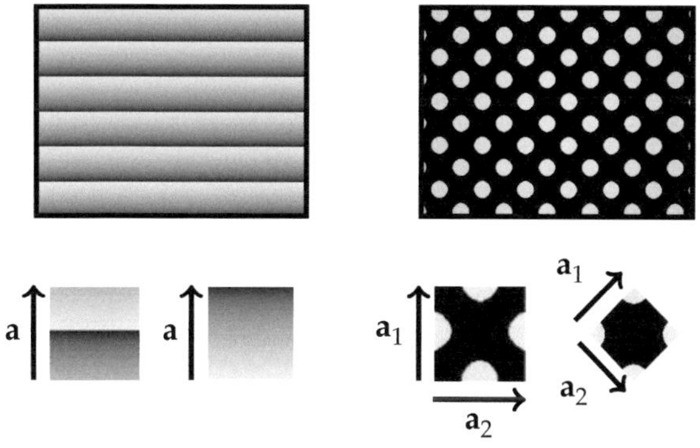

Figure 5.2 Properties of regular textures.

5.1.2 State of the art

Many methods have been proposed to sort textures. For this purpose, features are extracted from the image itself, or a modified version from it. Some features are extracted in space domain, while others are extracted in the space-frequency domain. Depending on the domain where the features are extracted, the methods can be roughly classified into two groups.

Gabor wavelets are commonly used to extract texture features in space-frequency domain. Manjunath and Ma propose in [92] a strategy to reduce the redundancy implied by Gabor wavelets. Furthermore, they propose a texture feature based on the information derived from the transformation with the Gabor wavelets and applied it to image retrieval. However, their proposed feature is not rotation invariant. This is considered by Zhang et al. in [151]. An overview and comparison over different texture features extracted from the information delivered by the Gabor wavelets can be found in [34]. Furthermore, the extraction of texture features based on the transformations achieved by the Gabor wavelets is also combined with the color information of the input image in [91, 106]. The Radon transform [20] combined with the wavelet transform is considered to analyze textures in [70, 71]. Based on the Radon transform and the wavelet transform, the ridgelet transform [27] has also won interest to analyze images, as it can deal better with edges. Do and Vetterli propose therefore the finite ridgelet transform for image representation in [44], whereas Gonde et al. use the ridgelet transform to extract features for content-based image retrieval purposes in [53]. Zhang et al. consider in [152] the curvelet transform, which they describe as an extension of the ridgelet transform, to extract rotation invariant features for region-based image retrieval.

On the other hand, many methods have also been proposed to extract features describing the characteristics of textures in space domain. Masotti and Campanini perform first the ranklet transform of the images to extract their features, which they use to classify textures in [95]. Afifi and Ashour combine features that represent the color information of the images with texture features extracted from the ranklet transform of the gray-level images in [4]. In [5] Afifi and Ashour extract only color features from the images, but as a pre-processing step they apply the ranklet transform to each color channel of the analyzed image. Several researchers have considered motifs to extract texture features [10, 72, 83, 129]. For this purpose, the input image is divided into 2×2 grids. Different motifs are assigned to the grids depending on the distribution of the intensity. Liu et al. extract in [85] texture features to sort the images according to their texton images. Ojala et al. propose in [110] local binary patterns for texture classification, whereas Ahonen et al. widen in [6] the local binary patterns to Fourier features also to classify textures.

Lin et al. concentrate in [84] in the retrieval of regular textures. For this purpose, two valid displacement vectors of the input texture are extracted with the help of the autocorrelation of the image. With the detected displacement vectors a parallelogram is spanned that describes a valid texel of the image. Five features are then extracted from the co-occurrence matrices of the detected texel to describe statistical components of the image. These features are used to sort the regular textures in the database.

However, perfectly regular textures are seldom found in images. Near-regular textures are more common. The detection of near-regular textures and the extraction of their appearance model is a challenging task with many application fields like geo-tagging [126] and texture sythesis [66, 86]. Liu et al. represent near-regular textures as a decomposition of geometric deformations, lighting variations, and color changes in [86]. Once the synthesis information of a near-regular texture has been extracted, new ones are created by replacing the texel information but maintaining all other extracted characteristics. However, in their work the interaction with a user is necessary. The user must give a pair of displacement vectors and adapt the lattice created from the two displacement vectors to the irregularities of the near-regular texture. Interest point or region detectors are used to automatically extract the regular texture information without the interaction with a user. Hays et al. propose in [64] the use of the MSER detector [96] to detect interest points and a cross-correlation method in case that the detected points are not enough to extract the characteristics of the near-regular textures. Schindler et al. extract SIFT features [88, 89] first and group them according to the similarity of their descriptors into N groups in [126]. As the features of the points in a group are similar, each group should contain points that span valid texels and are placed along the analyzed near-regular texture at positions with a similar environment.

Interest points extracted via a corner detector are used by Park et al. in [115]. These ones are clustered into groups of similar points using mean-shift [33, 35, 52], which has the advantage that no number of clusters must be defined in advance. However, in their work they use a window of fixed size along the detected interest points to extract the information of their environment, without considering changes due to scale and orientation. Hilsmann et al. combine the SIFT features with the mean-shift approach to automatically divide them into groups in [66]. The lattice of the analyzed near-regular texture is searched in their work starting from three neighboring characteristic points whose vectors are L-shaped. They are expanded to a lattice next.

5.2 Analysis, detection, and sorting of regular textures

As we can easily classify textures into regular and irregular ones, in this thesis the sorting of textures according to their type is considered. Although many features have been proposed in the literature to compare textures independently of their type, features adapted to the type of texture are not so common or even missing. Specially for regular textures many comparisons could be made from the two elements that describe it completely: the displacement vectors and the texel. Because of this, the focus is set on the detection of regular textures first (see Sec. 5.2.2), followed by the sorting of these type of textures (see Sec. 5.2.3). For this purpose, adapted features of regular textures are proposed that enable a direct comparison from properties of the textures like, e.g., their sizes, rotations, or structures appearing in their texels. A preliminary version of this work has been presented in [155].

Although many features can be presented to compare textures and sort them according to their similarity, the evaluation of their potential is a challenging task. The perception of similarity by humans is non-metric and subject dependent. However, signs of what is perceived by humans are necessary to be able to evaluate the proposed methods, implement new ones, and improve them. In Sec. 5.2.4 the extraction of a perception map of regular textures is therefore considered.

5.2.1 Extraction of the texel and its displacement vectors

Regular textures are completely described by a texel and its displacement vectors. In an idealized case we can consider the texture as continuous and of infinite extent in the space domain. The extraction of the texel and its displacement vectors in this idealized case is considered in Sec. 5.2.1.1. However, real images are discrete and limited in the space domain, which is why the extraction is considered for the real case in Sec. 5.2.1.2.

5.2.1.1 Ideal case

The properties of regular textures from the Fourier transform can be used to extract the displacement vectors of a regular texture [20]:

$$G(\mathbf{f}) \propto \begin{cases} T(\mathbf{f}) \sum\limits_{k\in\mathbb{Z}} \delta(\mathbf{f} - k\mathbf{l}_1) \cdot 1(\tilde{\mathbf{l}}) & \text{for 1-D textures, } \mathbf{l}_1 \perp \tilde{\mathbf{l}} \\ T(\mathbf{f}) \sum\limits_{(k_1,k_2)\in\mathbb{Z}^2} \delta(\mathbf{f} - k_1\mathbf{l}_1 - k_2\mathbf{l}_2) & \text{for 2-D textures.} \end{cases} \tag{5.2}$$

The convolution of the texel with the Dirac impulses at multiples of the displacement vectors in space domain (see Eq. 5.1) becomes a multiplication in frequency domain. The energy of the texture is therefore expected at multiples of the displacement vectors $\mathbf{l}$ (1-dimensional texture), $\mathbf{l}_k$, $k = 1, 2$ (2-dimensional texture), in frequency domain (see Fig. 5.3).

The relationship between the displacement vectors in space and frequency domain for two-dimensional textures is [20]

$$(\mathbf{a}_1, \mathbf{a}_2) = \begin{pmatrix} \mathbf{l}_1^{\mathrm{T}} \\ \mathbf{l}_2^{\mathrm{T}} \end{pmatrix}^{-1}. \tag{5.3}$$

To obtain the displacement vector of a one-dimensional texture in space domain from its corresponding displacement vector in frequency domain, an inversion of the vector's length is necessary, due to the properties of the Fourier transform:

$$\mathbf{a} = \frac{1}{\|\mathbf{l}\|^2} \cdot \mathbf{l}. \tag{5.4}$$

The concentration of the energy of the Fourier transform at Dirac impulses, placed at multiple combinations of the displacement vectors $\mathbf{l}$ (for 1-dimensional textures), $\mathbf{l}_k$, $k = 1,2$ (in case of 2-dimensional textures), makes an extraction of the displacement vectors easier than in space domain. Two bigger maxima are expected in $|G(\mathbf{f})|$ in case of two-dimensional regular textures, and one maximum is expected for a one-dimensional regular texture. The angles of the vectors are calculated from the radial projection of the magnitude of the Fourier spectrum $G(r, \varphi)$, considering frequencies along the f_2 coordinate and only the positive f_1 coordinate, as $|G(\mathbf{f})|$ is centrally symmetric. Due to the fact that higher energies are expected at lines with the same orientation as the displacement vectors and their linear combinations, the magnitude of the Fourier transform is integrated over all radii r per angle φ for the considered interval:

$$m(\varphi) = \int |G(r, \varphi)| \, \mathrm{d}r. \tag{5.5}$$

Local maxima are expected in $m(\varphi)$ at the orientations of the angles of the displacement vectors and their combinations. In case of a one-dimensional texture only one peak is expected at the angle of the displacement vector. On the other hand, in case of two-dimensional regular textures several local maxima may appear in $m(\varphi)$. The two angles of the displacement vectors are the ones that are local maxima in $m(\varphi)$ and possess the higher magnitude in $G(\mathbf{f})$ along its corresponding radial projection. This process is shown in Fig. 5.4 for the two-dimensional regular texture of Fig. 5.3.

The length of the displacement vectors is obtained from the maxima along the lines derived as radial projection of $G(\mathbf{f})$ with the orientations of the displacement vectors. The distance from the origin to the first considerable maximum is the length of the considered vector. Once the displacement vectors in frequency domain $\mathbf{l}_k$ have been extracted, the displacement vectors in space domain $\mathbf{a}_k$ are calculated via Eq. 5.3. In case of one-dimensional textures the displacement vector $\mathbf{a}$ is calculated via Eq. 5.4 from the extracted displacement vector $\mathbf{l}$ in frequency domain.

A valid texel $t(\mathbf{u})$ from the regular texture is finally extracted from the parallelogram spanned by the displacement vectors in space domain. In case of a one-dimensional regular texture the second vector $\tilde{\mathbf{a}}$ used to span the parallelogram is a vector orthogonal to the displacement vector $\mathbf{a}$.

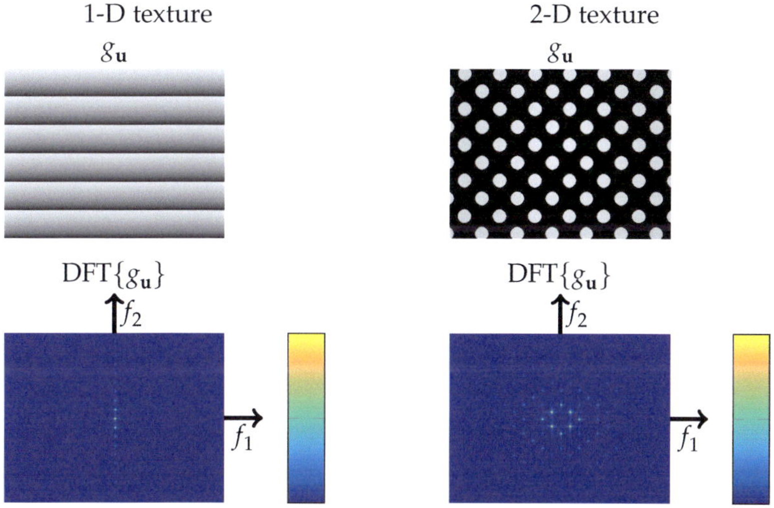

Figure 5.3 Properties of regular textures. The magnitudes of the Fourier transforms (lower row) are represented with pseudo-colors whose varying ranges are shown on the right of each plot.

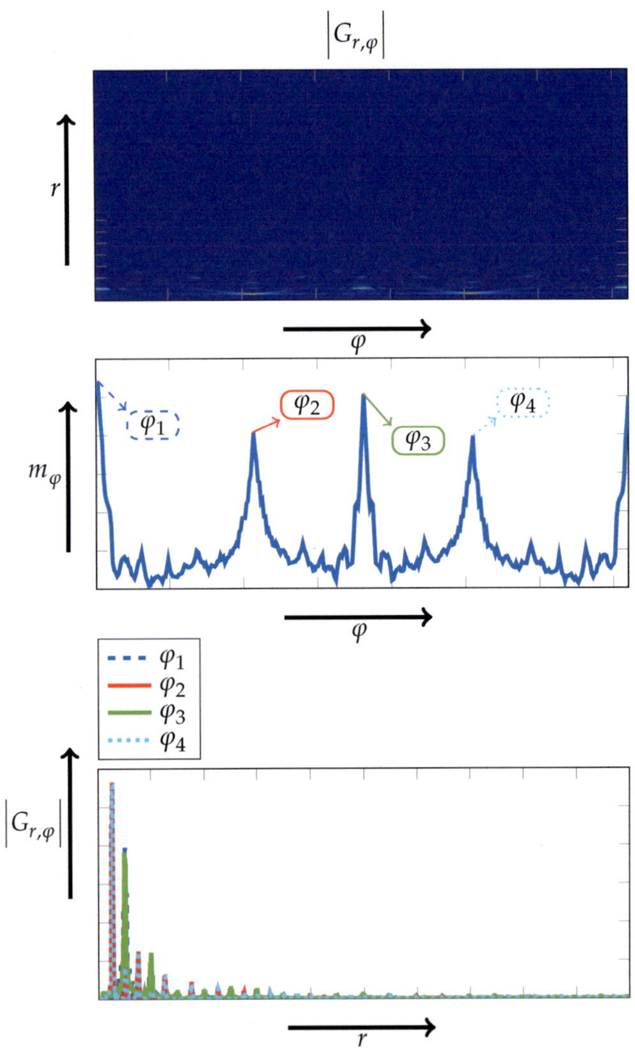

Figure 5.4 Properties of regular textures. $|G(r,\varphi)|$ (upper row) is represented with pseudo-colors.

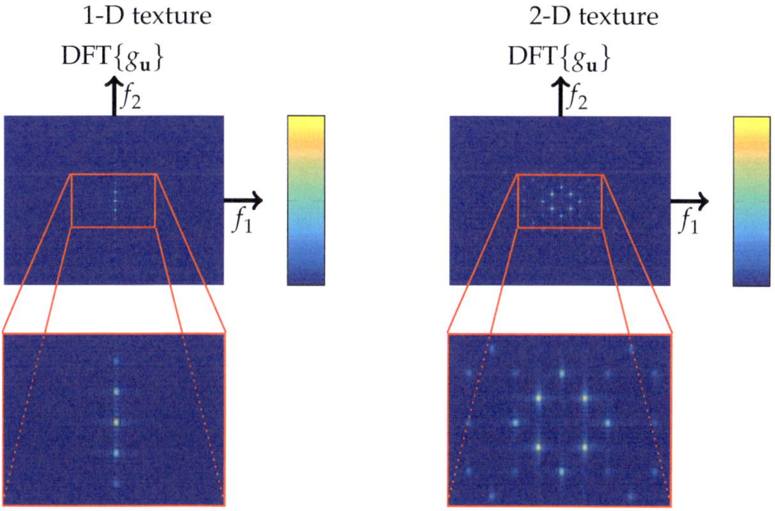

Figure 5.5 Detailed view of the magnitude of the Fourier transforms, represented with pseudo-colors, from Fig. 5.3. The varying ranges of the pseudo-colors are shown on the right of the upper plots.

5.2.1.2 Spectral leakage and discretization in the real case

Due to the fact that real images are discrete and limited in the space domain, spectral leakage and discretization errors have to be considered (observe that in Fig. 5.5 the energies do not appear at exact one point as it is expected from Dirac impulses, but they are blurred). Such kind of errors will distort the extraction of the displacement vectors and therefore also the extraction of the texel in the image. Perfectly regular textures are seldom found in real images due to, i.a., lighting variations and rounding errors at the discretization of linear combinations of the displacement vectors. Some of the alterations may be so small that they may not be noticed at a first glance. Furthermore, as explained in Sec. 5.1.1, there is no clear boundary between the types of textures. In this work, textures with insignificantly varying displacement vectors are considered as regular textures. Small stochastic changes of the texel representation due to, e.g., lighting conditions or varying boundaries are, however, allowed (see Fig. 5.6).

As the exact deterministic repetition of one unique texel over the whole image is not expected at real images, two texels are extracted per input image. The parallelograms spanned by the displacement vectors are a valid template of the area of the texels in the image. The first extracted texel $\overline{t_{\mathbf{u}}}$ is the mean texel from all the extracted ones in the image if the image is completely covered by repetitions of the template without them overlapping. The second considered texel $t_{\mathbf{u}}^{\mathrm{Det}}$ is the one extracted from only one template placed at one position in the image.

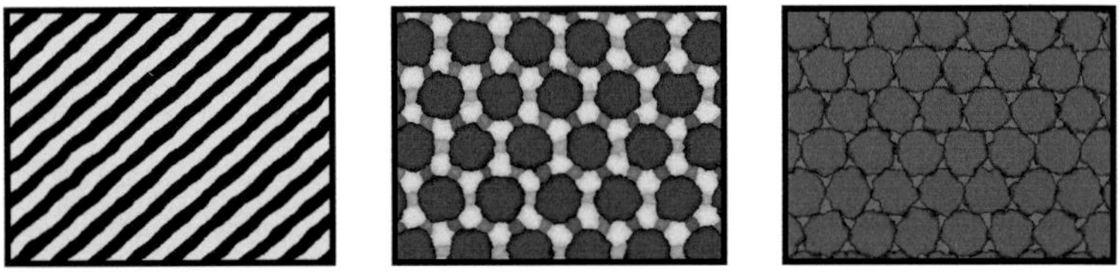

Figure 5.6 Examples of textures considered in this work as regular despite the stochastic changes of the texels.

To overcome the distortions caused by the impurity of the regular textures, fourteen window functions and three degrees of zero padding [20, 120] have been considered and are explained next. For this purpose, the input image is windowed first and padded with zeros before the magnitude of the two-dimensional Fourier transform is calculated, from which the displacement vectors are extracted. Furthermore, the extraction of the displacement vectors as in Sec. 5.2.1.1 implies the radial projection of the magnitude of the Fourier transform of the analyzed image. Two kinds of interpolations are examined to overcome discretization issues. In total 84 different combinations are studied to improve the extraction of the displacement vectors as a pre-processing step of the two-dimensional Fourier transform.

Window functions are widely used in signal processing tasks. As the discretization of the Fourier transform of discrete signals implies the repetition of both the analyzed signal and its spectrum (see Sec. 2.3.1), abrupt jumps between the repetitions of the signals should be attenuated. Several windows have been proposed for one dimensional signals in the literature [22, 29, 37, 61, 63, 109, 112, 113, 116]. In this work the following 14 one-dimensional window functions are considered.

- Modified Bartlett-Hann window [61]
- Blackman window [63, 112, 113]
- Bohman window [22, 63]
- Flat top window [37]
- Hann window [21, 63, 112, 113]
- Blackman-Harris window [63]
- Rectangular window [63, 112, 113] (see Eq. 2.13)
- Dolph-Chebyshev window [63]
- Hamming window [21, 63, 112, 113]
- 4-term window specified by Nuttal [109]
- Triangular window (similar to the Bartlett window [21, 63, 112, 113] but with no zero values at the end points)
- Kaiser window [74, 112, 113]
- De la Vallé-Poussin window [63, 116]
- Taylor window [29]

The input images are windowed by the two-dimensional window functions calculated from the one-dimensional ones as

$$w_{\mathbf{u}} = w_{u_1} \cdot w_{u_2}, \tag{5.6}$$

where $\mathbf{u} = \begin{pmatrix} u_1 & u_2 \end{pmatrix}^{\mathrm{T}}$ and w denotes the representation of one of the window functions used in the one-dimensional case. The considered two-dimensional window functions are shown in Figs. 5.7 – 5.9.

Zero padding is a method to increase the frequency resolution. For this purpose, the interval at which the signal is observed must be increased. In the case of two-dimensional signals this is done by padding the new unknown values to zero [20, 120]. The quality of the extraction of the displacement vectors has been tested for the input image (which may be a windowed one) with no zero padding and increasing its size by a factor of two and three.

Interpolation at the radial projection of the magnitude is necessary in real environments as these positions are discrete. The nearest neighbor interpolation assigns the value of the next existing neighbor to the predicted point. The bilinear interpolation is a linear interpolation of the next four neighboring points of the predicted one [20, 119]. Both interpolations are considered in this work.

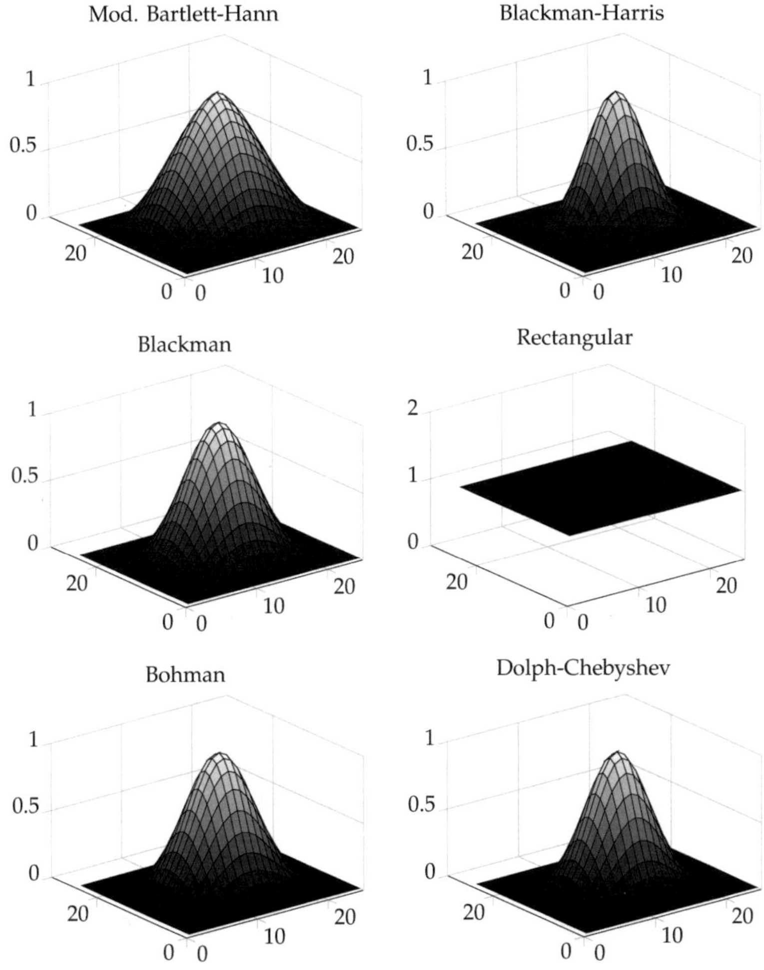

Figure 5.7 Two-dimensional window functions.

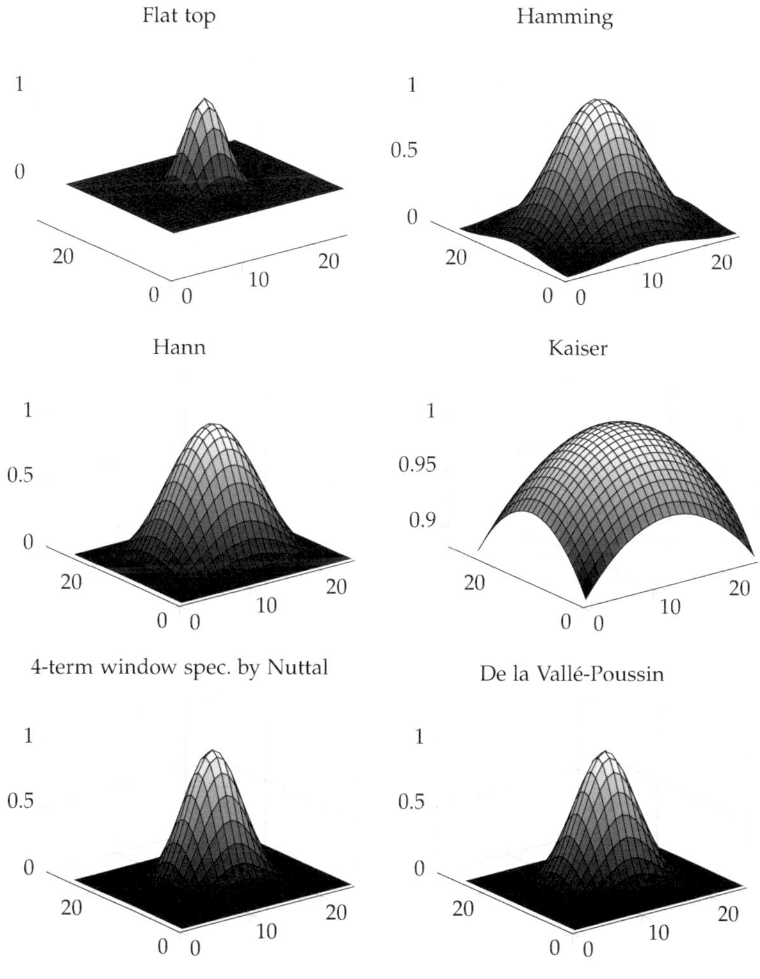

Figure 5.8 Two-dimensional window functions.

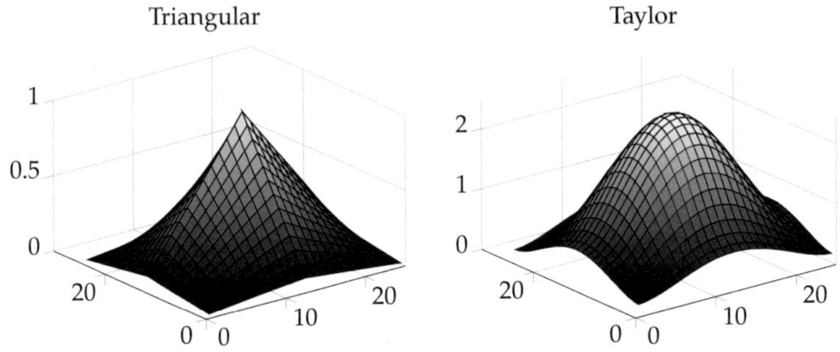

Figure 5.9 Two-dimensional window functions.

5.2.2 Detection of regular textures

The detection of regular textures in space (Sec. 5.2.2.1) (a preliminary version was presented in [155]) and frequency domain (Sec. 5.2.2.2) is considered in the following sections. To overcome the drawbacks from real images, a window function, zero padding, and an interpolation method may be used as explained in Sec. 5.2.1.2 to calculate the magnitude of the Fourier transform.

5.2.2.1 Detection in space domain

No matter which type of texture is analyzed, in this method it is always assumed that the texture is of regular type and its displacement vectors $\mathbf{a}$ (1-dimensional texture), $\mathbf{a}_k$ (2-dimensional texture), and mean texel $\overline{t_\mathbf{u}}$ are extracted from the input image $g_\mathbf{u}$ following the process of Sec. 5.2.1.1, whereas the arrangements of Sec. 5.2.2.2 may be used. At this juncture, the closest region to the origin of the Fourier spectrum is set to zero when the displacement vectors are extracted. This is done to overcome issues related to the real case like, e.g., the appearance of noise. If only one displacement vector is extracted from the input image, a one-dimensional regular texture is assumed. The length of the second vector $\tilde{\mathbf{a}}$, $\tilde{\mathbf{a}} \perp \mathbf{a}$, needed in this case to span the parallelogram for the texel extraction is set equal to the length of the extracted displacement vector. However, if the area of the parallelogram becomes too big in comparison with the total area of the input image, then the length of the second vector is set to the half of the length of the extracted displacement vector to be able to extract more texels from the input image. Using the extracted displacement vectors and the mean texel, the assumed regular texture $\tilde{g}_{\mathbf{u}}$ is reconstructed following Eq. 5.1:

$$\tilde{g}_{\mathbf{u}} = \begin{cases} \overline{t_{\mathbf{u}}} ** \sum\limits_{(k_1,k_2)\in\mathbb{Z}} \delta_{\mathbf{u}-k_1\mathbf{a}-k_2\tilde{\mathbf{a}}} & \text{for 1-D textures} \\ \overline{t_{\mathbf{u}}} ** \sum\limits_{(k_1,k_2)\in\mathbb{Z}^2} \delta_{\mathbf{u}-k_1\mathbf{a}_1-k_2\mathbf{a}_2} & \text{for 2-D textures.} \end{cases} \tag{5.7}$$

If the input texture $g_{\mathbf{u}}$ was from regular type, its reconstructed image $\tilde{g}_{\mathbf{u}}$ will be very similar. From the comparison of both images a detection of the type of texture (regular/irregular) is possible. Due to the quantization and the allowed small stochastic variations of the texels, the reconstructed image $\tilde{g}_{\mathbf{u}}$ will not be equal to the input one, even if the analyzed texture is perfectly regular. $d^{\mathrm{T},1}(g_{\mathbf{u}}, \tilde{g}_{\mathbf{u}})$, named in this work similarity distance, compares the input texture and the reconstructed one and is calculated by two-dimensional median filtering of the absolute difference between $g_{\mathbf{u}}$ and $\tilde{g}_{\mathbf{u}}$:

$$d^{\mathrm{T},1}(g_{\mathbf{u}}, \tilde{g}_{\mathbf{u}}) = \frac{\mu(\mathrm{med}\{|g_{\mathbf{u}} - \tilde{g}_{\mathbf{u}}|\})}{2 \cdot \sigma(g_{\mathbf{u}})}, \tag{5.8}$$

where $\mu(\mathrm{med}\{|g_{\mathbf{u}} - \tilde{g}_{\mathbf{u}}|\})$ is the mean value after median filtering the absolute differences between both images and $\sigma(g_{\mathbf{u}})$ the standard deviation of the gray values of the input image.

Due to quantization errors and small stochastic differences allowed between texels, $\mathrm{med}\{|g_{\mathbf{u}} - \tilde{g}_{\mathbf{u}}|\}$ will be bigger at texels containing bigger differences between their gray values. To overcome this problem, $d^{\mathrm{T},1}(g_{\mathbf{u}}, \tilde{g}_{\mathbf{u}})$ is calculated normalizing $\mathrm{med}\{|g_{\mathbf{u}} - \tilde{g}_{\mathbf{u}}|\}$ by $2 \cdot \sigma(g_{\mathbf{u}})$, whereas the factor 2 may be replaced by any other constant factor. As long as this factor remains equal across different images, the ratios of their $d^{\mathrm{T},1}(g_{\mathbf{u}}, \tilde{g}_{\mathbf{u}})$ will remain equal. However, the results presented in Sec. 8.4.1.3 are calculated setting this factor to 2.

If $d^{\mathrm{T},1}(g_{\mathbf{u}}, \tilde{g}_{\mathbf{u}})$ is smaller than a predifined threshold τ^{T3}, then the texture is detected as a regular one.

5.2.2.2 Detection in frequency domain

According to Eq. 5.2 the energy of regular textures is expected in frequency domain at linear combinations of the displacement vectors $\mathbf{l}$ (1-dimensional textures), $\mathbf{l}_k$ (2-dimensional textures). If every texture is assumed of regular type and their displacement vectors are extracted, then the energy distributed at the linear combinations of the extracted displacement vectors compared to the energy distributed along the whole frequency domain will be a good feature to detect regular textures, as the energies should be equal. However, we have to deal with the real case instead of the ideal one as noise may appear and the images are discrete and limited. Spectral leakage, discretization errors, and random noise must be considered. For this purpose, seven different templates are proposed to extract the energy at the linear combinations of the displacement vectors. Eight regions in frequency domain, and two different features are also considered.

As a first step, every considered texture is assumed of regular type and their displacement vectors $\mathbf{l}$ (1-dimensional texture), $\mathbf{l}_k$ (2-dimensional texture), are extracted according to Sec. 5.2.1.1, whereas the arrangements of Sec. 5.2.1.2 may be adopted. If the lengths of the displacement vectors in frequency domain are too short, the length of their corresponding displacement vectors in space domain will be too long, without even allowing enough repetitions along the textured image. In such cases the analyzed texture will be directly classified as irregular, as in Sec. 5.2.2.1 where the detection in space domain is considered. Next, the linear combinations of the extracted displacement vectors are detected and their energy is extracted.

Templates $t_{k,\mathbf{f}}^{\text{temp}}$, $1 \leq k \leq 7$, can be used to attenuate the issues related to real images. Due to spectral leakage and discretization, the energy in frequency domain may not be exactly at the linear combinations of the displacement vectors but close to them or even spread over several frequencies. Seven different templates are therefore set at the linear combinations of the displacement vectors to extract the energy, creating a texture dependent window function $w_{k,\mathbf{f}}$. The templates are shown in Fig. 5.10. Template 1 is the only one which considers only one discrete frequency. All of the other templates extract the energy at several discrete frequencies. Templates 2 to 5 normalize the total extracted amount of energy per considered position in contrast to the templates 6 and 7. Furthermore, templates 3 and 5 take into consideration the distance of the discrete frequency from which the energy is extracted to the expected position of the linear combinations of the displacement vectors, by weighting the energy extracted at the expected positions stronger than the energy extracted at their neighbors.

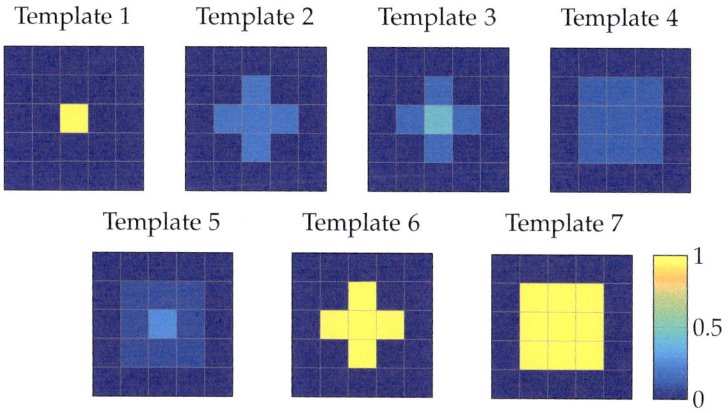

Figure 5.10 Representation of the seven templates considered to extract the energy in frequency domain.

Regions in frequency space are considered at the extraction of the energy. The higher the number of times that the displacement vectors are combined, the higher the uncertainty will be. This implies a bigger probability of a faulty detection of the positions where the local maxima should be. As the propagation of the uncertainty corresponds with the distance to the origin in frequency space, only this closest area should be considered. However, no hard boundaries should be given to the considered area in frequency space, as the positions of the peaks depend on the length of the displacement vectors. The considered area $\mathcal{U}$ is a rectangle. The lengths of the sides of the rectangle are entire multiples of the maximal lengths of the projected displacement vectors along the axis to consider the same number of harmonics along each axis:

$$\mathcal{U} = \left\{ \mathbf{f} \left| \begin{array}{l} |f_1| < k_1 \cdot |l_1| \text{ and } |f_2| < k_1 \cdot |l_2| \\ \hfill \text{for 1-dimensional textures} \\ |f_1| < k_1 \cdot \max\left(|l_{1,1}|, |l_{2,1}|\right) \text{ and } |f_2| < k_1 \cdot \max\left(|l_{1,2}|, |l_{2,2}|\right) \\ \hfill \text{for 2-dimensional textures} \end{array} \right. \right\}, \tag{5.9}$$

where $\mathbf{f} = \begin{pmatrix} f_1 & f_2 \end{pmatrix}^{\mathrm{T}}$, $\mathbf{l} = \begin{pmatrix} l_1 & l_2 \end{pmatrix}^{\mathrm{T}}$ (for 1-dimensional textures), $\mathbf{l}_1 = \begin{pmatrix} l_{1,1} & l_{1,2} \end{pmatrix}^{\mathrm{T}}$ and $\mathbf{l}_2 = \begin{pmatrix} l_{2,1} & l_{2,2} \end{pmatrix}^{\mathrm{T}}$ (for 2-dimensional textures), $k_1 \in \{2, 3, 4, \infty\}$. $k_1 = \infty$ considers the whole frequency space.

Four more combinations of the regions in frequency space are taken into consideration by suppressing the energies situated immediately close to the origin, as these energies are much bigger than the other ones and can therefore distort the comparison (see Fig. 5.11).

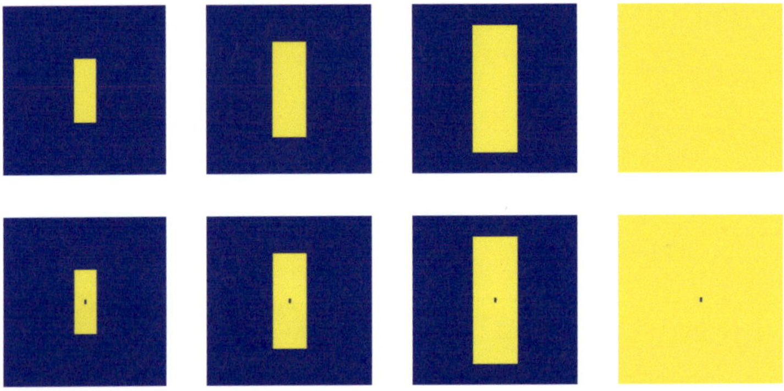

Figure 5.11 The considered regions in frequency space are marked in yellow.

Features are extracted from the magnitudes in frequency domain and used for the detection of regular textures. Two different features $m^{\mathrm{T1}}, m^{\mathrm{T2}}$ are proposed to detect the type of texture. For both features a window function $w_{k,\mathbf{f}}$ is obtained first depending on the selected template to extract the energy:

$$w_{k,\mathbf{f}} = \sum_{(k_1,k_2)\in\mathbb{Z}^2} t_{k,\mathbf{f}}^{\mathrm{temp}} ** \delta_{\mathbf{f}-k_1\mathbf{l}_1-k_2\mathbf{l}_2}. \tag{5.10}$$

The first feature compares in the considered frequency environment the magnitude of the windowed spectrum to the not windowed one:

$$m^{\mathrm{T1}} = \frac{\sum_{\mathbf{f}\in\mathcal{U}} w_{k,\mathbf{f}} \cdot |G_{\mathbf{f}}|}{\sum_{\mathbf{f}\in\mathcal{U}} |G_{\mathbf{f}}|}. \tag{5.11}$$

Furthermore, the second feature also considers the relationship between the area allowed by the window function and the considered region in frequency domain, to punish textures whose projection of the displacement vectors in frequency domain along one of the axis is very small:

$$m^{\mathrm{T2}} = \frac{\frac{\sum\limits_{\mathbf{f}\in\mathcal{U}} w_{k,\mathbf{f}}\cdot|G_{\mathbf{f}}|}{\sum\limits_{\mathbf{f}\in\mathcal{U}} |G_{\mathbf{f}}|}}{\frac{\sum\limits_{\mathbf{f}\in\mathcal{U}} w_{k,\mathbf{f}}}{|\mathcal{U}|}}. \tag{5.12}$$

Such kind of textures are more likely to be of irregular type, but their corresponding window function will extract energy from a big area of the selected environment. This implies that the relationship considered in feature m^{T1} will be high, as expected from regular textures.

The higher the values of the features $m^{\mathrm{T1}}, m^{\mathrm{T2}}$ are, the higher the expectation for a texture of regular type will be.

5.2.3 Sorting of regular textures

If an input image has been detected as a regular texture following one of the approaches in Sec. 5.2.2, it will be compared with the previously detected regular textures stored at the database. The input image will be compared with each image in the database to define a similarity value s between the compared textures. For this purpose, one-dimensional textures will only be compared with one-dimensional textures and two-dimensional textures with two-dimensional ones. The images in the database will then be sorted depending on their similarity to the input image.

Eight different similarity features s_k, $1 \leq k \leq 8$, are explained here that were presented in [155]. As similarity perception is human- and task-dependent, the strength of the similarity features s_k can be independently selected w_k. Their combination yields the total similarity between the compared textures:

$$s = \prod_k s_k^{w_k},\ w_k \in [0,1], \tag{5.13}$$

meaning $s = 1$ a maximum similarity and $s = 0$ no similarity. The features s_k can be classified into two groups: texel's properties (Sec. 5.2.3.1) and displacement properties (Sec. 5.2.3.2).

5.2.3.1 Texels' features

Five similarity features $s_1, \ldots, s_5$ are extracted from the texels of the regular textures. The extracted mean texel of the texture $\overline{t_{\mathbf{u}}}$ and one extracted texel per image $t_{\mathbf{u}}^{\mathrm{Det}}$ will be used. The input image will be characterized with the index I and the image in the database with the index O.

Three features s_1, s_2, s_3 compare the intensities that appear in the texels. s_4 and s_5 extract information about the similarity of the content of the texels.

Brightness s_1: The mean brightness between the textures are compared via the mean gray values $\mu(\overline{t_{\mathbf{u}}})$ of the extracted mean texels of the textures. The smaller mean value is divided by the bigger one to get a normalized feature:

$$s_1 = \frac{\mu\left(\overline{t_{\mathbf{u}}^{c_1}}\right)}{\mu\left(\overline{t_{\mathbf{u}}^{c_2}}\right)}, \tag{5.14}$$

where $\{c_1, c_2\} \in \{\mathrm{I}, \mathrm{O}\}, c_1 \neq c_2$, and $\mu\left(\overline{t_{\mathbf{u}}^{c_1}}\right) \leq \mu\left(\overline{t_{\mathbf{u}}^{c_2}}\right)$ must apply.

Homogeneity of the Brightness s_2: The range of intensities appearing in the texels is compared in s_2. For this purpose, the standard deviations of the mean texels $\sigma(\overline{t_{\mathbf{u}}})$ of the images are divided yielding a normalized value:

$$s_2 = \frac{\sigma\left(\overline{t_{\mathbf{u}}^{c_1}}\right)}{\sigma\left(\overline{t_{\mathbf{u}}^{c_2}}\right)}, \tag{5.15}$$

where $\{c_1, c_2\} \in \{\mathrm{I}, \mathrm{O}\}, c_1 \neq c_2$, and $\sigma\left(\overline{t_{\mathbf{u}}^{c_1}}\right) \leq \sigma\left(\overline{t_{\mathbf{u}}^{c_2}}\right)$ must apply.

Distribution of the Brightness s_3: The feature s_3 is a measure for the similarity of the distribution of the intensities appearing in the texels. Histograms of the appearing gray values in the texels $\mathbf{h}^{\mathrm{Bright}}$ are computed first and compared using the quadratic-form distance next [108, 122] (see Sec. 2.1):

$$s_3 = 1 - \sqrt{\left(\mathbf{h}^{\mathrm{Bright,I}} - \mathbf{h}^{\mathrm{Bright,O}}\right)^{\mathrm{T}} \mathbf{B} \left(\mathbf{h}^{\mathrm{Bright,I}} - \mathbf{h}^{\mathrm{Bright,O}}\right)}, \tag{5.16}$$

where

$$\mathbf{b}_{ij} = 1 - \frac{d_{ij}}{d_{\max}} \tag{5.17}$$

is an element of the matrix **B** and d_{ij} denotes the distance between the gray values of the center bin i and j. $d_{\max}$ is the length of the maximum range spanned by the gray values.

Structure s_4: The similarity of the structure of the texels is measured by the feature s_4 based on the edges that appear in the texels of the regular textures that are extracted at a certain point from the original images $t_{\mathbf{u}}^{\mathrm{Det}}$. The edges are detected here filtering the texels $t_{\mathbf{u}}^{\mathrm{Det}}$ with the Canny operator [20, 28]. s_4 is obtained from two comparisons: the number of edges orientations $s_{4,1}$ and their relative angles $s_{4,2}$:

$$s_4 = s_{4,1} \cdot s_{4,2}. \tag{5.18}$$

In the Fourier transform of the image filtered with the Canny operator the edges will appear as straight lines passing through the origin. Following the approach described in Sec. 5.2.1.1 the straight lines can be detected. The comparison of the number of detected lines yields

$$s_{4,1} = \frac{n^{\mathrm{Line},c_1}}{n^{\mathrm{Line},c_2}}, \tag{5.19}$$

where $\{c_1, c_2\} \in \{\mathrm{I}, \mathrm{O}\}, c_1 \neq c_2$, and $n^{\mathrm{Line},c_1} \leq n^{\mathrm{Line},c_2}$ must apply. From the slopes of the lines in frequency domain, the orientations of the edges φ_k, $1 \leq k \leq n^{\mathrm{Line}}$, are extracted and sorted from higher to lower value. The difference from each edge orientation to the next smaller one is represented by $\Delta\varphi_k$. If $\Delta\varphi_k$ is bigger than $\frac{\pi}{2}$, then the difference to $\frac{\pi}{2}$ is calculated and set as $\Delta\varphi_k$. $s_{4,2}$ is the quotient of the mean differences of the orientation angles per image:

$$s_{4,2} = \frac{\mu\left(\Delta\varphi_k^{c_1}\right)}{\mu\left(\Delta\varphi_k^{c_2}\right)}, \tag{5.20}$$

where $\{c_1, c_2\} \in \{\mathrm{I}, \mathrm{O}\}, c_1 \neq c_2$, and $\mu\left(\Delta\varphi_k^{c_1}\right) \leq \mu\left(\Delta\varphi_k^{c_2}\right)$ must apply. If many edge orientations are detected in a texture, then almost circular structures can be assumed. This implies that the mean difference $\mu(\Delta\varphi_k)$

will become very small. Consequently, $s_{4,2}$ and s_4 will become close to zero and with them the total similarity s independently of the other similarity features. To avoid this, in such cases $\mu(\Delta\varphi_k)$ is set to $\frac{\pi}{18}$.

Regions s_5**:** This feature compares the regions that possess an almost constant intensity. For this purpose, the regions in the texel must be determined first. Such regions are detected using a watershed filling method [54] in a similar way to the MSER detector [96]. The texel extracted at a determined position in the texture is compared with an increasing threshold $\boldsymbol{\tau} = \left(\tau_1, \tau_2, \ldots, \tau_K\right)^{\mathrm{T}}$ that varies from the minimal possible intensity to the maximum one, to obtain thresholded texels $t_{k,\mathbf{u}}^{\text{Thresh}}$, $1 \leq k \leq K$. Each pixel in the texel is marked at the compared threshold intensity if its value is smaller than the threshold value:

$$t_{k,\mathbf{u}}^{\text{Thresh}} = \begin{cases} 1 & \text{if } t_{\mathbf{u}}^{\text{Det}} < \tau_k \\ 0 & \text{otherwise.} \end{cases} \tag{5.21}$$

The thresholded images are then compared with the ones at the next threshold value:

$$\Delta t_{k,\mathbf{u}}^{\text{Thresh}} = t_{k,\mathbf{u}}^{\text{Thresh}} - t_{k+1,\mathbf{u}}^{\text{Thresh}}. \tag{5.22}$$

Closed regions with an almost constant intensity are considered those, whose area does not vary considerably over a minimum number of consecutive thresholds. Due to the fact that regions detected at higher threshold values will overlap with smaller regions detected at smaller thresholds, the regions from the smaller thresholds will be removed from the bigger ones, as non-overlapping regions are searched. The texels of regular textures are displaced all over the plane, so detected regions at the contours of the texel $t_{\mathbf{u}}^{\text{Det}}$ may have been extracted separately. However, as the texel will be repeated all over the image plain, such regions are not separated in the real image. In a final step those regions are grouped together.

Once the gray-level regions in the texel have been extracted, two comparisons are taken between the images to compare their content: the number of detected regions $s_{5,1}$ and the size of the regions $s_{5,2}$:

$$s_5 = s_{5,1} \cdot s_{5,2}. \tag{5.23}$$

The number of regions between the images is compared via the normalized quotient of the number of detected regions n^{Region} per image:

$$s_{5,1} = \frac{n^{\text{Region},c_1}}{n^{\text{Region},c_2}}, \tag{5.24}$$

where $\{c_1, c_2\} \in \{\text{I}, \text{O}\}, c_1 \neq c_2$, and $n^{\text{Region},c_1} \leq n^{\text{Region},c_2}$ must apply. Per image, a histogram of the area of the regions normalized over the whole area of the texel $\mathbf{h}^{\text{Area}}$ is calculated first. The histograms are compared next using the quadratic-form distance [108, 122] (see Sec. 2.1):

$$s_{5,2} = 1 - \sqrt{\left(\mathbf{h}^{\text{Area,I}} - \mathbf{h}^{\text{Area,O}}\right)^{\text{T}} \mathbf{B} \left(\mathbf{h}^{\text{Area,I}} - \mathbf{h}^{\text{Area,O}}\right)}, \tag{5.25}$$

where

$$\mathbf{b}_{ij} = 1 - d_{ij} \tag{5.26}$$

is an element of the matrix $\mathbf{B}$ and d_{ij} denotes the distance of the represented relative areas at the center bins i and j.

5.2.3.2 Displacement features

The bases for the features comparing the similarity between the lattices of regular textures are their displacement vectors. From now on $\mathbf{a}^{\text{I}}$ (for one-dimensional textures), $\mathbf{a}_k^{\text{I}}$, $k \in \{1, 2\}$ (for two-dimensional textures), are the displacement vectors of the input texture and $\mathbf{a}^{\text{O}}$ (for one-dimensional textures), $\mathbf{a}_k^{\text{O}}$, $k \in \{1, 2\}$ (for two-dimensional textures), the vectors of the compared image in the database. Three features, s_6, s_7, and s_8, are presented to compare the lattices of two-dimensional textures. Two features, s_6 and s_7, are used in case of one-dimensional textures.

Scale s_6: Variations of the scale at regular textures imply variations of the lengths of the displacement vectors. In case of one-dimensional textures the quotient of the vector lengths is used as similarity feature between the scales. To obtain a normalized feature, the length of the smaller vector is divided by the length of the bigger one:

$$s_6 = \frac{\left\|\mathbf{a}^{c_1}\right\|_2}{\left\|\mathbf{a}^{c_2}\right\|_2}, \tag{5.27}$$

where $\{c_1, c_2\} \in \{\mathrm{I}, \mathrm{O}\}, c_1 \neq c_2$, and $\left\|\mathbf{a}^{c_1}\right\|_2 \leq \left\|\mathbf{a}^{c_2}\right\|_2$ must apply. When dealing with two-dimensional textures, the displacement of the texel along the image is represented via two displacement vectors. The scale similarity is also obtained by comparing the lengths of the displacement vectors. In this case the length of the smallest displacement vector from the input texture (e.g., $\mathbf{a}_2^{\mathrm{I}}$) is compared to the smallest displacement vector of the texture in the database (e.g., $\mathbf{a}_1^{\mathrm{O}}$). Respectively, the lengths of the remaining bigger vectors are also compared. Following the example, let's assume that $\left\|\mathbf{a}_1^{\mathrm{O}}\right\|_2 \geq \left\|\mathbf{a}_2^{\mathrm{I}}\right\|_2$ and $\left\|\mathbf{a}_1^{\mathrm{I}}\right\|_2 \geq \left\|\mathbf{a}_2^{\mathrm{O}}\right\|_2$, then

$$s_6 = \sqrt{\frac{\left\|\mathbf{a}_2^{\mathrm{I}}\right\|_2}{\left\|\mathbf{a}_1^{\mathrm{O}}\right\|_2} \cdot \frac{\left\|\mathbf{a}_2^{\mathrm{O}}\right\|_2}{\left\|\mathbf{a}_1^{\mathrm{I}}\right\|_2}}. \tag{5.28}$$

Rotation s_7: The similarity of the rotation between two features is extracted depending on the dimension of the compared textures.

If the textures are one-dimensional, then the angles α spanned via their displacement vectors and the horizontal axis are calculated per texture. For this purpose, the angles must point into the positive u_1-axis, using their projection over the origin if this is not the case. The rotation similarity between the two one-dimensional textures is calculated as

$$s_7 = \begin{cases} 1 - \frac{\left|\alpha^{\mathrm{I}} - \alpha^{\mathrm{O}}\right|}{\frac{\pi}{2}} & \text{if } \left|\alpha^{\mathrm{I}} - \alpha^{\mathrm{O}}\right| \leq \frac{\pi}{2} \\ 1 - \frac{\pi - \left|\alpha^{\mathrm{I}} - \alpha^{\mathrm{O}}\right|}{\frac{\pi}{2}} & \text{otherwise.} \end{cases} \tag{5.29}$$

If the textures are two-dimensional, then the angles α spanned by their displacement vectors and the u_1-axis are also calculated first, as in the one-dimensional case. From the two obtained angles α per image, only the smaller one will be further considered (e.g., $\alpha_2^{\mathrm{I}}, \alpha_2^{\mathrm{O}}$). These angles are used to calculate the absolute rotation γ per image as the remainder of its division by the angles $\angle(\mathbf{a}_1, \mathbf{a}_2)$ spanned by their corresponding displacement vectors $\mathbf{a}_k$:

$$\gamma^c = \alpha_2^c \mathrm{rem}\left(\angle\left(\mathbf{a}_1^c, \mathbf{a}_2^c\right)\right), \tag{5.30}$$

where $c \in \{\mathrm{I}, \mathrm{O}\}$ and $\angle(\mathbf{a}_1, \mathbf{a}_2)$ is the smallest angle spanned by the displacement vectors, whereas its difference to $\frac{\pi}{2}$ is considered in case that the angle is bigger than $\frac{\pi}{2}$. The similarity parameter is obtained by comparing the absolute rotation of the textures taking into consideration the relative angles between the displacement vectors of the input image:

$$s_7 = \begin{cases} 1 - \frac{\left|\gamma^{\mathrm{I}} - \gamma^{\mathrm{O}}\right|}{\frac{\angle\left(\mathbf{a}_1^{\mathrm{I}}, \mathbf{a}_2^{\mathrm{I}}\right)}{2}} & \text{if } \left|\gamma^{\mathrm{I}} - \gamma^{\mathrm{O}}\right| \leq \frac{\angle\left(\mathbf{a}_1^{\mathrm{I}}, \mathbf{a}_2^{\mathrm{I}}\right)}{2} \\ 1 - \frac{\frac{\angle\left(\mathbf{a}_1^{\mathrm{I}}, \mathbf{a}_2^{\mathrm{I}}\right)}{2} - \left(\left|\gamma^{\mathrm{I}} - \gamma^{\mathrm{O}}\right| \mathrm{rem}\left(\frac{\angle\left(\mathbf{a}_1^{\mathrm{I}}, \mathbf{a}_2^{\mathrm{I}}\right)}{2}\right)\right)}{\frac{\angle\left(\mathbf{a}_1^{\mathrm{I}}, \mathbf{a}_2^{\mathrm{I}}\right)}{2}} & \text{otherwise.} \end{cases} \tag{5.31}$$

As the similarity parameter s_7 for two-dimensional textures depends on the relative angle of the displacement vectors of the input image, it is not a symmetric feature.

Orientation s_8: The orientation feature s_8 is only extracted from two-dimensional textures by comparing the relative angles between the displacement vectors:

$$s_8 = \frac{\angle\left(\mathbf{a}_1^{c_1}, \mathbf{a}_2^{c_1}\right)}{\angle\left(\mathbf{a}_1^{c_2}, \mathbf{a}_2^{c_2}\right)}, \tag{5.32}$$

where $\{c_1, c_2\} \in \{\mathrm{I}, \mathrm{O}\}, c_1 \neq c_2$, and $\angle\left(\mathbf{a}_1^{c_1}, \mathbf{a}_2^{c_1}\right) \leq \angle\left(\mathbf{a}_1^{c_2}, \mathbf{a}_2^{c_2}\right)$ must apply. For this purpose, the smaller angles spanned by the respective displacement vectors are used. If the angles are bigger than $\frac{\pi}{2}$, then their differences to $\frac{\pi}{2}$ are defined as the relative angles.

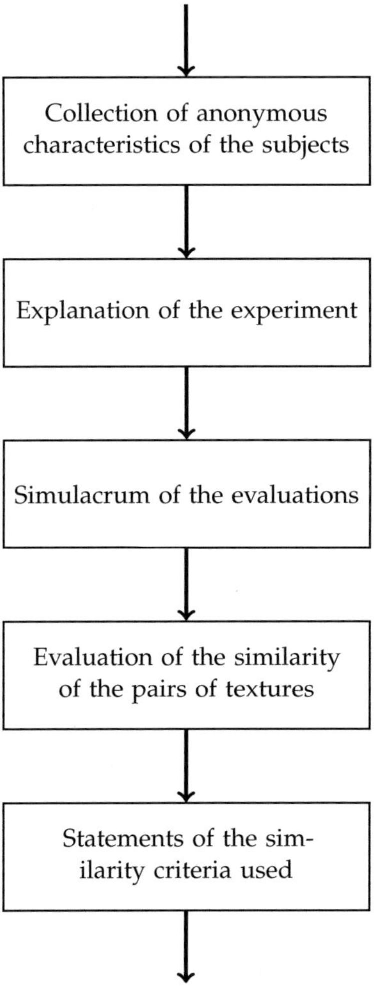

Figure 5.12 Sequence of the experiment performed with humans.

5.2.4 Perception map of regular textures

Appropriate methods are necessary to sort images according to their similarity. The knowledge of human perception is important to be able to compare, evaluate, and improve these methods. However, this is a challenging task as human perception is subjective. Since in this thesis the sorting of textures is considered depending on their type and that the sorting of regular textures has been especially focused, the creation of a perception map [82] of regular textures is interesting to evaluate the sorting results of the method proposed in Secs. 5.2.2 and 5.2.3. Furthermore, such a perception map will also enable us to evaluate if the proposed sorting method is reasonable or useless.

With the help of psychologists an experiment has been drafted. Its procedure is presented in Sec. 5.2.4.1. The analysis of the data obtained from the experiment to extract the perception map of regular textures is explained in Sec. 5.2.4.2.

5.2.4.1 Experimental procedure

With the help of an experiment, statements of subjects about the relationship between different regular textures are collected. The evaluation of the similarity of pairs of regular textures turned out to be an appropriate approach for a good trade-off between the collection of many statements to different regular textures and a fast and simple question for the subjects to answer. For this purpose, pairs of textures are consecutively shown to the subjects and the similarities between the pairs are evaluated by a numerical rating scale. Every texture must be compared with every other considered one to be able to analyze the data (see Sec. 5.2.4.2), which means $\frac{k\cdot(k+1)}{2}$ pair comparisons for k textures. As the number of pairs of textures that must be compared increases enormously with the number of considered textures and the experiment must be done in a reasonable time to avoid fatigued subjects, a representative selection is necessary to build the pairs of textures. Furthermore, the experiment should be repeated to several subjects to become generalized perception maps.

Twenty subjects participated in the experiment, which took place for all of them always at the same computer in the same room. The experiment's sequence is shown in Fig. 5.12. In a first step the subjects must answer some questions that may alter the results, e.g., if they possess any defective sight. Next, the rating of the similarity of pairs of textures is explained with the help of text. This is the scope of the experiment. Five pairs of textures are consecutively shown to enable the subjects to become familiar with the type of textures that are compared. Subsequently, a simulacrum of the experiment is done. For this purpose, five pairs of textures are consecutively shown, and the subjects must evaluate after the display of the corresponding pair of textures in a six-point scale how similar the compared textures are. The only information told to the subjects about the scale is that one indicates very dissimilar and six very similar. The evaluation of the similarity of every pair of textures is continued with the question to the subjects of how confident they are, rated on a four-point scale. The information of one as very unsure and four as very sure was the only one transmitted to the subjects about this rating scale. The subjects themselves were the ones who set the velocity of the experiment, as they could decide per click on the computer's mouse when to answer and continue with the next pair of textures. Every subject evaluated the same pairs of textures, but their order at the evaluation was randomly chosen to overcome fatigue over the subjects or possible dependencies across consecutive pairs of textures. At the end of the experiment the subjects were asked to explain their criteria used for the similarity evaluation. Ten of the evaluated pairs of textures (the same for all subjects) were shown to the subjects on the monitor and also on a paper to help them remember the kind of pairs of textures they analyzed. These ones could also be used as support when the subjects explained their evaluation criteria.

5.2.4.2 Data analysis

The data can be analyzed once it has been collected in form of similarity statements between pairs of textures. The goal is to obtain a perception map of regular textures, in which the analyzed textures are represented as points in a multidimensional space [82]. The distance between the points in space should correlate with the similarity between their respective represented textures. Exactly this kind of problems are addressed by multidimensional scaling [11, 48], which is commonly applied in psychology and market research problems [11, 48]. The non-metric multidimensional scaling [48, 78, 79] is considered, which can be applied to the collected data directly. For this purpose, the Euclidean distance is selected as distance function and the dimensions of the space, in which the textures are represented, are limited to two.

Over all subjects one similarity statement is calculated per pair of textures. These ones are obtained from the median value over all similarity statements of all subjects of the corresponding pair of textures.

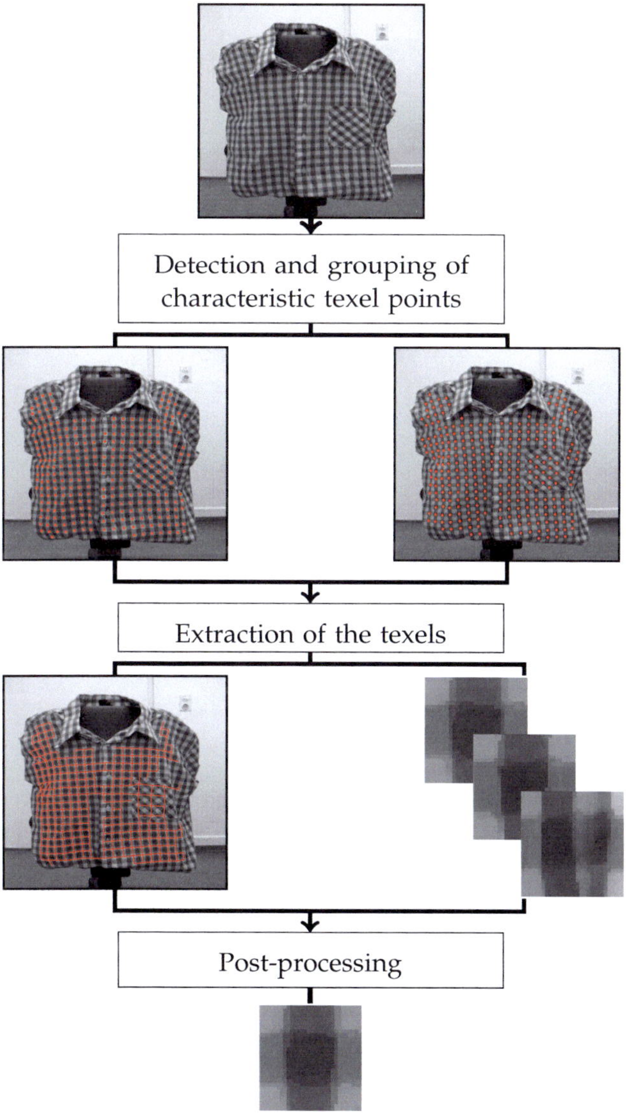

Figure 5.13 Overview of the procedure to extract regular textures from near-regular ones.

5.3 Detection of near-regular textures and extraction of their regular texture

Regular textures are seldom found in digital images due to lighting variations and the projection of the three-dimensional world onto the two-dimensional image plain. Near-regular textures (see Sec. 5.1.1) are therefore more common in digital images. In the following sections the detection and extraction of regular textures from near-regular ones is considered. An overview of the procedure is shown in Fig. 5.13. This modus operandi is inspired by [66]. However, different options are proposed for the resolution of the goal of each block that may even be fused. First, regions or points of interest are detected in the image and grouped according to their similarity (Sec. 5.3.1). Per cluster a lattice over the input image is spanned to extract the average texel of the texture (Sec. 5.3.2). Finally, the suppression of faulty extracted texels, as well as the fusion of repeated extracted texels, is considered in Sec. 5.3.3. Note that no previuos segmentation of the image is needed to detect near-regular textures in images with the presented methods. A preliminary version of this work has been presented in [159].

5.3.1 Detection and grouping of characteristic texel points

The detection of characteristic points or regions of interest in an input image is considered in Sec. 5.3.1.1 and their grouping into clusters with similar characteristics in Sec. 5.3.1.2. In Sec. 5.3.1.3 the obtained clusters are further processed to assure spatially compact points and discard clusters that do not describe a valid near-regular texture.

5.3.1.1 Detection of points of interest

As a near-regular texture is composed of a repetition of a texel, regions or points of interest detected at texels will be repeated all over the texture. Due to the fact that variations of the displacement vectors and the texel appear at near-regular textures, the detectors should be robust to lighting variations and affine transformations. The SURF detector [14, 15] and the MSER detector [96] are considered here to respectively detect points and regions of interest.

Whereas the SURF detector yields points in the image, the MSER detector yields regions. As in [102], every MSER region is approximated in this work by an ellipse whose second moments are equal to the ones of the region. The center of the ellipse is then named as the point of interest obtained via the MSER detector.

5.3.1.2 Clustering the detected points of interest

Once points of interest have been detected at the input image, their SURF features are extracted and compared [14, 15]. Near-regular textures are created from a texel that is repeated over the texture, so similar features are expected at repeated detected points of the texels. Clusters are therefore expected in the extracted SURF features dividing the points according to the similarity of the regions described by their features. The division of the detected points into clusters is an unsupervised learning problem with unknown number of expected clusters. In [159] the following sorting method was proposed to detect the clusters instead of the mean-shift approach [33, 35, 52], which is commonly used in the literature for such purposes [66, 115].

The **proposed sorting method** is based on a graph representation of the input image. A graph of the input image is used to sort the detected points of interest. For this purpose, every point of interest is represented as a node in the graph and connected by an edge to every node whose point possesses a similar feature. The similarity between the SURF features is measured using the Euclidean distance (see Sec. 2.1). The connected graphs containing a minimum number of nodes are the clusters of similar points of interest. This method can be understood as a simplified version of the DBSCAN algorithm [47], because the number of nodes with which every node is considered similar is not taken in care here.

In extension to [159] the detected points of interest may be processed. Several points of interest lying spatially very close to each other may be detected by the detectors. Such kind of points will all describe the same region, but as they are detected separately, they will count as independent points. This may be therefore a source of future mistakes. Due to the fact that they represent very similar regions, they will be grouped into the same cluster. To avoid future misleading, such points are replaced in this extension by their spatially mean point.

5.3.1.3 Post-processing of the clustered points of interest

An immediate post-processing of the extracted clusters is profitable to correct clusters and remove those that do not contain adequate points to describe a valid lattice of a near-regular texture.

Spatially compact point clouds are required from the clustered points to improve the detection of the near-regular texures. An image may contain several objects with a similar texture. The detected points of similar textures will be grouped into the same clusters, as no spatial localization is considered when the points are grouped. To extract the correct lattices of all textures in the image, the spatially separated points should therefore be located at different clusters. For this purpose, every point in a cluster is represented as a node of a graph. Every node is connected by an edge to its n^{T1} spatially closest points that belong to its cluster. If a cluster consists of several points that belong to spatially separated similar textures, several connected graphs (see Sec. 2.2.1) are expected at its graph representation. Each connected graph is therefore considered as an extra cluster to assure that the points are spatially agglomerated at one place.

The **suppression of clusters of points situated merely along edges** is considered next. A valid lattice of a near-regular texture may be extracted from every cluster containing enough points of interest. However, some clusters may only consist of points displaced along the contours or edges from regions in the image. The sooner such clusters are discarded, the better, most of all due to time consumption, it is. From the points in a cluster $\mathbf{p}_k, 1 \leq k \leq K$, $\mathbf{p}_k = \begin{pmatrix} u_{1,k} & u_{2,k} \end{pmatrix}^{\mathrm{T}}$, the ones that spatially envelop all points and compactly describe the spatial boundary $\mathbf{p}_{k_1}^{\mathrm{Bound}}, 1 \leq k_1 \leq K_1, K_1 < K$, are searched first. Their spatial distance to the center of the cluster $\overline{\mathbf{p}_k}$ is calculated next, and the minimum distance is compared via a division by the mean distance of the points in the boundary to the center of the cluster:

$$d^{\mathrm{Bound}}(\mathbf{p}_k) = \frac{\min\limits_k(\|\mathbf{p}_k - \overline{\mathbf{p}_k}\|_2)}{\mu\left(\left\|\mathbf{p}_{k_1}^{\mathrm{Bound}} - \overline{\mathbf{p}_k}\right\|_2\right)}. \tag{5.33}$$

If $d^{\mathrm{Bound}}(\mathbf{p}_k)$ is higher than a predefined threshold, then the cluster is discarded as it merely contains points situated at an edge.

5.3.2 Extraction of the texels

For the extraction of the representative texels of the near-regular textures in images, every cluster is independently taken into consideration. For each cluster texels will be extracted from the input image and median filtered to obtain the representative texels of the near-regular textures in the image.

Per cluster a starting lattice is extracted first (Sec. 5.3.2.1) that spans a local and almost regular texture. As the textures in the image are rather near-regular, the starting lattice is expanded next over the image to describe the lattice of the near-regular texture (Sec. 5.3.2.2). Every cell of the lattice describes a potential valid texel (Sec. 5.3.2.3). To compare all potential texels in the lattice, they have to be projected onto quadrangles of equal shape and normalized intensity, as the texels in the input image may vary, i.a., in gray values, size, shear, and rotation (Sec. 5.3.2.4). The texels in the quadrangles should finally be processed to suppress faulty texels and avoid averaging along different texel representations (Sec. 5.3.2.5). Finally, the representative texels of the near-regular textures are obtained after filtering the valid potential texels in the quadrangles with a median filter, whereas all valid texels or a random selection may be used, depending on the desired accuracy and especially time consumption.

5.3.2.1 Starting lattice

The starting lattice is composed of cells that span a local and almost regular texture. The cells describe hereby texels of the texture. The higher the number of cells in the starting lattice is, the higher the probability that the lattice of an almost regular texture has been detected and therefore the higher the probability of extracting real texels from the texture will be. This also implies smaller errors at the expansion of the starting lattice over the whole texture in the next section.

Valid neighbors to the points in the cluster must be defined first to extract the starting lattice. Every point can be assigned up to four neighbors from its cluster that must fulfill the following criteria, whereas the spatially closest point with a similar gray value will become the first neighbor:

- Neighboring points must have a similar gray value.
- The vectors spanned between a considered point and its neighbors must lie each in a different quadrant with origin at the considered point.
- The spatially closest points to the considered point that fulfill the above conditions are selected.

To extract the starting lattice, the points in the cluster are represented as nodes in a graph. Only points with four neighbors are further considered. As the texel of a regular texture can be spanned by a parallelogram, the vectors spanned from a considered point to its four neighbors can be divided into two groups of almost anti-parallel vectors with similar vector lengths. These vectors can be considered in regular textures as the displacement vectors. For every point in the cluster that fulfills these criteria, edges to its neighboring points are set in the graph. The biggest connected graph may be used as the starting lattice for further processing as in [159]. However, as vectors between neighboring points are not compared between each other, the displacement vectors may vary depending on the considered point, and the lattice will not necessarily span a regular texture. This will propagate uncertainty when the lattice is expanded in the next section. An example of a starting lattice obtained by this method is shown on the left side of Fig. 5.14. The points of interest are highlighted by the blue and green dots. The displacement vectors between neighboring points are represented in the image by the red lines. Notice the green highlighted points. Due to the fact that their displacement vectors pointing to the four neighboring points can be divided into the two sets of almost anti-parallel vectors with similar lengths, they form part of the starting lattice. However, their displacement vectors are not similar to the displacement vectors of their neighboring points.

The **consideration of the similarity of the vectors between neighboring points** allows another possibility to extract the starting lattice. For this purpose, only the points in the cluster with four neighbors, whose vectors spanned from the point to its neighbors can be divided into the two sets of almost anti-parallel vectors with similar vector lengths, are represented as nodes in the graph. An edge will only be set between the nodes if they are neighbors and their displacement vectors are similar. By these means two features are assigned per node. The first feature $f^{\mathrm{NT},1}$ is the relationship of the lengths of the displacement vectors. The average length of the anti-parallel vectors are therefore calculated and the smallest one is divided by the bigger one to obtain $f^{\mathrm{NT},1}$. The second feature β is the absolute difference between the smallest angles between not anti-parallel vectors. The displacement vectors between neighboring points are considered similar (an edge is therefore set in the graph between their nodes) if the relationships of their displacement vectors' lengths and angles are similar:

- $f^{\mathrm{NT},1} > \tau^{\mathrm{T1}}$
- $\beta < \tau^{\mathrm{T2}}$.

The biggest component graph is the starting lattice. However, due to the further consideration of the similarity of the vectors from the points to their neighbors, the probability of extracting local regular textures is higher (see Fig. 5.14 right).

5.3.2.2 Expansion of the starting lattice

Once the starting lattice has been detected at a local regular texture, it is expanded along the texture. Bigger variations between the displacement vectors are now allowed along the lattice. In [159] a method was proposed to expand the starting lattice and it is explained next. The goal in [159] was the extraction of the regular texture from the near-regular one, which is possible after extracting the correct texel of the texture. A perfect extraction of the lattice of the texture is, however, not indispensable. A second method is further presented here to also improve the correctness of the extracted lattice.

The basis for both methods is a graph whose nodes are all points of interest in the considered cluster. The nodes that form part of the starting lattice are connected by a directed edge if they are neighbors. From now on $v_k^{\mathrm{latt}} (1 \leq k \leq K)$ are the nodes that form part of the lattice, $[v_{k_1}^{\mathrm{latt}}, v_{k_2}^{\mathrm{latt}}], (k_1, k_2) \in K^2$, is a directed edge from node $v_{k_1}^{\mathrm{latt}}$ to $v_{k_2}^{\mathrm{latt}}$, meaning that $v_{k_2}^{\mathrm{latt}}$ is considered in the lattice as a neighbor of $v_{k_1}^{\mathrm{latt}}$, and $\mathcal{N}^+(v_k^{\mathrm{latt}})$ is the set of all outneighbors of v_k^{latt} (see Sec. 2.2.2).

As the lattice will be expanded now over a near-regular texture, variations in the lighting conditions are expected, so new added neighbors to the lattice do not need to have a similar gray value in contrast to the conditions imposed for neighbors at the starting lattice (see Sec. 5.3.2.1).

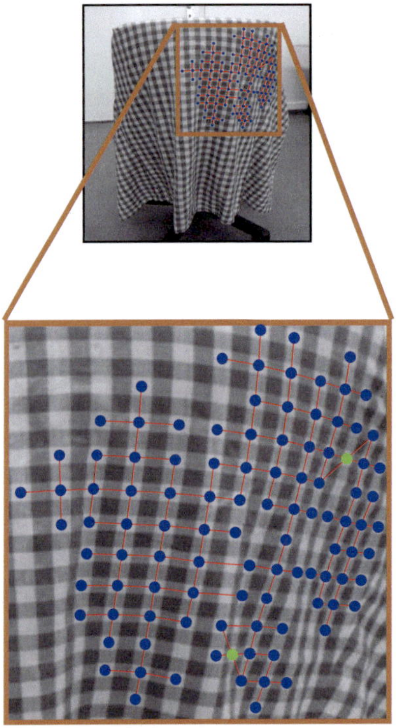

Figure 5.14 The starting lattices for an input image, without taking into consideration the similarity of the displacement vectors of neighboring points (left) and considering it (right). The dots are the points of interest in the starting lattice and the red lines connect neighboring points.

Based on [159] the starting lattice is expanded as explained next. Every node in the graph with less than four outneighbors ($|\mathcal{N}^+(v_k^{\text{latt}})| < 4$) is further considered to expand the starting lattice. For this purpose, new outneighbors are searched in the points that belong to the cluster. The potential outneighbors must lie only in an environment of the position where the point will be if the texture were regular. In case that several points in the cluster fulfill these criteria, then the closest point of interest to the expected position will become the outneighbor of the searched node and a directed edge will be therefore set (e.g., in Fig. 5.15

upper row left, the point $\mathbf{p}_1^{\text{poss}}$ will become part of the lattice instead of $\mathbf{p}_2^{\text{poss}}$). The expected position is calculated from the vectors spanned by the inneighbors of the considered node to their respective outneighbors. As a node can have several inneighbors and the texture is not regular, different vectors will be used to obtain the proposed new outneighbors. Because of this, a node may have more than four outneighbors.

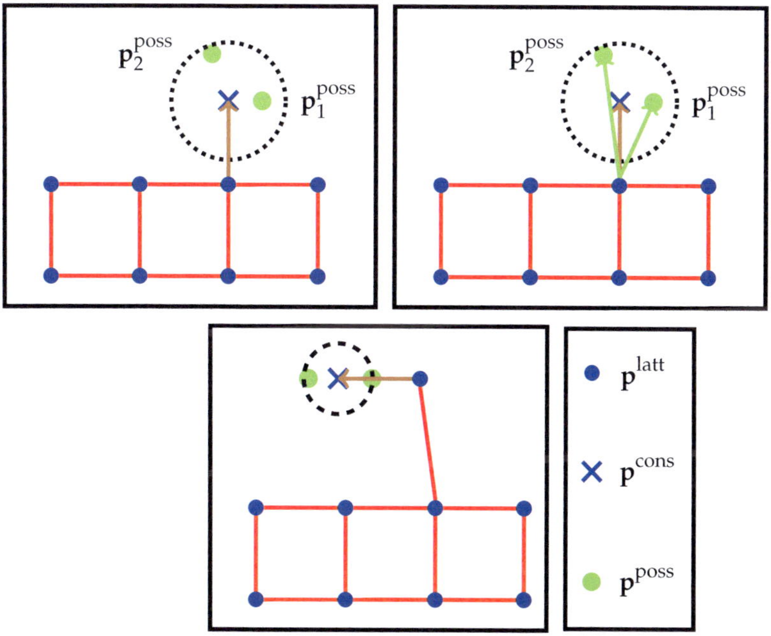

Figure 5.15 Illustration of the selection of new points for the lattice. The method based on [159] will select $\mathbf{p}_1^{\text{poss}}$ in the upper configuration as new point, whereas the other proposed approach will select $\mathbf{p}_2^{\text{poss}}$.

Considering the maximum number of outneighbors per node, the starting lattice is expanded as follows. Every node in the graph with less than four outneighbors $(|\mathcal{N}^+(v_k^{\text{latt}})| < 4)$ is also considered in this approach to expand the starting lattice. However, the number of allowed outneighbors per node is restricted in this version of the expansion of the starting lattice to four. Similar to the previous approach, outneighbors will be searched from points in the cluster that lie in an environment where the point is expected if the texture were regular.

The expected position will also be calculated from the vectors spanned from the inneighbors to the considered node, but, in contrast to the previous approach, they will not be considered independently. Average vectors will be calculated from the parallel vectors and used for the search. Furthermore, if several points of interest $\mathbf{p}_{k_1}^{\text{poss}}$, $1 < k_1 \leq K_1$, in the cluster lie in the allowed environment, the closest point to the expected one will not be necessarily selected anymore. In this version, the vectors spanned from the point of the considered node $\mathbf{p}^{\text{cons}}$ to the points $\mathbf{p}_{k_1}^{\text{poss}}$ representing the new possible outneighbors are compared. The candidate point in the cluster whose vector becomes more similar to the expected one will be selected (e.g., in Fig. 5.15 upper row right, the point $\mathbf{p}_2^{\text{poss}}$ will become part of the lattice instead of $\mathbf{p}_1^{\text{poss}}$). The similarity is measured by taking into consideration the angles of the vectors and their lengths. For this purpose, the following cost function is minimized:

$$m_{k_1}^{\text{T3}} = \frac{\left\|\mathbf{p}_{k_1}^{\text{poss}} - \mathbf{p}^{\text{cons}}\right\|_2}{\mu\left(\left\|\mathbf{p}_{k_1}^{\text{poss}} - \mathbf{p}^{\text{cons}}\right\|_2\right)} \cdot \left|\measuredangle\left(\mathbf{p}_{k_1}^{\text{poss}}\right) - \measuredangle\left(\mathbf{p}^{\text{cons}}\right)\right|, \tag{5.34}$$

where $\measuredangle(\mathbf{p})$ denotes the angle spanned by the vector $\mathbf{p}$ and the u_1-axis. In case that the spanned vectors of several candidate points have a similar angle to the angle of the expected vector, then the point with the smallest spatial distance to the considered point will be selected (e.g., in Fig. 5.15 down, the right green point will be selected instead of the left one) to avoid springing interest points along the direction.

Finally, vectors whose outneighbors have already been searched but still have less than four outneighbors will be considered again if they become inneighbors of a new considered node. Note that in this approach the number of outneighbors per node is restricted to a maximum of four, but the number of inneighbors that a node may possess is not restricted.

5.3.2.3 Detection of potential texels

Once the lattice of the near-regular texture has been detected, potential texels are searched. They are found at every closed cell in the expanded lattice (see Fig. 5.16 upper row left). As a consequence, every node in the lattice with outneighbors is considered (see Fig. 5.16 upper row right).

The vectors spanned from a node to its outneighbors are calculated and grouped into orthogonal pairs (see Fig. 5.16 lower row left). If the outneighbors in a pair of orthogonal vectors have an outneighbor in common that is not the analyzed node, then a cell is set with the common outneighbor as the fourth point of the cell (see Fig. 5.16 lower row right). This cell contains one potential texel.

To increase the probability of extracting the correct texels of the near-regular texture, every detected texel in the lattice becomes a weight. The weight is given by the number of times that the cell will be found if the nodes that make up the cell are used as the starting search node.

5.3.2.4 Projection into quadrangles of equal shape with normalized intensities

The detected potential texels of the texture must be compared independently of lighting and displacement variations along the image plane. For this purpose, the detected texels are transformed first into squared texels of equal lengths. At this point the assumption is made that the transformation can be described by an affine transformation. The six degrees of freedom [54, 107] $\mathbf{A}^{\mathrm{Aff}}, \mathbf{v}^{\mathrm{Aff}}$ are obtained from the correspondences of the four points that span the cell $\mathbf{p}_{k_1}^{\mathrm{grid}}$ with the four corresponding points of the corresponding quadrangle $\mathbf{p}_{k_1}^{\mathrm{grid,2}}$ (see e.g., Fig. 5.17 left):

$$\mathbf{p}_{k_1}^{\mathrm{grid}} = \mathbf{A}^{\mathrm{Aff}} \cdot \mathbf{p}_{k_1}^{\mathrm{grid,2}} + \mathbf{v}^{\mathrm{Aff}} \qquad 1 \leq k_1 \leq 4. \tag{5.35}$$

Note that a correct enumeration of the four points that span a cell is very important to be able to compare affinely transformed texels in the quadrangles space directly. This system of equations is overdetermined as no perfect affine transformation exists to warp the texels in image plane into the quadrangles. Furthermore, the assumption of an affine transformation is not always real, as cells may not be a parallelogram.

The parameters of the affine transformation are therefore estimated by the least-squares method [59]:

$$\begin{pmatrix} \mathbf{p}_1^{\text{grid}} \\ \mathbf{p}_2^{\text{grid}} \\ \mathbf{p}_3^{\text{grid}} \\ \mathbf{p}_4^{\text{grid}} \end{pmatrix} = \underbrace{\begin{pmatrix} p_{1,1}^{\text{grid},2} & p_{1,2}^{\text{grid},2} & 0 & 0 & 1 & 0 \\ 0 & 0 & p_{1,1}^{\text{grid},2} & p_{1,2}^{\text{grid},2} & 0 & 1 \\ p_{2,1}^{\text{grid},2} & p_{2,2}^{\text{grid},2} & 0 & 0 & 1 & 0 \\ 0 & 0 & p_{2,1}^{\text{grid},2} & p_{2,2}^{\text{grid},2} & 0 & 1 \\ p_{3,1}^{\text{grid},2} & p_{3,2}^{\text{grid},2} & 0 & 0 & 1 & 0 \\ 0 & 0 & p_{3,1}^{\text{grid},2} & p_{3,2}^{\text{grid},2} & 0 & 1 \\ p_{4,1}^{\text{grid},2} & p_{4,2}^{\text{grid},2} & 0 & 0 & 1 & 0 \\ 0 & 0 & p_{4,1}^{\text{grid},2} & p_{4,2}^{\text{grid},2} & 0 & 1 \end{pmatrix}}_{\boldsymbol{\Phi}} \cdot \begin{pmatrix} a_{11}^{\text{Aff}} \\ a_{12}^{\text{Aff}} \\ a_{21}^{\text{Aff}} \\ a_{22}^{\text{Aff}} \\ v_1^{\text{Aff}} \\ v_2^{\text{Aff}} \end{pmatrix} \tag{5.36}$$

$$\rightarrow \begin{pmatrix} \hat{a}_{11}^{\text{Aff}} \\ \hat{a}_{12}^{\text{Aff}} \\ \hat{a}_{21}^{\text{Aff}} \\ \hat{a}_{22}^{\text{Aff}} \\ \hat{v}_1^{\text{Aff}} \\ \hat{v}_2^{\text{Aff}} \end{pmatrix} = \left(\boldsymbol{\Phi}^{\text{T}} \cdot \boldsymbol{\Phi}\right)^{-1} \cdot \boldsymbol{\Phi}^{\text{T}} \cdot \begin{pmatrix} \mathbf{p}_1^{\text{grid}} \\ \mathbf{p}_2^{\text{grid}} \\ \mathbf{p}_3^{\text{grid}} \\ \mathbf{p}_4^{\text{grid}} \end{pmatrix}, \tag{5.37}$$

where $\mathbf{p}_{k_1}^c = \left(p_{k_1 1}^c \quad p_{k_1 2}^c\right)^{\text{T}}$, $1 \leq k_1 \leq 4$, $c \in \{\text{grid}, \text{grid}, 2\}$, a_{ij} is a component of the matrix $\mathbf{A}^{\text{Aff}}$, $i, j \in \{1, 2\}$, and $\mathbf{v}^{\text{Aff}} = \left(v_1^{\text{Aff}} \quad v_2^{\text{Aff}}\right)^{\text{T}}$. With these equations the corresponding positions of the points of the texel in the quadrangle can be calculated in the image plane to adopt their image values and therefore transform the detected texels to the quadrangles $t_{\mathbf{u}}^{\text{Aff}}$ that are robust to affine transformations.

Finally, the affinely transformed texels must also become lighting independent. For this purpose, the transformed texels are all normalized by the following equation in contrast to [159]:

$$t_{\mathbf{u}}^{\text{ind}} = \frac{t_{\mathbf{u}}^{\text{Aff}} - \min\limits_{\mathbf{u}}\left(t_{\mathbf{u}}^{\text{Aff}}\right)}{\max\limits_{\mathbf{u}}\left(t_{\mathbf{u}}^{\text{Aff}}\right) - \min\limits_{\mathbf{u}}\left(t_{\mathbf{u}}^{\text{Aff}}\right)}. \tag{5.38}$$

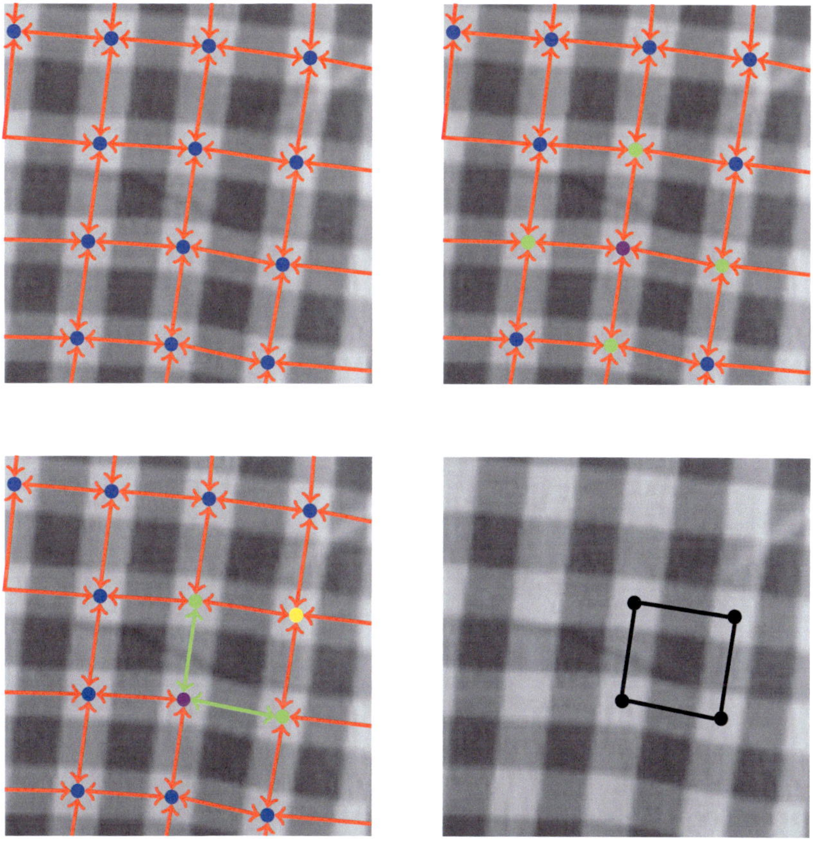

Figure 5.16 Illustration of the extraction of potential texels. An extracted lattice over a texture is shown (upper row left), whereas the interesting points are the blue dots and their relationship to their neighbors is given by the red arrows. The outneighbors (green dots) of a considered point (violet dot) are selected first (upper row right). Two outneighbors with orthogonal vectors are selected next (green) and their common outneighbor (yellow dot) is searched (lower row left). The cell spanned by the four selected points is a potential texel (lower row right).

5.3.2.5 Extraction of the representative texel

The representative texel $t_{\mathbf{u}}^{\text{rep}}$ of the detected near-regular texture is the median texel from the extracted ones projected onto the quadrangles $t_{k_1,\mathbf{u}}^{\text{ind}}$, $1 \leq k_1 \leq K_1$. However, as shown in [159], processing the texels in the quadrangles before the filtering step will improve the quality of the representative texel. On the one hand, the suppression of inappropriate texels minimizes errors when the median value is calculated. For this purpose, outliers in the set of extracted texels, as well as texels with no repetitions at the contours, are considered here. On the other hand, different texels may have been extracted at one cluster, e.g., if the image consists of two textures, one occluded by the other one, with similar detected points of interest. In such cases the texels of both textures may be correctly extracted, but the median filtering over them will reveal a wrong texel of the textures. However, the detection of the different texel groups will allow to separate them and extract different average texels, one per texture. All of these methods may be performed or only a selection of them. For simplification purposes, the methods will be explained with $t^{\text{ind}}_{k_1,\mathbf{u}}$, $1 \leq k_1 \leq K_1$.

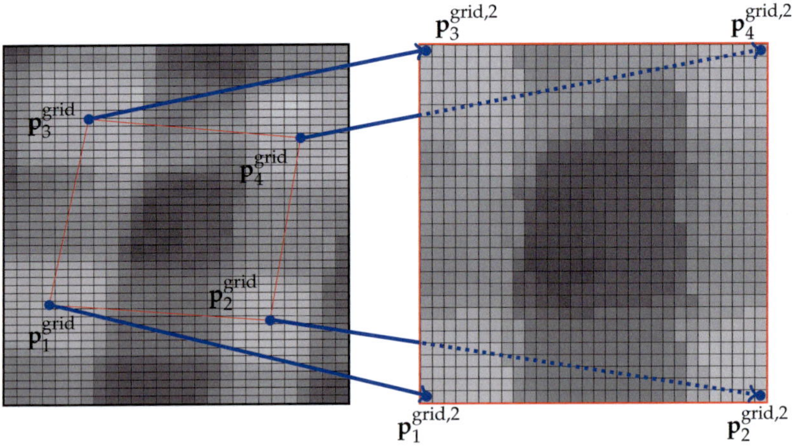

Figure 5.17 Projection of the texels into a quadrangle.

The **occlusion of outliers** is considered via the principal component analysis [45]. The eigentexels $e^{\text{PCA}}_{\mathbf{u}}$ and eigenvalues λ^{PCA} are extracted from all texels $t^{\text{ind}}_{k_1,\mathbf{u}}$, $1 \leq k_1 \leq K_1$. These are approximated in a second step using only the eigentexels with the τ^{PCA} strongest eigenvalues:

$$\hat{t}^{\text{ind}}_{k_1,\mathbf{u}} = \sum_{k}^{\tau^{\text{PCA}}} c_k^{\text{PCA}} \cdot e^{\text{PCA}}_{\mathbf{u},k} + \overline{t^{\text{ind}}_{\mathbf{u}}}, \tag{5.39}$$

where c_k^{PCA} denotes the k-th strongest principal component and $\overline{t^{\text{ind}}_{\mathbf{u}}}$ the average texel over all texels in the quadrangles $t^{\text{ind}}_{k_1,\mathbf{u}}$. All of the texels $t^{\text{ind}}_{k_1,\mathbf{u}}$ that vary significantly from their reconstructed ones $\hat{t}^{\text{ind}}_{k_1,\mathbf{u}}$ via the principal component analysis method are discarded, as they can be assumed as outliers.

The **repeatability of the texels at the contours** is considered next. As the texel of the texture is repeated over the texture, the texel should have similar boundaries. This condition has already been used in [66] and in [159] to discard faulty texels. Here the condition is implemented as in [159], where the correlation coefficient (see Sec. 2.1) of the left and right contour, respectively top and lower contour

- $r\left(t^{\text{ind}}\left[\begin{pmatrix}1\\k\end{pmatrix}\right], t^{\text{ind}}\left[\begin{pmatrix}1\\U_2-k\end{pmatrix}\right]\right)$
- $r\left(t^{\text{ind}}\left[\begin{pmatrix}k\\1\end{pmatrix}\right], t^{\text{ind}}\left[\begin{pmatrix}U_1-k\\1\end{pmatrix}\right]\right)$

has to be high, where $1 \leq k \leq n^{\text{T},2}$, U_1 is the number of columns in the texel and U_2 the number of rows. However, if the compared contours are of an almost homogeneous gray value, then the texels would not be classified as faulty.

The **grouping of texels according to their similarity** is considered to improve the extraction of the representative texels. Different texels may be extracted at one cluster if the characteristic points of different textures are not separated. Faulty texels may be extracted, i.a., due to the simplification of the assumption of an affine transformation of the texels to project them onto the quadrangles. Therefore clusters and isolated texels may be obtained at the extracted texels from the image if the similarity of their content is compared. To detect such cases, all of the extracted texels are represented by a node in a graph and pairwise compared using the correlation coefficient $r(t^{\text{ind}}_{k_1,\mathbf{u}}, t^{\text{ind}}_{k_2,\mathbf{u}})$ (see Sec. 2.1).

Similar texels will have a correlation coefficient close to one and their corresponding nodes will be therefore connected by an edge. Clusters of similar texels are every connected graph. Isolated vertices or connected graphs with a small number of nodes are extracted texels that are probably not a real texel of the image, as they appear seldom. Due to this fact, only the connected graphs containing a minimum number of nodes will further be considered. Representative texels will be extracted from every cluster group via median filtering and will represent the textures in the image.

If more than one representative texel $t_{\mathbf{u}}^{\text{rep}}$ is extracted per cluster, then the expanded lattice may also be divided, so that every lattice is composed from cells that are similar to only one of the obtained representative texels. However, in this case the texels of every cell in the original expanded lattice must be transformed to the quadrangles robust to affine transformations and lighting variations, and finally compared, e.g., using the correlation coefficient, to the extracted representative texels.

5.3.3 Post-processing

The extracted representative texels $t_{\mathbf{u}}^{\text{rep}}$ of the image represent the near-regular textures detected at the input image. Due to the fact that there is not a unique texel per texture (see Sec. 5.1.1), some of the extracted representative texels $t_{\mathbf{u}}^{\text{rep}}$ may represent the same texture. In Sec. 5.3.3.1 the detection of texels that represent the same texture is considered.

Furthermore, some of the extracted representative texels $t_{\mathbf{u}}^{\text{rep}}$ may not belong to a valid texture in the image at all. The average texels may result from more than one texel. A method to detect such overdetermined texels is explained in Sec. 5.3.3.2.

Finally, the repeatibility at the contours of the texels may also be tested for the extracted representative texels $t_{\mathbf{u}}^{\text{rep}}$ as explained in Sec. 5.3.2.5.

5.3.3.1 Fusion of similar texels

Points of interest with different corresponding features may be extracted from one texture. This will lead after the clustering of the points of interest according to their features to different clusters and therefore to different extracted texels of the same texture. Redundant information is therefore obtained, as the same texture is extracted several times from one near-regular texture. New texels from a texture are obtained in general by a cyclic displacement of the texel (e.g., see Fig. 5.18). To fuse similar texels, all of the extracted representative texels are pairwise compared to detect if they represent the same texture. For this purpose, the correlation coefficient is obtained from the compared pairs $t^{\mathrm{rep}}_{\mathbf{u},k_1}, t^{\mathrm{rep}}_{\mathbf{u},k_2}$, but one of the texels is cyclically displaced at this point:

$$\max_{\mathbf{k}\in\mathbb{Z}^2}\left(r\left(t^{\mathrm{rep}}_{\mathbf{u},k_1}, t^{\mathrm{rep}}_{\mathbf{u}+\mathbf{k},k_2}\right)\right). \tag{5.40}$$

Every pair of texels is compared as many times as needed until the cyclically displaced texel is similar to its undisplaced one, taking into consideration all possible cyclic displacements of the texel. Texels that represent the same texture and possess a similar correlation coefficient are finally merged.

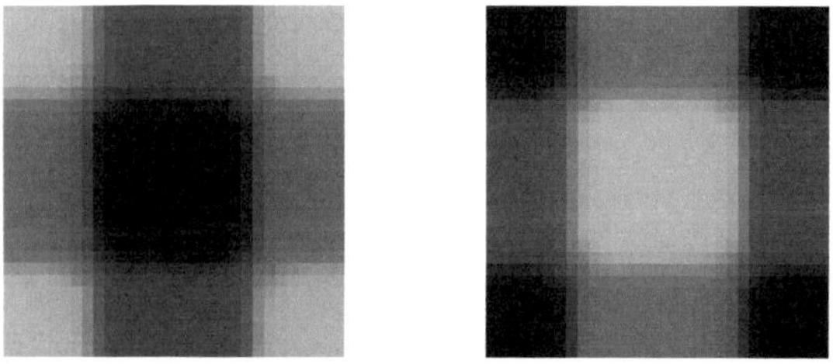

Figure 5.18 Example of two extracted representative texels that are similar but cyclically displaced.

The presented approaches in the previous Secs. 5.3.1 – 5.3.2 for the detection and extraction of near-regular textures do not use the color information. Spatially displaced textures with the same structure but different colors may be very similar in the gray-level image and therefore grouped and fused to the same texel in Eq. 5.40. Such a fusion can be overcome if the color is taken into consideration. For this purpose, the texels projected onto the quadrangles that are most similar to their corresponding representative texel of their textures are determined. From their color information the color signatures from Sec. 3.2 are extracted and compared using the earth mover's distance [122].

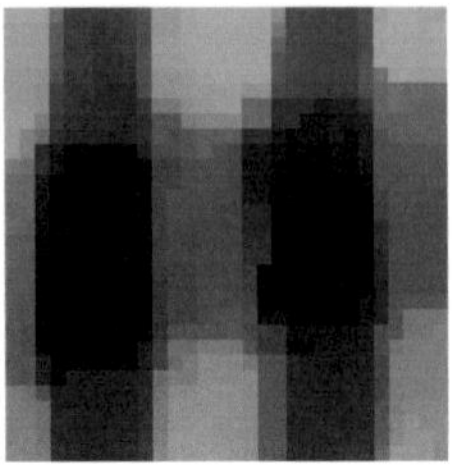

Figure 5.19 Example of an overdetermined texel.

5.3.3.2 Detection of overdetermined texels

Extracted representative texels resulting from several valid texels (overdetermined) distort the result. To detect and discard them, a regular texture is created for every extracted representative texel $t_{\mathbf{u}}^{\mathrm{rep}}$ following Eq. 5.1 as

$$g_{\mathbf{u}} = \sum_{(k_1,k_2)=(1,1)}^{(K_1,K_2)} t_{\mathbf{u}}^{\mathrm{rep}} ** \delta\left[\mathbf{u} - k_1 \cdot U_1 \begin{pmatrix}1\\0\end{pmatrix} - k_2 \cdot U_2 \begin{pmatrix}0\\1\end{pmatrix}\right], \qquad (5.41)$$

where U_2 is the height and U_1 the width of the quadrangles on which the detected texels in the image plane are projected. The Fourier transform of this image is according to Eq. 5.2

$$G_{\mathbf{u}} \propto T_{\mathbf{f}}^{\mathrm{rep}} \sum_{(k_1,k_2)}^{(K_1,K_2)} \delta_{\mathbf{f}-k_1\mathbf{l}_1-k_2\mathbf{l}_2}, \qquad (5.42)$$

where

$$\begin{pmatrix}\mathbf{l}_1^{\mathrm{T}}\\ \mathbf{l}_2^{\mathrm{T}}\end{pmatrix} = \begin{pmatrix}U_1 & 0\\ 0 & U_2\end{pmatrix}^{-1}. \qquad (5.43)$$

If the first considerable peaks of $|G_{\mathbf{u}}|$ do not appear at the expected positions, then the extracted average texel is discarded.

6 Detection of regions

The recognition of connected regions due to stable colors or a repeating pattern is a very important task in image processing. Otherwise, the extraction of the color, shape, and texture features presented in the previous chapters can be distorted if different regions contribute to them. The detection of such regions should be robust to affine transformations, as the regions should be detected independently of their scale, rotation, shear, or position in the image. This step is considered in this chapter.

This chapter is organized as follows. An introduction to the detection of regions and to the state of the art is given in Sec. 6.1. The structure of the proposed region detectors is presented in Sec. 6.2. It can be divided into two steps, the detection of color regions in images (Sec. 6.3) and the detection and extraction of patterns (Sec. 6.4). The results achieved by the proposed region detectors are shown in Sec. 8.5.

6.1 Introduction to the detection of regions

The division of an image into meaningful areas is called segmentation [20, 54]. For this purpose, every pixel in the image is assigned to a region, whereas the regions must be spatially connected and must not overlap between each other. Two types of methods exist to segment images: edge-oriented methods, where edges between the regions are searched, and region-oriented methods, where neighboring pixels with similar characteristics are grouped into regions [20, 54].

The detection of regions robust to affine transformations and lighting conditions (up to a certain variation) in images and the representation of their neighborhood is another way of describing the information in images. However, in this case not all of the pixels in an image are used. Only interesting points or regions are searched first. Typically, the neighborhood of the detected points and even the detected regions are approximated by an ellipse [102], from which the characteristics are extracted.

Due to noise and distortions in the images, e.g., compression artifacts, the need to assign every pixel to a region may alternate the properties of the meaningful areas in the image. Every pixel in the image may not be necessary for the image processing or not even improve it. On the other hand, the description of the image information with the neighborhood of interesting points may contain information of different objects appearing in the image. Because of this, the detection and extraction of meaningful regions is considered. Regions in the input images are searched, whose pixels possess either a similar color or form a pattern of alternating colors. However, the assignment of every pixel to a region is not forced in this thesis.

6.1.1 State of the art

Many segmentation methods have been proposed in the literature. A brief overview of some of the segmentation methods that consider color and texture information and do not need interaction with humans is presented first. Wang et al. segment in [139] the image block-wise instead of pixel-wise. For this purpose, they partition the image into 4×4 pixel blocks. A feature vector is then assigned to each block that contains information about the average color in the block and the average coefficients of their wavelet transform. With the help of the k-means algorithm [45] the image is segmented. The JSEG method is proposed by Deng and Manjunath in [42]. This segmentation method works in two steps. First, the colors appearing in the images are quantized. In the second step homogenous areas are searched. The homogeneity is measured at different scales taking into consideration the spatial distribution of the quantized values of the pixels. Carson et al. present Blobworld in [30], where the image is segmented into regions using the color and texture properties of the pixels plus their spatial location. To extract the texture properties, an appropriate scale is selected per pixel.

Furthermore, several detectors have been proposed for the detection of points and regions of interest in images. An overview and comparison between some of them can be found in [101, 102]. They can be roughly classified into their search aim, "points of interest" or "regions of interest." In case of detectors searching for points, prominent points are desired. Tuytelaars and Van Gool use in [134] local invariants to describe the neighborhood of points of interest. For this purpose, they represent affinely invariant regions as a parallelogram obtained at corner points using their adjacent edges. In [135] Tuytelaars and Van Gool search for affinely invariant regions from maxima intensities instead of using corner points. Furthermore, the affinely invariant regions are represented with the help of ellipses instead of parallelograms. Mikolajczyk and Schmid consider the detection of scale and affinely invariant interest points in [98–100]. The Harris detector [62] is therefore combined with automatic scale selection. Lowe also considers an automatic scale selection to detect points of interest in [88, 89]. For this purpose, the Hessian matrix is used instead of the Harris detector. A descriptor for the local image regions at the detected interesting points is also proposed. The descriptor is the histogram of the orientation of the gradients around the interest point. The *Speeded Up Robust Features* (SURF) detector and descriptor are presented by Bay et al. in [14, 15]. The detection of points of interest is also based on a scale-space analysis. An approximation of the second order of the Gaussian derivatives is used together with integral images [36, 136] to improve the performance when the points are being detected. The descriptor also considers the gradients around the interest point, but in this case the wavelet transform is used. The area around the interest point (its size is dependent on the scale at which the interest point was detected) is subdivided into regions, from which the descriptor is extracted.

The second type of detectors tries to detect regions of interest in images, like the *Maximally Stable Extremal Regions* (MSER) detector [96]. This one analyzes gray-level images by comparing the intensity values of all pixels with an increasing threshold value. Along the iterations the pixels with an intensity smaller than the threshold value are marked and grouped into connected regions. If two regions are connected in a new iteration, then the smaller one is added to the bigger one. Stable regions are those whose area remain similar during different threshold values. The *Maximally Stable Colour Regions* (MSCR) detector extends the idea of the MSER detector to color images [50]. The color differences between neighboring pixels are calculated first. In [50] the use of the Chi-squared distance is preferred to the Euclidean distance. Like the MSER detector, the color differences between the pixels are iteratively compared with an increasing threshold value, which is obtained from the expected distribution between neighboring pixels. Stable regions are selected according to the area of the obtained regions at different thresholds and their threshold values. Furthermore, Chavez and Gustafson also study the extension of the MSER detector to color images in [32]. Three functions of the color information are defined to separate red, green and blue pixels from dissimilar pixels. The MSER detector is then run on every new channel information plus on the gray-level image and its inverse. Marques et al. propose in [93, 94] the extraction of regions of interest in images using visual attention models. They focus on the detection of regions that acquire a rapid and involuntary visual attention.

6.2 Structure of the proposed region detectors

The structures of the region detectors proposed in the following sections are similar, as color areas in the image are searched in a first step (Sec. 6.3) and combined next (Sec. 6.4) to find patterns in the input images. An overview of this modus operandi is shown in Fig. 6.1. A preliminary version of a region detector working this way has been presented in [156].

6.3 Detection of color regions in images

Two different paths are followed for the detection of non-overlapping color regions in images. The first path (Sec. 6.3.1) uses the representation in the CIELAB color space (see Sec. 3.1.1) and has been presented in [156]. The second path (Sec. 6.3.2) follows the psychologically inspired color representation using humans' color categories (see Sec. 3.3).

6.3.1 Extraction of non-overlapping stable color regions

Analog to the stable regions in the MSER detector [96], the detection of stable color regions is introduced in Sec. 6.3.1.1 inspired by [50]. However, the stable color regions may overlap, as a pixel in an image can belong to different regions, which implies a redundant information of the pixels in the image. A method to obtain non-overlapping stable color regions from an image is therefore presented in Sec. 6.3.1.2.

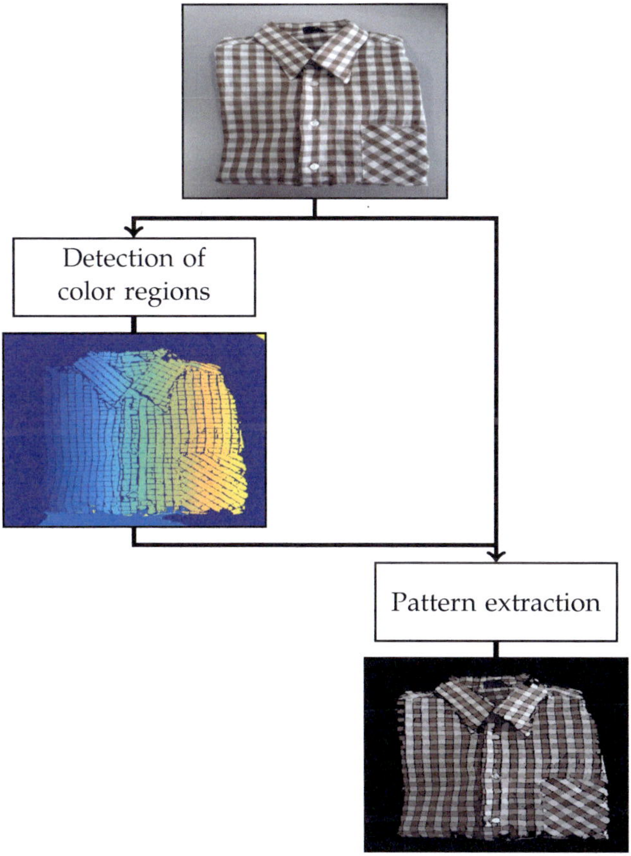

Figure 6.1 Modus operandi of the proposed region detectors.

6.3.1.1 Stable color regions

According to the MSCR detector [50], the color difference between neighboring pixels is calculated first. However, the ℓ_2-norm (see Sec. 2.1) is used for this purpose instead of the chi-squared distance recommended in [50]:

$$d_{\mathbf{u}}^{\mathrm{SCR}} = \left\| \mathbf{g}_{\mathbf{u}} - \mathbf{g}\left[\mathbf{u} + \begin{pmatrix}1\\0\end{pmatrix}\right]\right\|_2 + \left\| \mathbf{g}_{\mathbf{u}} - \mathbf{g}\left[\mathbf{u} + \begin{pmatrix}0\\1\end{pmatrix}\right]\right\|_2 . \qquad (6.1)$$

The difference image $d_{\mathbf{u}}^{\mathrm{SCR}}$ is iteratively compared with the increasing values of a threshold vector. The values of the vector were obtained empirically from the inversed cumulative distribution function of the difference image $d_{\mathbf{u}}^{\mathrm{SCR}}$ of some test images [156]. The maximally stable color regions are then further determined as in [50].

In order to reduce noise, two difference images $d_{\mathbf{u}}^{\mathrm{SCR},1}, d_{\mathbf{u}}^{\mathrm{SCR},2}$ are obtained per input image. From both difference images the maximally stable color regions are extracted. $d_{\mathbf{u}}^{\mathrm{SCR},1}$ and $d_{\mathbf{u}}^{\mathrm{SCR},2}$ are obtained after filtering the input image with a Gaussian filter. However, in $d_{\mathbf{u}}^{\mathrm{SCR},2}$ the color values of the real input image are kept at edges that are detected by the Canny operator [20, 28]. Pixels that already belong to a maximally stable color region extracted with the difference image $d_{\mathbf{u}}^{\mathrm{SCR},2}$ are suppressed from the maximally stable color regions obtained from $d_{\mathbf{u}}^{\mathrm{SCR},1}$ to reduce the number of stable color regions that a pixel may belong to.

Stable color regions of an input image are all maximally stable color regions from $d_{\mathbf{u}}^{\mathrm{SCR},1}$ and $d_{\mathbf{u}}^{\mathrm{SCR},2}$ with a minimum size.

6.3.1.2 Non-overlapping stable color regions

The stable color regions extracted in Sec. 6.3.1.1 can have pixels in common and therefore overlap (see Fig. 6.2 top, the boundaries of the extracted stable color regions are displayed in black). However, non-overlapping color regions are essential for the algorithm to detect patterns in Sec. 6.4 and to avoid redundant information. To obtain non-overlapping stable color regions, a graph representation is used. The extracted stable color regions are represented as nodes v_k from the graph. Edges are set between the nodes if they overlap and no other stable color region exists being part of the bigger stable color region and containing the smaller one (e.g., (v_5, v_4) and (v_5, v_1)) in Fig. 6.2). Although in Fig. 6.2 the stable color region v_2 is part of v_5, it is not directly connected with it by an edge because v_4 contains v_2 and is part of v_5. Another exemplary graph representation is shown in the left of Fig. 6.3. The methods used to obtain non-overlapping color regions explained next will be exemplified with this graph.

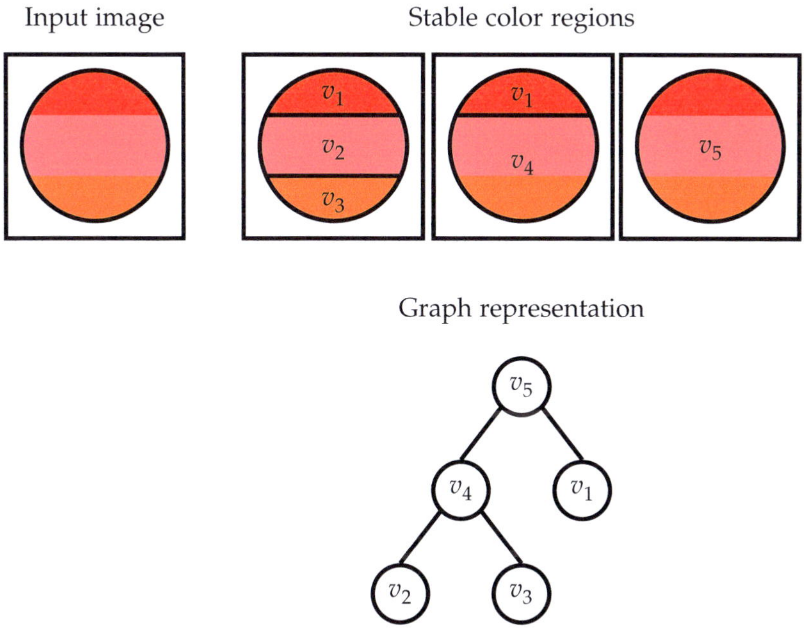

Figure 6.2 Graph representation of the extracted color regions. Five stable color regions are extracted from the input image (top left) and their boundaries are displayed in black in the illustrations (top). v_5 is a stable color region that contains the whole circle and all the other extracted color regions. However, v_5 is not directly connected with v_2 and v_3 in the graph representation (bottom), as v_4 contains v_2 and v_3 and is itself contained in v_5.

For every input image, the graph of the stable color regions will contain isolated vertices for the stable color regions that do not overlap (e.g., v_1, v_8 in Fig. 6.3 left) and trees with the color regions that overlap (e.g., $v_2, \ldots, v_7$ in Fig. 6.3 left). Therefore, to obtain non-overlapping stable color regions, the trees in the graph must be processed until the graph consists only of isolated vertices.

From now on vertices connected by an edge to a smaller color region will be denoted as a parent and the smaller color region as a child. By these means, a child may also be a parent of another stable color region and vice versa. For every parent in the graph, the set of pixels that belong to the parent but not to its children is determined first. From these pixels connected areas with a minimum size are determined. Each connected area that is big enough will be added as new node in the graph (ν_k), as a child of the considered parent node v_k (see Fig. 6.3 right ν_5, ν_7). The remaining pixels that do not form a big connected area in the image are considered at its corresponding node v_k as ω_k ($\omega_3, \omega_5, \omega_7$ in Fig. 6.3 right). The trees in the graph representation are further processed until isolated vertices are left. For this purpose, every parent node will be iteratively considered starting with the corresponding one to the smallest color region. Depending on the number of children that a parent node has, different approches are used. These are exemplified in Fig. 6.4 for the red squared color regions in Fig. 6.3 right.

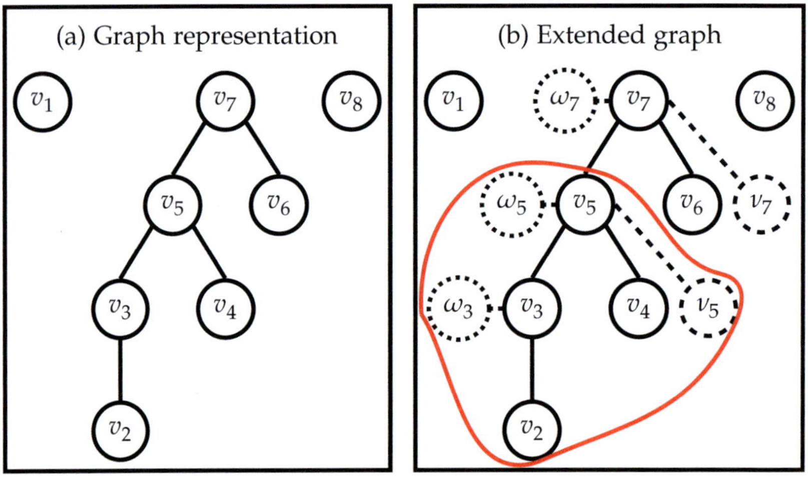

Figure 6.3 Exemplary graph representation of the extracted color regions.

If the considered node has only one child (e.g v_3 in Fig. 6.4 top left), then the child will be discarded and the original color region of the parent kept, including its pixels in ω_k. For example, v_3 is kept in our example graph and v_2 discarded (see Fig. 6.4 top right). However, if a parent has more than one child, then the relationship between the children must be considered to process the tree. To this end, an auxiliary graph is used, whose nodes are the children (see Fig. 6.4 bottom left). The children in the auxiliary graph will be connected by an edge if their mean colors of their stable color regions calculated in CIELAB color space are similar, and they are spatially connected (v_3, ν_5 in Fig. 6.4 bottom left). To prove the spatial connection, the pixels in ω_k (from the parent node) are considered. If the auxiliary graph is connected, then in the original graph the parent will be kept and their children discarded. On the other hand, if the auxiliary graph is not connected, then the parent will be removed from the original image and its children kept. However, children that were connected by an edge in the auxiliary graph will be merged in the original graph (see Fig. 6.4 bottom). When a parent is removed from the original graph, the nodes that will replace it become children from their original grandparent. In our example the node v_5 is removed from the original graph (see Fig. 6.5 left) and replaced by its child v_4 and the new node v_9 (see Fig. 6.5 right). These nodes become children from their original grandparent v_7 (see Fig. 6.5 right). These methods are further processed until the graph representing the stable color regions of the image consists uniquely of isolated nodes.

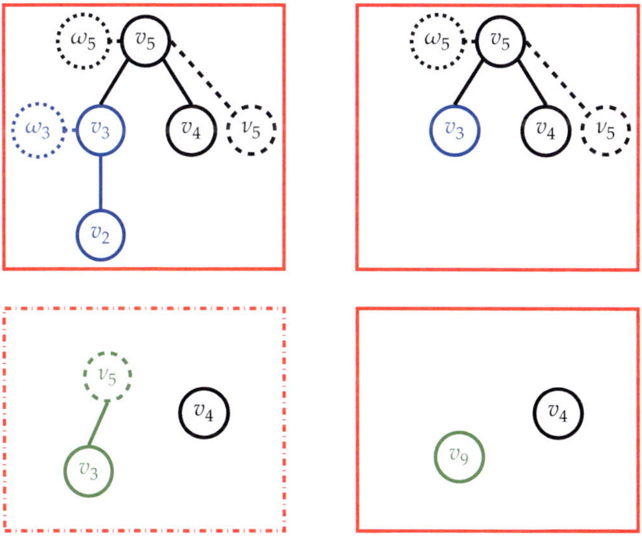

Figure 6.4 Exemplary graph representation of the extracted color regions.

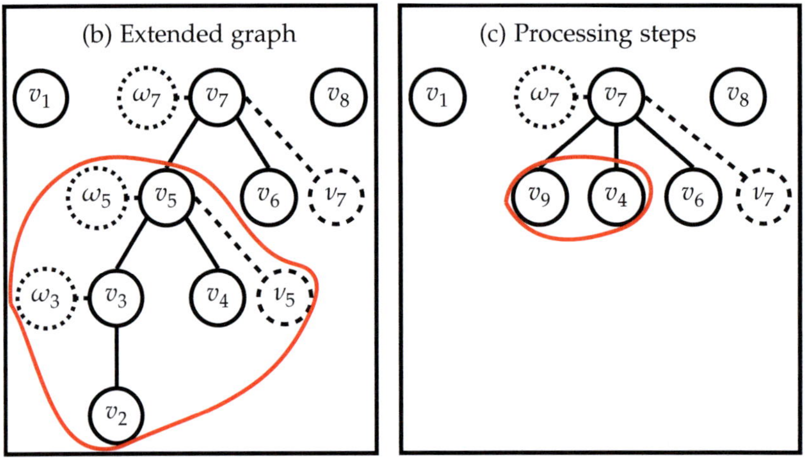

Figure 6.5 Exemplary graph representation of the extracted color regions.

6.3.2 Extraction of color regions in images using humans' color categories

The extraction of color regions in images using the extracted humans' color categories from Sec. 3.3 is considered in the following sections. A preliminary version has been published in [160].

Neighboring pixels with a similar color are expected to have a similar distribution over the extracted color categories $c_k^{\text{Color}}(\mathbf{g_u}), \mathbf{c}^{\text{Color}}(\mathbf{g_u})$. Because of this, the comparison of the color representation of neighboring pixels can be used to detect regions of colors in images. However, if the pixels are compared with their direct neighbors, errors may occur due to blur. To reduce such kind of errors, the colors of the pixels are compared with their direct neighbors in Δ distance along the u_1 and u_2 direction and the analyzed image may be a filtered version of the input image. Two different distance comparisons are considered (Sec. 6.3.2.1). Once the distances to the neighboring pixels in Δ distance have been calculated for all pixels in the image, color regions are extracted as in Sec. 6.3.2.2. Though the comparison of every pixel with its neighbors in Δ distance reduces artifacts due to blur, some color regions may be extracted from the input image containing different colors that are not clearly separated between each other via an edge. Methods to overcome such problems, to increase the areas of the detected color regions, and to reduce the number of detected color regions are described in Sec. 6.3.2.3.

6.3.2.1 Color relationship between pixels

Two distances are proposed to measure the color relationship between neighboring pixels in Δ distance, whereas their color information is represented with the extracted humans' color categories. The first distance $d_{\mathbf{u}}^{\mathrm{CC},1}$ is based on the correlation coefficient (see Sec. 2.1) and therefore the colors of the pixels are represented over the color categories via the probability distribution $c_k^{\mathrm{Color}}(\mathbf{g}_{\mathbf{u}})$ (see Eq. 3.9). The second distance to measure the color similarity is based on the ℓ_2-norm (see Sec. 2.1) and uses the vector representation $\mathbf{c}^{\mathrm{Color}}(\mathbf{g}_{\mathbf{u}})$ (see Eq. 3.10).

Color relationship based on the correlation coefficient: The probability distribution $c_k^{\mathrm{Color}}(\mathbf{g}_{\mathbf{u}})$ of the color of a pixel at the position $\mathbf{u}$ over the color categories is interpreted for the first distance measure $d_{\mathbf{u}}^{\mathrm{CC},1}$ as a random variable with the color categories k as the elementary events. Therefore the colors between neighboring pixels in Δ distance can be compared using the correlation coefficient. Two comparisons are done per pixel to consider its direct neighbors in Δ distances along the u_1- and u_2-axis:

$$r_{\mathbf{u}}^{CC} = \frac{r_{1,\mathbf{u}}^{CC} + r_{2,\mathbf{u}}^{CC}}{2}, \tag{6.2}$$

where

$$r_{1,\mathbf{u}}^{CC} = r\left(c_k^{\mathrm{Color}}(\mathbf{g}_{\mathbf{u}}), c_k^{\mathrm{Color}}\left(\mathbf{g}\left[\mathbf{u} + \begin{pmatrix}\Delta\\0\end{pmatrix}\right]\right)\right) \tag{6.3}$$

$$r_{2,\mathbf{u}}^{CC} = r\left(c_k^{\mathrm{Color}}(\mathbf{g}_{\mathbf{u}}), c_k^{\mathrm{Color}}\left(\mathbf{g}\left[\mathbf{u} + \begin{pmatrix}0\\\Delta\end{pmatrix}\right]\right)\right) . \tag{6.4}$$

The color distances between the neighboring pixels, and therefore a complementary measure of the probability of the pixels of being at a same color region, is given by

$$d_{\mathbf{u}}^{\mathrm{CC},1} = 1 - r_{\mathbf{u}}^{CC}. \tag{6.5}$$

Color relationship based on the ℓ_2-norm: If the vector representation of the color of the pixels $\mathbf{c}^{\text{Color}}(\mathbf{g_u})$ is used (see Sec. 3.3), then the distance of the colors of neighboring color pixels can be calculated using the ℓ_2-norm:

$$d_{\mathbf{u}}^{\text{CC},2} = \frac{d_{1,\mathbf{u}}^{\text{CC},2} + d_{2,\mathbf{u}}^{\text{CC},2}}{2}, \tag{6.6}$$

where

$$d_{1,\mathbf{u}}^{\text{CC},2} = \left\| \mathbf{c}^{\text{Color}}(\mathbf{g_u}) - \mathbf{c}^{\text{Color}}\left(\mathbf{g}\left[\mathbf{u} + \begin{pmatrix}\Delta\\0\end{pmatrix}\right]\right) \right\|_2 \tag{6.7}$$

$$d_{2,\mathbf{u}}^{\text{CC},2} = \left\| \mathbf{c}^{\text{Color}}(\mathbf{g_u}) - \mathbf{c}^{\text{Color}}\left(\mathbf{g}\left[\mathbf{u} + \begin{pmatrix}0\\\Delta\end{pmatrix}\right]\right) \right\|_2 . \tag{6.8}$$

6.3.2.2 Extraction of the color regions

Let $d_{\mathbf{u}}^{\text{CC}} \in \{d_{\mathbf{u}}^{\text{CC},1}, d_{\mathbf{u}}^{\text{CC},2}\}$ be one of the distances used to compare the colors between neighboring pixels in Δ distance. Over all positions in the image, the calculated color distances are compared with a threshold value τ^{CC}. A new binary image $g_{\mathbf{u}}^{\text{bin}}$ is created as

$$g_{\mathbf{u}}^{\text{bin}} = \begin{cases} 1 & \text{if } d_{\mathbf{u}}^{\text{CC}} < \tau^{\text{CC}}, \\ 0 & \text{otherwise.} \end{cases} \tag{6.9}$$

The connected components in the binary image are the extracted color regions of the input image $\mathbf{g_u}$.

6.3.2.3 Post-processing of the extracted color regions

The more homogenous the color, the bigger the area, and the lower the number of extracted color regions are, the more accurate and faster future processing will be. To improve the three conditions, three different approaches are explained next to increase the areas, increment the homogeneity of the color within the color regions, and reduce the total number of extracted color regions.

The **expansion of color regions** is considered first. The detection of color regions following the procedure proposed in the previous sections is based on the color distance of pixels with their neighbors in Δ distances. The color distance $d_{\mathbf{u}}^{\mathrm{CC}} \in \{d_{\mathbf{u}}^{\mathrm{CC},1}, d_{\mathbf{u}}^{\mathrm{CC},2}\}$ between the pixel at the position **u** and its neighbors in Δ distance is calculated and assigned to the pixel at the position **u**. However, when the color regions are extracted, the connected areas in $d_{\mathbf{u}}^{\mathrm{CC}}$ are searched with a small assigned color distance. The pixel at the position **u** may belong to a color region but its neighboring pixel, e.g., at the position $\mathbf{u} + \begin{bmatrix} 0 \\ \Delta \end{bmatrix}$, not if its color distance to its respective neighbors in Δ distance is too high. The extracted color regions will be therefore smaller than the real ones in the input image. The morphological dilation [20] of the extracted color regions will increment their size. This is done via the following structuring element with cardinality $(\Delta + 1)^2$:

$$\mathcal{S} = \left\{ \begin{pmatrix} u_1 \\ u_2 \end{pmatrix} \middle| \, |u_1| \leq \frac{\Delta + 1}{2} \text{ and } |u_2| \leq \frac{\Delta + 1}{2} \right\}. \tag{6.10}$$

Pixels that already belonged to a color region before the dilation step will also belong to the same color region after the dilation. The color regions will only be expanded by the pixels that did not belong to a color region before the dilation but formed part of the area of a dilated color region.

The **incrementation of the color homogeneity** within a color region is considered next. Although the color distances are compared between pixels at Δ distance when the color regions are extracted, some color regions may contain different colors due to blur or no clear boundaries between the colors. To detect such color regions and divide them into several new color regions, which increments the color homogeneity within the color regions, a reconstructed image $\mathbf{g}_{\mathbf{u}}^{\mathrm{R}}$ is created first. The color regions in $\mathbf{g}_{\mathbf{u}}^{\mathrm{R}}$ are represented by the average color of their pixels in the analyzed image (calculated in the CIELAB color space). Unassigned pixels to color regions are represented with a black color, but they will not influence the process. The colors of the pixels in the reconstructed image are compared, using the correlation function, with the colors of the input image $r\left(c_k^{\mathrm{Color}}(\mathbf{g}_{\mathbf{u}}), c_k^{\mathrm{Color}}\left(\mathbf{g}_{\mathbf{u}}^{\mathrm{R}}\right)\right)$. To this end, the colors of the pixels are represented over the color categories via the probability distribution function $c_k^{\mathrm{Color}}(\mathbf{g}_{\mathbf{u}})$. Connected pixels whose colors in the reconstructed image vary significantly from the input image are detected and if they span big connected areas, they are separated from their assigned color regions to create new color regions.

For the **reduction of the total number of extracted color regions,** the reconstructed image $\mathbf{g}_{\mathbf{u}}^{\mathrm{R}}$ that assigns every pixel the mean color of its color region is also used. Neighboring color regions in the reconstructed image with a similar assigned mean color are detected and grouped together to form a bigger color region. Color regions are neighbors if they possess neighboring pixels. 4-neighbors and 8-neighbors of a pixel (see [54]) are therefore considered. The comparison of the color similarity between the color regions is done by representing the assigned color of the regions via the normalized probabilities over the extracted humans' color categories and calculating their distances via the correlation coefficient.

6.4 Detection and extraction of patterns

As in Sec. 6.3, two different paths are followed to extract the patterns from images depending on the way that the color is processed. Along the first path discussed in Sec. 6.4.1 the color information of the detected color regions is directly processed and compared in the CIELAB color space (see Sec. 3.1.1), whereas in the second path presented in Sec. 6.4.2 color categories (see Sec. 3.3) are used for color representation and processing. Although the methods in Sec. 6.4.1 compare the color directly in the CIELAB color space, the extracted color regions from Sec. 6.3.2 using the color categories can also be used as extracted color areas. Furthermore, the color regions from Sec. 6.3.1 can also be used as input information for the pattern recognition using the methods of Sec. 6.4.2.

No matter which kind of the mentioned color representation and processing method is selected, both approaches to extract patterns follow a similar modus operandi which can be visualized in Fig. 6.6 and has been already used in [156]. The goal of each block is briefly explained next. However, the methods to resolve the goals of each block vary depending on the selected color representation method, with the exception of the extracted information based on the space-frequency analysis, which is therefore explained in detail next.

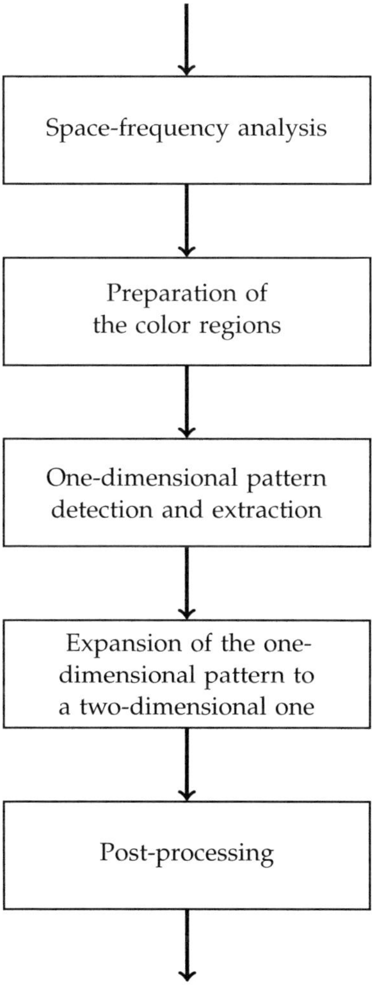

Figure 6.6 Modus operandi to detect and extract patterns.

Space-frequency analysis is a powerful tool to roughly detect the place of repetitions in signals. In this work, the two-dimensional wavelet transform (see Sec. 2.3.4) is used to analyze the input images, as higher energies at certain frequencies are expected at the image where repetitions of alterations of color regions are located. The goal of this block is the detection of candidate color regions involved in patterns.

To consider the color information, the wavelet transform is calculated. Per color channel three matrices with the detail signals for the different structure types (horizontal, vertical, and diagonal) are obtained at each stage. The detail signals at every stage and orientation are independently projected back onto the original space domain. Per orientation (horizontal, vertical, and diagonal) and stage a two-dimensional signal of equal size to the analyzed input signal is obtained. For each pixel the maximum per orientation over all stages and color channels is stored at its corresponding location and orientation in $\mathbf{F}_{\mathbf{u}}^{k}$, $k \in \{\text{horizontal, vertical, diagonal}\}$. After filtering these signals with a Gaussian filter [20], a measure is obtained which describes the probability of a pixel to belong to a pattern. Every color region from Sec. 6.3 containing a pixel with a high measure of probability to belong to a pattern that is not situated at its contour is further considered as a candidate color region of a pattern. The limit from which pixels are considered to have a high degree of probability to belong to a pattern is automatically set depending on the considered input image to allow a dynamic adjustment of the algorithm.

As different images may possess different sizes, an automatic selection of the number of stages is necessary to assure equal conditions. Furthermore, as the height and width of the images can be different, different stages are reasonable depending on the kind of structures (horizontal, vertical, diagonal) that are analyzed. Let l be the minimal length that alternating structures along a line of length L have that must be detected and H the height and B the width of the input image (see Fig. 6.7). The normalized frequencies that the highest stage of the wavelet transform in horizontal and vertical direction must pass along the band-pass filter is given by

$$f^{\text{norm,ver}} = \frac{L}{l} \cdot \frac{1}{H} \quad \text{and} \quad f^{\text{norm,hor}} = \frac{L}{l} \cdot \frac{1}{B}. \tag{6.11}$$

The number of stages along the horizontal and vertical analysis is respectively given from the first stage at which these normalized frequencies are passed through the corresponding band-pass filter. The number of considered stages for the analysis of diagonal structures is set equal to the minimum of the number of stages needed for horizontal and vertical structures.

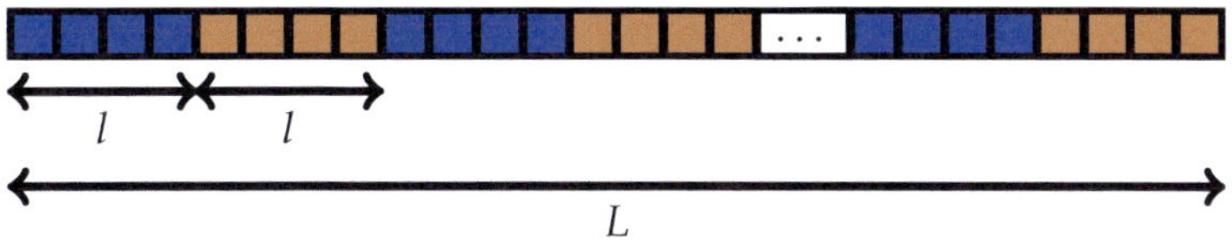

Figure 6.7 Automatic selection of the number of stages of the wavelet transform.

The **preparation of the color regions** obtained by the methods presented in Sec. 6.3 for the pattern detection and extraction is the goal of this block. The assignment of neighbors to the color regions is a necessary feature for the pattern detection and extraction independently of the path followed to process the color. The following three conditions are considered for this purpose.

1. For every pixel at the contour of an analyzed color region its spatially closest color region becomes a neighbor.
2. Spatially close color regions become neighbors.
3. If a color region is a neighbor of another color region, then this second color region is also a neighbor of the first color region.

At this point the smallest spatial distance between color regions is given by the smallest distance between two boundary pixels of the considered color regions. The third condition is necessary to assure a symmetric relation. An additional preparation of the color regions is required depending on the path selected for the processing of color information and is therefore explained in detail in Sec. 6.4.1.1 and Sec. 6.4.2.1.

The **one-dimensional pattern detection and extraction** is the basis for the pattern recognition along the image. Every color region classified as candidate of a pattern due to the space-frequency analysis is therefore considered, starting with the one containing the pixel with the highest measure of probability to belong to a pattern. The goal of this block is to detect if the color regions form part of a one-dimensional pattern and its extraction if this is the case. For this purpose, parallel lines are set along the considered color region. The orientation of the lines along which the one-dimensional pattern is searched depends on the expected orientation (horizontal, vertical, or diagonal) of the pattern according to the space-frequency analysis (see Fig. 6.8 top). Along the lines the next similar color region to the analyzed one is searched. The criterion used to measure the similarity depends at this juncture on the followed path explained in the next sections. The use of several lines reduces wrong detections, as the color regions are actually two dimensional and may therefore have different sizes. A single line could not even contain a valid part of the searched pattern. If several similar regions are found along the lines, the line containing less number of color regions in-between the similar color regions is selected for the further extraction of the pattern along the line (the one-dimensional pattern extraction). Note that the number of colors in the detected pattern is equal to the number of regions in-between the similar ones plus one (see Fig. 6.8 top).

A basic unit of the pattern formed from one color region per color appearing in the pattern can be detected from the estimated number of colors in the pattern together with the color region that is being analyzed due to the space-frequency analysis (see Fig. 6.8 middle). In order to avoid overhead, new patterns will not be searched in future iterations from the color regions that become part of a basic unit of a pattern. The reason is that possible patterns from these color regions are already considered in the current iteration. Once the basic unit has been detected (which depends on the path followed for color processing, see Sec. 6.4.1 and Sec. 6.4.2), the pattern can be extracted along the selected line considering the similarity of the color regions along the line to the ones that form the detected basic unit of the pattern and considering also the sequence in which the colors appear. For this purpose, the use of graph representations is useful. As many graphs are necessary as number of colors expected in the pattern (see Fig. 6.8 down). Nodes of the graphs are the color regions along the line placed at whole multiples of the expected number of colors in the pattern. In every graph the nodes are connected by an edge if they are similar and exactly placed at the expected number of colors in the pattern from each other. However, edges are removed from the graphs if the color regions that they represent are not connected by a path in their corresponding graphs to one of the nodes of the color regions that form the basic unit of the pattern. The one-dimensional pattern along the line is extracted from the graph representations as the color regions whose corresponding nodes are connected by a valid path to one of the nodes of the color regions that form the basic unit of the pattern (see Fig. 6.8 down).

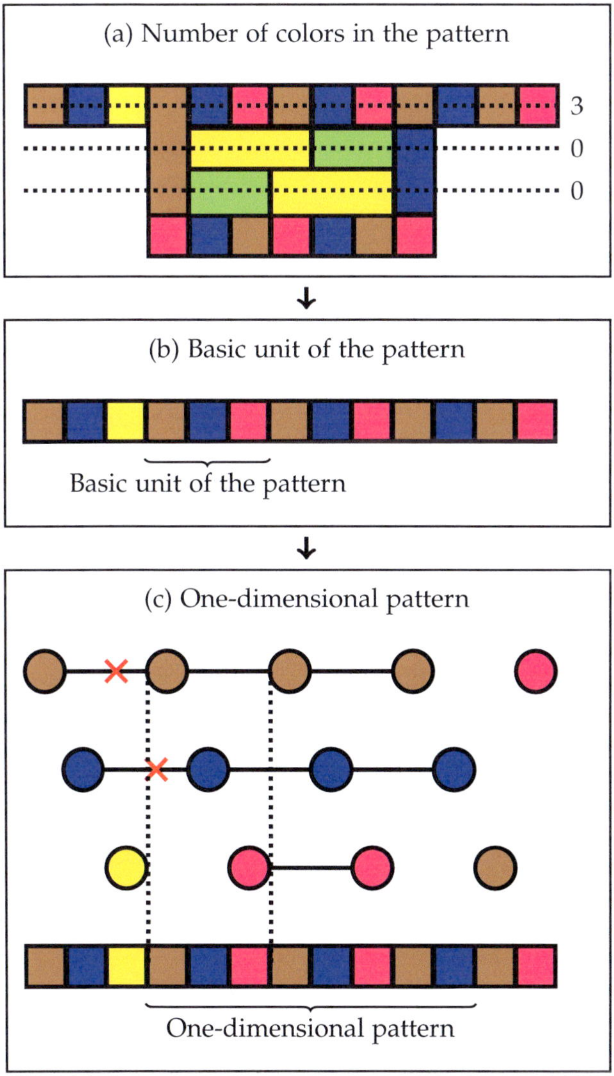

Figure 6.8 Overview of the detection and extraction of the patterns along one dimension.

Once more, the similarity between color regions depends on the selected path for the processing of the color information and is therefore explained in detail in the next sections (Sec. 6.4.1.2 and Sec. 6.4.2.2).

The **expansion of the one-dimensional pattern to a two-dimensional one** is the goal of this block. For this purpose, the expansion of the one-dimensional pattern along the whole image is considered. Only one-dimensional patterns that have at least one color region per color in the pattern and at least two colors in the pattern formed from two color regions are expanded to a two-dimensional pattern. Similar neighboring color regions to the ones that already form the detected pattern are included to the pattern. For this purpose, the colors appearing in the pattern are consecutively considered. Per considered color of the pattern, its neighboring color regions that do not belong to the pattern are detected. If they are similar to the color regions in the pattern of the next expected color, then they are included in the pattern. This process is iteratively repeated until no new regions are added to the pattern. The definition of similarity between the regions is strongly dependent on the followed path to compare and process the color information and is therefore explained in the following sections (Sec. 6.4.1.3 and Sec. 6.4.2.3).

The **post-processing** of the extracted patterns may improve the results. The fusion of similar extracted patterns, the merger of concatenated patterns, and the suppression of some color regions (e.g., merely frames) from the pattern can improve the extracted patterns and reduce duplicates. These optional methods are explained in detail in the following sections (Sec. 6.4.1.4 and Sec. 6.4.2.4) as they depend on the selected color representation and processing.

6.4.1 Detection and extraction of patterns based on the CIELAB color space

The CIELAB color space (see Sec. 3.1.1) is used for color representation and processing in this version of the region detector. Color dissimilarities are measured using the ℓ_2-norm (see Sec. 2.1) of the CIELAB values along all of the steps of the detector. A preliminary version of this region detector has been presented in [156].

6.4.1.1 Preparation of the color regions

Although any of the extracted color regions from the image following the methods in Sec. 6.3 may be used, this version of the algorithm focuses on the direct representation and processing of color in the CIELAB color space. The results in Sec. 8.5.1 show that the color regions extracted by the method presented in Sec. 6.3.1 using the CIELAB values directly do not cover on average almost all of the image. Small color regions that appear stable at a first sight might not be found as color regions due to, e.g., compression artifacts. As part of the preparation of the color regions for the pattern detection, such kind of missing intermediate regions are searched. For this purpose, the color of a color region is obtained from the mean color over all pixels that belong to it, calculated in CIELAB color space. Missing intermediate regions are typically found between two color regions that are neighbors, have a similar color, and several pixels with a high measure of probability to belong to a pattern due to the space-frequency analysis. If such regions do not have a common neighbor or the minimal spatial distance for most of the pixels on the boundaries is between each other, then an intermediate region is probably missing. To detect the missing region, all of the pixels between the two color regions that have not been assigned to a color region yet are taken into consideration. Pixels with a similar color to one of the two neighbor regions are discarded, as they do not produce an alternation between the colors. Out of the possible remaining pixels the biggest spatially connected area is added as a new color region if it reaches a minimium size and a minimum measure of the probability to belong to a pattern. As the new potential color region was not detected in Sec. 6.3, the color between the pixels will be different, but their measure of probability to belong to a pattern is still high. Because of this, the measure of probability for such potential color regions to belong to a pattern is calculated per orientation from the average value of the maxima measure of probability to belong to a pattern over all its pixels.

Due to the fact that new color regions are added, the neighbors between the color regions may change. These ones must be therefore assigned again (as defined in Sec. 6.4) after the inclusion of the new regions. However, the accuracy of the assigned neighborhoods must further be considered because two regions may become neighbors even if they are spatially far away from each other. This is possible because the first condition to assign neighbors in Sec. 6.4 does not consider the amount of spatial distance between the color regions, together with the fact that the results show (see Sec. 8.5.1) that not almost all of the image is covered by the stable color regions extracted using the CIELAB values for the processing of the color as shown in Sec. 6.3.1. To avoid defining as neighbors color regions that are far from each other but also take into consideration the proportion of the distance between the regions to their sizes, an average extent is defined per color region. If the minimal spatial distance between two pixels on the boundaries of the neighboring regions is bigger than the mean average extents of the corresponding regions, then the regions will only still be considered as neighbors if the color of the pixels in-between (that were not assigned to a color region) are similar to one of the colors of the considered regions or their CIELAB color value lay between the CIELAB color values of the colors of the regions. Spatially separated regions by a color gradient of themselves that were not assigned to a color region will be therefore maintained as neighbors.

Color clusters formed from neighboring color regions with a similar color, as well as background regions, are identified at this step in order to consider them in the following steps when the pattern is detected and extracted. A background region may be any color region or color cluster placed mainly in a defined frame of the image. For this purpose, the rows and columns of the regions are taken into consideration independently of each other.

6.4.1.2 One-dimensional pattern detection and extraction

The specific details to detect and extract the one-dimensional pattern following the trend from Sec. 6.4 considered in this version of the algorithm are explained next.

An **initial manipulation of the selected line** containing the minimal number of colors for a pattern is necessary for the detection of the basic unit of the pattern (see Sec. 6.4 and Fig. 6.8) and, furthermore, for the extraction of the one-dimensional pattern. As the main focus of this version of the algorithm relies on the direct process of color in the CIELAB color space and the results show that the extracted color regions based on the color representation in CIELAB color space do not cover almost all of the input image (see Sec. 8.5.1), color regions may be spatially separated by a big number of pixels that were not assigned to a color region. To avoid the inclusion of such kind of regions in the basic unit of the pattern and in the one-dimensional extracted pattern, the selected line must be processed. To this end, all color regions along the line that are separated by a long chain of unassigned pixels from the color region that is being analyzed are suppressed from the line. Next, every pixel along the line that was not assigned to a color region is removed from the line, as patterns are searched between color regions and undefined pixels will always be between their contours.

Due to the fact that the size of the color regions is not considered when the similarity between them is compared and that in many images background regions are much bigger than the regions belonging to patterns (e.g., sky or floor), background regions should be removed from the line as in [156]. However, a valid pattern may be placed or expanded over the frames of an image and therefore over the defined background regions. To fulfill both considerations, in contrast to [156], the background regions appearing at the start and end of the line are detected. Color regions between the start of the line and the first detected background region, as well as between the last detected background region of the line and the end of it, are suppressed from the line together with the two detected background regions.

The **detection of the basic unit of the pattern** is considered next. Once the number of colors in the pattern has been detected and the line manipulated, the basic unit is detected. This one consists of so many neighboring color regions along the line as colors expected in the pattern, whereas the color region that initialized the search of the one-dimensional pattern is always part of it. Its color distance (measured using the ℓ_2-norm in CIELAB color space) to its next neighbors is respectively calculated and added (as many as missing in the basic unit) along the left hand side of the line and the right hand side. The side with the biggest cumulative difference contains the color regions that complete the basic unit of the pattern.

The **similarity criteria for the one-dimensional pattern extraction** is obtained from the color dissimilarity calculated using the ℓ_2-norm of the color values in CIELAB color space. Every pair of color regions whose ℓ_2-norm of their colors is smaller than a predefined threshold is considered similar. Furthermore, if the distance is bigger than the threshold but still small enough, then the colors of the regions will be considered similar if their values along the channels considering the difference between green and red colors and blue and yellow vary only slightly. This is done to overcome brightness differences, as these ones are described by the other channel. Finally, two color regions will not be considered similar independently of the similarity of their color if both of them have a color region between them in the line with a similar color to them.

6.4.1.3 Expansion of the one-dimensional pattern to a two-dimensional one

For the expansion of the one-dimensional pattern to a two-dimensional one, the colors appearing in the pattern are compared to the potential new color regions of the pattern. For this purpose, a color of the pattern is defined as the mean color values calculated in CIELAB color space from all color regions in the pattern that belong to the considered color. As the pattern is iteratively expanded, the colors of the pattern are also updated with each new added color region.

The similarity between the color regions and the color of a pattern is calculated as in the one-dimensional case (see Sec. 6.4.1.2). For this purpose, the potential new color region of the pattern is compared to the considered color of the pattern. Additionally, the new potential color region of the pattern is compared to every color region that already belongs to the pattern for the considered color, to avoid impreciseness due to the arithmetic mean. If a high similarity is found at any of the above mentioned comparisons, then the new potential color region will be added to the pattern.

However, for the incorporation of background regions to the pattern a stricter condition must apply to avoid incorporating big frame regions to the pattern. To be incorporated to the pattern, background regions must fulfill the above mentioned similarity criterion, but also its size must be adequate to the size of the pattern. If the considered background regions form part of a color cluster, then the adequate size is proved for the whole color cluster.

Finally, if a color region that belongs to a color cluster is part of the extracted pattern, then all color regions belonging to the color cluster are also added to the pattern and assigned to the same color of the pattern. This is the reason why the appropriateness of the size of the whole color cluster is considered when a background region that belongs to a color cluster becomes a possible color region of a pattern.

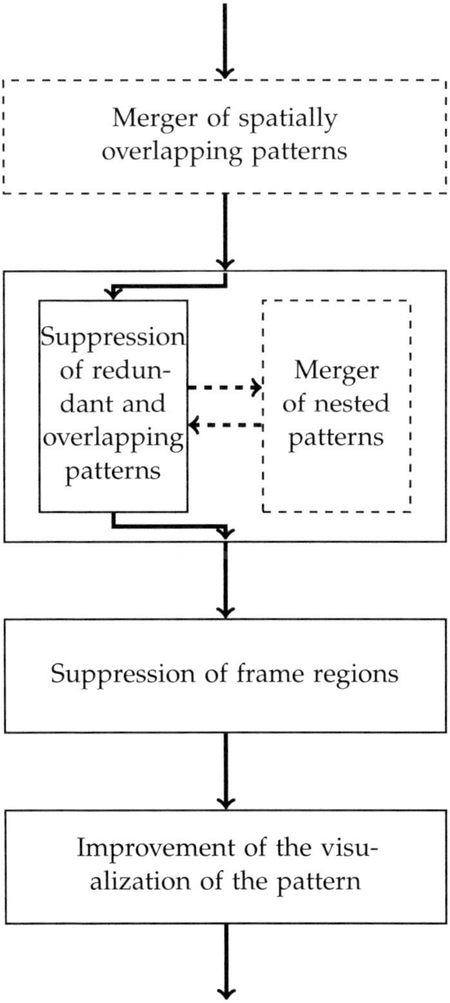

Figure 6.9 Flow-chart of the post-processing step.

6.4.1.4 Post-processing

Many patterns and pattern combinations are possible. The extracted patterns from Sec. 6.4.1.3 must be therefore processed and selected in a final step. The merger of spatially overlapping patterns, the suppression of redundant and overlapping patterns, the merger of nested patterns, the suppression of merely frame regions, and the improvement of the pattern representation is therefore considered. All of these approaches can be considered independently or combined. A flow-chart is shown in Fig. 6.9, in which dotted squares represent optional processing steps.

The **merger of spatially overlapping patterns** improves their extraction and also reduces their total number. The pattern detection and extraction with the methods proposed so far are based on the number of colors expected in the pattern, which is given from the minimal number of color regions along the selected line until a similar color region to the one that initiated the search of the pattern is found. However, the approximation of the two-dimensional pattern to a one-dimensional one along a single line may not describe the real pattern completely, so that the number of colors in the original pattern is not completely detected. This will result in the extraction of several patterns with a lower number of colors than the real one. An example for such kind of patterns is shown in Fig. 6.10. The goal of this approach is the detection of such patterns as well as the detection of patterns whose number of colors has been correctly detected and that spatially overlap, and merge the patterns to improve the pattern extraction and reduce the number of extracted and redundant patterns.

For this purpose, all of the extracted patterns are compared between each other and represented as nodes in a graph. Edges are set between the corresponding nodes of patterns whose area spanned by their respective convex hulls highly overlap. The common area of both convex hulls is normalized by their biggest area to perform a normalized comparison. Furthermore, to avoid the merger of patterns whose convex hulls highly overlap but do not represent the pattern spatially good enough (e.g., when the convex hull includes big areas that are not in the pattern), only patterns whose areas compared to the areas of their convex hulls are high enough are considered for the comparison. Once the graph that contains the relationships about the spatial overlap between the patterns exists, all patterns whose nodes can be reached by a valid path are merged. If the patterns that are merged have similar colors, which are calculated as explained in Sec. 6.4.1.2 and compared using the ℓ_2-norm, then the color regions of the patterns that belong to the corresponding colors are merged together to form one color of the new merged pattern; otherwise, the number of colors of the merged patterns increases.

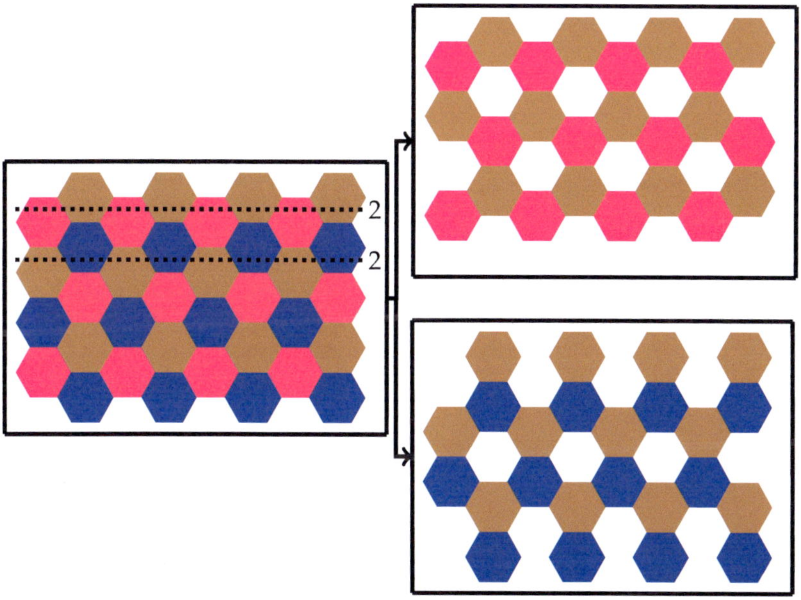

Figure 6.10 Demonstrative representation of the need of a spatial merger. In the pattern of the left the lines will only recognize two colors along the one-dimensional pattern instead of the three present in the two-dimensional pattern. In this regard, the two patterns of the right side can be detected but not the whole one.

The **suppression of redundant and overlapping patterns** is a very important step of the post-processing. As color regions in patterns are likely to have a high probability to belong to the pattern, several start color regions will be found for each pattern. This will lead to a redundant extraction of patterns. Nonetheless, the repeatedly extracted patterns may vary in the color regions that they possess due to color variations of the color regions. Furthermore, a color region should belong to maximal one extracted pattern, as a pattern is associated with an object. The processing of the extracted patterns so far is necessary to assure non-overlapping patterns.

First of all, patterns included in bigger ones are deleted, as they do not contain additional information of the extracted pattern of the image. This is the case if all of the color regions of the smaller pattern are included in a bigger one, and the number of colors in the pattern is equal for both patterns. If the number of colors is not equal, then the smaller pattern will not be discarded, as it describes another pattern than the bigger one.

To merge similar extracted patterns that refer to the same pattern in the image, the neighboring color regions of every pattern are needed. These are color regions that do not belong to the pattern but are neighbors of the color regions in the pattern. If two patterns have a color region in common or if a neighboring color region of a pattern is part of the color regions of the other pattern, then the patterns are merged if they have the same number of colors and the colors are similar. The similarity is obtained as in Sec. 6.4.1.2 from the distances of the colors of the pattern. At this juncture, the pattern detected first (the order is given by the probability of the pixels to belong to a pattern) is amplified with the other one.

Patterns detected later (lower probability to find a pattern) are more likely to repeat already extracted patterns. Because of this, every pattern containing per color at least one color region that already belongs to a different pattern is suppressed. In contrast to [156], here the condition is proved that the color regions that are already part of another pattern also belong to different colors in the other patterns. As these color regions may appear in various patterns in different colors, the color group of the pattern with which these color regions appeared first are the ones considered for this purpose. Furthermore, color regions that appear in different patterns are always considered as if they belong to different colors in the patterns.

Non-overlapping patterns are obtained from the assignment of the color regions that are part of different extracted patterns to only one pattern. For this purpose, the extracted patterns that were detected first (and possess therefore a higher probability to describe a real pattern in the image) will maintain these color regions. As color regions are now suppressed from some patterns, other color regions may remain in the pattern that are not spatially connected with the described pattern anymore. Such kind of regions are detected easily, as their neighboring color regions are not included in the pattern. These color regions are suppressed from the pattern. The suppression of color regions may reduce the number of colors in a pattern or produce patterns that are not spatially connected. For the first case, the number of colors in the pattern is updated together with the assigned color values in CIELAB color space. In case of patterns that are spatially separated, these ones will be separated into new independent and spatially connected patterns. At this juncture the number of patterns increases. They are therefore sorted according to the highest assigned measure of probability of their color regions to belong to a pattern.

The manipulation of the different patterns to reduce redundant information and assure non-overlapping patterns can deliver some non-valid patterns, like, e.g., patterns containing less number of color regions as colors expected in the pattern or less than two colors. Such invalid patterns are suppressed.

The appropriateness of color clusters in the remaining patterns is proved next. At the two-dimensional extraction of the patterns (see Sec. 6.4.1.3) color regions belonging to a color cluster were automatically added to a pattern if at least one of its color regions belonged to the pattern. If the number of color regions assigned to the color of a pattern that do not belong to the considered color cluster is higher than the number of color regions in the color cluster, then their suitability is proved. If the mean color, calculated in CIELAB color space, of the color regions that belong to the color cluster differs considerably from the mean color formed from the other color regions, then the color cluster is suppressed from the pattern.

For every pattern which is morphologically dilated [20] and not spatially connected, only one of its spatially connected regions is considered as the pattern for further processing. For this purpose, the spatially connected region with the biggest area that possesses a valid pattern (contains at least two different colors) is kept.

The **merger of nested patterns** is an optional approach to permit the detection and extraction of nested patterns. Nested patterns are different overlapping patterns with some common colors and one pattern spatially including the other one (an example is shown in Fig. 6.11). Such kind of patterns cannot be detected by the one-dimensional detection and extraction, nor by the two-dimensional expansion and must be therefore considered. This optional approach to detect and merge them is a supplement to the above presented method to suppress redundant and overlapping regions and is executed after the suppression of patterns whose colors contain at least one color region that already belongs to other patterns and before the explicit assignment of every color region to exact one pattern to assure non-overlapping patterns.

Nested patterns are detected between extracted pairs of patterns when the following conditions apply:

1. The color of every pattern is formed from at least two color regions, which may be the same.

2. One of the patterns is included in the closed filled area of the other pattern.

3. The area of both patterns overlap.

If several patterns are extracted from the input image, then the search for nested patterns is done between every extracted pair of patterns. Every pattern is then represented as a node in a graph and connected by an edge to the respective node of another pattern if they are nested. All of the patterns whose corresponding nodes can be reached via a valid path in the graph are then merged. For this purpose, the colors of the patterns that are going to be merged are compared and merged in case of similarity.

As the patterns have changed the number of colors, a new extraction of the pattern along the two-dimensions, like at the expansion of the pattern from the one-dimensional case to the two-dimensional one, is reasonable. However, to avoid redundant information, the new merged patterns that describe the same pattern are merged first as explained above. Furthermore, the color regions are assigned to only one pattern to reduce redundant processing. After the expansion of the patterns, patterns describing similar patterns are merged. In this case, the pattern found later (lower measure of probability for a pattern) is included to the pattern found earlier. For this purpose, extracted patterns describe similar patterns in the input image if they have the same number of colors, a high percentage of overlapping color regions, and all of the non-overlapping color regions of the later detected pattern have a similar color with one of the colors of the pattern.

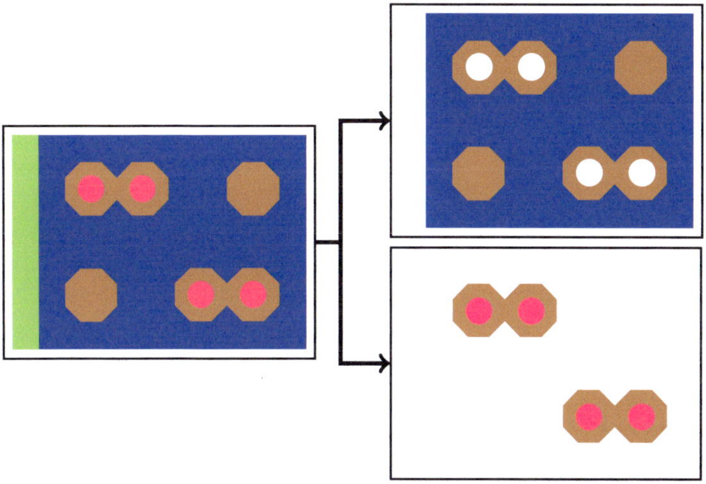

Figure 6.11 Example of a nested pattern (left), which is composed from two patterns (right).

The **suppression of frame regions** is an approach to improve the quality of the extracted patterns. Up to now the color and neighborhood between color regions are the only conditions used by the algorithm to detect, extract, and post-process the patterns. The relationship of their sizes has only been considered if one of the color regions was also classified as a background region. As a consequence, real patterns in the input image surrounded by a color region whose color is similar to one of the colors of the pattern will be extracted together as one pattern. Such kind of color regions that are incorporated in the extracted pattern but do not belong to the real pattern are called from now on frame regions, as they are a frame of the real pattern.

To detect frame regions, a similar procedure is used as for the detection of the background regions (see Sec. 6.4.1.1). Horizontal and vertical lines are set along the pattern. Starting from the outside boundary of the pattern every line along the pattern running through only one color region is selected, until the first line appears running through more than two color regions. Along the selected lines, the length of the pattern is compared to the mean length of the pattern along all horizontal or vertical lines, depending on the considered orientation. From the selected lines, those whose corresponding pattern length is almost as big as the mean length of the pattern along the considered orientation are further processed for the detection of frame regions. The remaining lines to be considered run each through only one color region. These color regions represent potential frame regions of the pattern. Per line, if the maximal length or height (depending on the considered orientation) of its corresponding color region is big enough compared to the maximal length, respectively height, of the pattern, then it is kept as a potential frame region. In a final step these potential color regions are compared to all other color regions in the pattern that are associated with the same color of the pattern. If the maximal length or height (depending on the considered orientation) of the potential color region is much bigger than respectively the maximal length or height over all other color regions, then a frame region exists and it is suppressed from the extracted pattern.

If a pattern is formed from one color containing other ones, then the color region of the outer color may be detected as a frame region and suppressed, involving a false extraction of the pattern. To avoid this case, if the first color region found at the boundary of the analyzed pattern contains many color regions in its holes that belong to the pattern, then no frame regions will be searched.

To **improve the visualization of the pattern,** the pixels that have not been assigned to a color region and are situated in the closed area spanned by the pattern are considered. Unassigned pixels to a color region typically appear at the transition between color regions. However, their incorporation to the pattern will improve the quality impression of the extracted pattern. Because of this, all unassigned pixels having a similar color to the pixels that belong to the pattern are incorporated for visualization purposes to the pattern if they are spatially connected to the pattern, either directly or via a chain of unassigned pixels. Furthermore, every color region that is completely in the closed area of the extracted pattern and describes a color transition between color regions of the pattern is also incorporated to improve the quality of its visualization.

6.4.2 Detection and extraction of patterns based on the humans' color categories

This path of the pattern detection and extraction focuses on the processing of color with the use of color categories (see Sec. 3.3).

6.4.2.1 Preparation of the color regions

Due to the fact that the color regions obtained based on the humans' color categories cover almost all of the image (see Sec. 8.5.1), the neighbors assigned with the criteria of Sec. 6.4 are considered valid and no further processing is necessary in contrast to the path followed in Sec. 6.4.1, as we can assume that no color regions that are spatially far away from each other will become neighbors.

For the pattern detection and extraction a color must be assigned to each color region. As color regions contain pixels with a similar color, the color is calculated from the average values in CIELAB color space over all pixels. However, when the color between color regions is compared, the representation over color categories is used. For this purpose, the color of the regions must be presented via the normalized likelihoods over the color categories (see Sec. 3.3.3).

Furthermore, the size, in pixels, must also be assigned to each color region to be able to detect and extract the pattern with the presented method.

In contrast to the preparation of the color regions for the version of the algorithm processing the color directly in CIELAB color space (see Sec. 6.4.1), the detection of background regions is not necessary here, as the size and color similarity is considered when the one-dimensional pattern is detected and extracted.

6.4.2.2 One-dimensional pattern detection and extraction

The specific details for the one-dimensional pattern detection and extraction using color categories are presented in this section.

The **initial manipulation of the selected line** for this version of the algorithm is done by the suppression of unassigned pixels to color regions. As the results of the obtained color regions processing the color information via the color categories show that almost all of the image is covered by the extracted color regions (see Sec. 8.5.1), no long sequences of unassigned pixels are expected along the line in contrast to the processing of color directly in CIELAB color space (see Sec. 6.4.1).

The **similarity criteria for the one-dimensional pattern detection and extraction** between two color regions considers their color and size. Any of the color distance functions presented in Sec. 6.3.2.1 can be used to compare the colors. The size of color regions is compared by their quotient. To obtain a normalized value, meaning a score close to one a high similarity, the smaller size will be always divided by the bigger one.

The **basic unit of the pattern** consists of one representative color region per expected color in the pattern, whereas the color region that initiated the search of the one-dimensional pattern is always part of it. Along the line the similarity of this region is compared to its next neighbors on the left and right hand side of the line separated exactly by the number of expected colors in the pattern minus one. If similarity only applies for one of the sides of the line, then the color regions in-between are the missing representatives of the colors of the pattern in its basic unit. Otherwise, the color distances per side of the line are calculated between the regions in-between and the color region already belonging to the basic unit of the pattern. The regions in-between that have a bigger cumulative color distance are the ones that complete the basic unit of the pattern in this case.

6.4.2.3 Expansion of the one-dimensional pattern to a two-dimensional one

When the appropriateness of new candidate color regions to the pattern is evaluated, four different similarity comparisons considering their color information, their size, or both characteristics are presented. This allows four versions of the algorithm. From now on the similarity comparison of new possible color regions of the pattern with the color regions of the pattern that represent one of its colors is considered.

An **approximation of the colors** in the pattern is considered in this case. To this end, every color in the pattern is defined as the mean color value in CIELAB color space over the color of all its corresponding color regions. The color distance between the new candidate color region and the considered color of the pattern can be calculated with any of the functions presented in Sec. 6.3.2.1. For this purpose, the color assigned to the pattern is represented with the normalized likelihoods over the color categories (see Sec. 3.3.3). As the number of color regions belonging to a color of the pattern increases iteratively, the color of the pattern must be updated.

An **approximation of the colors and sizes** of the color regions belonging to the pattern is considered in this version. New color regions will only be added to the detected pattern if they have a similar color and size to the color regions forming the considered color of the pattern. The color similarity is calculated as in the above explained version, where the approximation of the colors of the pattern is considered. For the size similarity, the mean size over the color regions forming the color of the pattern is calculated first and compared to the size of the candidate color regions via their quotient. To obtain a normalized measure, the smaller value will be divided by the bigger one. Similarity due to the size is only present in case of a high quotient.

An **exact color** comparison between the color regions that form a color of a pattern and its new possible color regions is considered now. Potential color regions will be added to the pattern if they have a similar color to at least one of the color regions that form the considered color of the pattern. For this purpose, the color distance between the color regions can be measured using any of the color distances presented in Sec. 6.3.2.1. The comparison of the similarity of the color here avoids inaccuracies due to the calculation of the average value. Furthermore, it also fulfills the condition that the CIELAB color space is rather reasonable for smaller color differences than for bigger ones.

An **exact color and size** comparison between the color regions that form a color of a pattern and its new possible color regions is considered for the similarity measure in this version. New possible color regions will only be added to the pattern if they have a similar color and size to the color regions that form the considered color of the pattern. The color similarity is measured as explained in the above version of the exact color comparison. For the size similarity, the size of the new possible color region is compared to the size of every color region that belongs to the considered color of the pattern, by building their quotient, whereas the smaller value is divided by the bigger one to obtain a normalized value. The new possible color region is considered similar in size if its size is similar to at least the size of one of the color regions in the pattern.

Finally, an optional processing approach is presented to detect patterns that actually represent the same pattern in the image and to merge them. For this purpose, the area spanned by the convex hull of the actually expanded pattern along the two dimensions is compared with the convex hulls spanned by every pattern that has already been expanded over the two-dimensions. Patterns with highly overlapping areas spanned by their convex hulls are merged as in Sec. 6.4.1.4 (merger of spatially overlapping patterns). However, to detect if the patterns that are merged have similar colors, the colors of the pattern and also the sizes of the color regions that form each color are considered. The color information is processed in this version using the color categories representation from Sec. 3.3. The colors of the pattern are represented via the normalized likelihoods over the color categories of the mean colors, calculated in CIELAB color space, of the color regions that form each color. The color similarity is obtained according to Sec. 6.4.2.2. On the other hand, per color appearing in the pattern the mean size over its color regions is calculated. Between different patterns, the sizes of their colors are considered similar if the quotient of the smallest mean size divided by the biggest mean size is large enough. The color regions forming colors of patterns detected as similar are merged to form only one color of the pattern.

6.4.2.4 Post-processing

After the detection and extraction of the pattern along one dimension and its expansion over two dimensions, many pattern combinations describing the same pattern in the input image may be possible. Because of this, post-processing becomes necessary to avoid redundant patterns and also to improve the quality of the extracted ones.

In a first step invalid patterns are detected and suppressed. These are patterns not containing an enough number of color regions compared to the number of colors that are expected in the pattern.

Two approaches are considered to detect extracted patterns describing the same pattern in the input image. On the one hand, overlapping patterns with a high percentage of area in common are detected. For this purpose, the extracted patterns are pairwise compared. The total number of pixels belonging to both compared patterns is respectively divided by the total number of pixels in the one pattern and the other one. If any of the calculated quotients is high, then the areas of the patterns highly overlap and the patterns are merged into one. On the other hand, patterns with highly overlapping areas spanned by their convex hulls are detected and merged. At this juncture, the relations for the detection of patterns describing the same one in the input image are transitive. This means that if, e.g., the first and second extracted patterns highly overlap and the second and third patterns too, then all of the three patterns are merged into one.

7 Fusion of the methods

In the previous chapters several properties have been considered related to the sorting of images according to the similarity of their content. The detection and extraction of regions with a similar color together with the detection and extraction of patterned regions in images (Sec. 6), the detection of near-regular textures together with the extraction of their regular textures (Sec. 5.3), and the extraction and comparison of color (Sec. 3), shape (Sec. 4), and texture (Sec. 5) properties have been considered. The fusion of these methods is considered in this chapter to enable a content-based image retrieval environment. The detection and extraction of significant patterned regions is considered in Sec. 7.1, which results from the fusion of the detected and extracted color regions, patterned regions, and near-regular textures. The method to sort images considering color, shape, and texture information is then presented in Sec. 7.2. The results yielded by the methods proposed in this chapter are shown in Sec. 8.6.

7.1 Significant patterned regions

A pattern is a generalized concept of a near-regular texture. Whereas a near-regular texture is always a valid pattern, a pattern is not always a near-regular texture. The detection and extraction of near-regular textures and patterned surfaces has been considered in Secs. 5.3 and 6.4. The following conclusions can be drawn from the results (Secs. 8.4.2 and 8.5.2) of the presented methods:

1. A high percentage of the near-regular textures from the tested database (up to 98.08 %) is detected.

2. The extraction of the areas spanned by the near-regular textures are limited to the areas spanned by a whole number of the detected texels. The area of the objects containing the near-regular textures cannot be approximated perfectly.

3. All of the near-regular textures in the database (100 %) are part of at least one of the extracted patterns. However, several patterns are extracted that contain parts of near-regular textures that are already part of another pattern.

4. Many patterns that do not contain a near-regular texture are detected.

In this section the fusion of the results achieved by the methods to detect and extract near-regular textures and patterns is considered to select significant patterned regions in the images that will be used in Sec. 7.2.2 in a content-based image retrieval environment. The procedure used to fuse the methods is shown in Fig. 7.1 and explained next.

From the detected near-regular textures a mask per surface is estimated. For this purpose, all of the points of interest extracted from the input image that belong to the same cluster from which the near-regular texture was detected are considered. From this point cloud, their alpha-shape [46] is calculated. This one is obtained from the straight lines that connect alpha-neighbors. Two points of the point cloud are alpha-neighbors if they lie on the boundary of a disc (or its complement depending on the sign of alpha) that contains all of the points. The radius of the disc depends on the selected alpha. In this work, alpha is adapted for every point cloud to the value that produces the tightest fitting alpha shape that encloses all of the interest points. The area spanned by this boundary together with the boundary itself is the mask of the near-regular texture. If more than one near-regular texture is detected per image and one of them covers the borders of the image, its corresponding mask will be spread over almost the whole image. To avoid such cases, its corresponding mask will be spread over almost the whole image apart from the regions, where masks from other detected near-regular textures are already placed.

The **fusion of the masks of the near-regular textures with the extracted color regions** from Sec. 6.3 is considered next. For this purpose every detected color region whose area lies mostly at the mask of the near-regular texture is added to a new broadened mask. The mask is broadened with the color information of the image. Areas in the mask that are not covered by a color region lying mostly at the mask are not incorporated to the broadened mask.

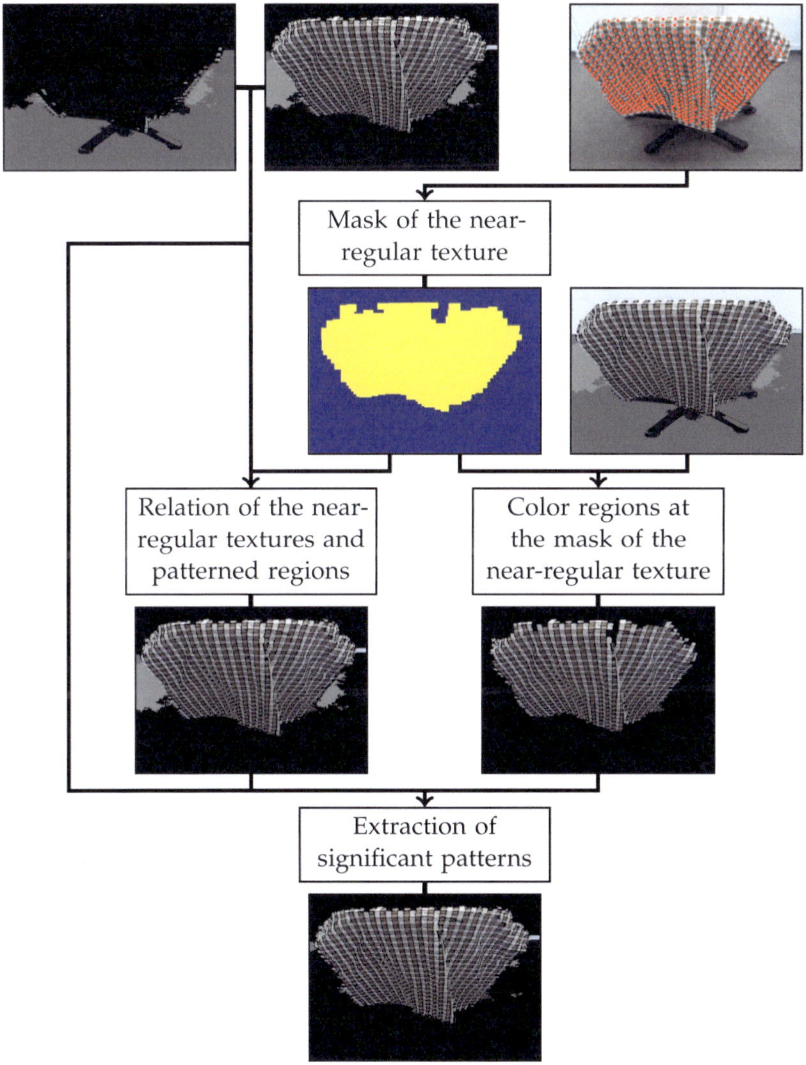

Figure 7.1 Extraction of significant patterned regions.

The **masks of the near-regular textures are also fused with the extracted patterns.** For this purpose, extracted patterns that lie at the mask of a near-regular texture are fused, as well as masks of near-regular textures that lie at an extracted pattern. The information extracted from the near-regular texture is also incorporated to the common extracted patterns.

In a final step, **significant patterns** are extracted by fusing every available information. Significant patterns can come from two different paths. On the one hand, every extracted pattern that lies mostly at the mask of a near-regular texture is the basis of a future significant pattern. However, the areas spanned by the broadened mask and the extracted pattern are usually not equal. A fusion of both possibilities is therefore necessary. For this purpose, their appropriateness is valued first. If the considered pattern and broadened mask of the near-regular texture have only a small percentage of the color regions in common, then the extracted pattern is directly considered as a significant pattern. The reason is that the extracted near-regular textures cannot be approximated perfectly. However, if the percentage of color regions in common is high, then the sizes of the color regions in common are compared to the sizes of the color regions that only form part of the extracted pattern. Color regions that only form part of the extracted pattern and whose sizes vary considerably from the sizes of the color regions in common are suppressed. The improved version of the extracted patterns are considered as significant patterns.

On the other hand, every extracted pattern that contains a big number of color regions is directly considered as a significant pattern.

7.2 Image sorting according to their similarity fusing color, shape, and texture information

Once the significant patterned regions have been detected and extracted, the images can be sorted. The problem of sorting the content of the images according to their similarity is transferred to the problem of sorting the detected significant patterns according to their similarity.

Therefore, the assumption is made that the most important content of the image is given by the significant patterns.

The adjustment of the color (Sec. 3), shape (Sec. 4), and texture (Sec. 5) methods proposed in the previous sections to the detected and extracted significant patterns (Sec. 7.1) is considered next. For this purpose, the extraction of the features is considered in Sec. 7.2.1 and the sorting of the images considering all three properties in Sec. 7.2.2.

7.2.1 Feature extraction

Adequate features describing the significant patterned regions are necessary for their comparison. The color, shape, and texture information is separately considered per significant region. Their extraction is briefly explained next and results as a fusion with the methods already presented in Secs. 3, 4, and 5.

As **color feature** the compact color signature proposed in Sec. 3.2 is used. However, this one is not directly extracted from the color values of the pixels in the input image that belong to the patterned regions but from the mean colors of their corresponding detected color regions. Nevertheless, the sizes of every detected color region in the considered significant pattern is still considered in its respective compact color signature.

The **shape feature** of a significant pattern is the normal angular descriptor from Sec. 4.2.1 of its boundary. The determination of the boundary of a significant patterned region is a challenging task, as the patterned regions must not be a connected component. At the contours of color regions pixels are expected that do not belong to a color region and will not be part of the considered significant patterned region. To overcome this problem, a mask of the surface spanned by the considered significant patterned region is created. Every pixel with a spatial distance smaller than a given threshold τ^{SP1} is added to the mask, including of course all pixels that belong to the significant patterned region. As this process increases the area, a morphological erosion [20] is subsequently performed. The boundary of the mask is then determined. In case that the mask still consists of more than one connected component, then the boundary is extracted from the one with the biggest area.

The **texture information** is only used for the detected significant patterned regions that contain at least one of the detected near-regular textures. The sorting of regular textures has been exhaustively considered in Sec. 5.2.3. This method has to be adjusted now for regular textures that have been extracted from near-regular ones. As the color information is separated from the texture information, the gray-level near-regular texture is considered to extract the features.

All of the eight similarity features proposed in Sec. 5.2.3 are also used to compare near-regular textures. The mean texel of the regular texture, one extracted texel, and its displacement vectors are the three characteristics needed in Sec. 5.2.3 to compare regular textures. These characteristics must be defined now for near-regular textures. The representative texel of the near-regular texture is used to obtain the corresponding features extracted from the mean texel in case of regular textures. Among all extracted texels from the near-regular texture, the most similar one to the extracted representative texel is used to calculate the similarity feature s_4, which compares the structure between the texels. Furthermore, the similarity parameter s_5 that compares the regions with an almost constant intensity between texels is calculated from a sharpened version of the extracted texel that is most similar to the representative one. The sharpening is performed by the unsharp masking method [54]. This is necessary to improve the detection of the regions, which is based on a watershed filling method, as the transformation of the extracted texel to the quadrangles robust to affine transformations and lighting variations often implicates the loss of sharpness.

The vectors spanned by the sides of the extracted texels are used to obtain the displacement vectors that are assigned to the near-regular texture for comparison purposes. The vectors are divided into two groups, where each group contains the vectors corresponding to the parallel sides of the texels. At this point it is important to consider only parallel vectors per group. The median value per dimension and group yields the displacement vectors which are used for the extraction of the similarity features comparing the displacement between near-regular textures.

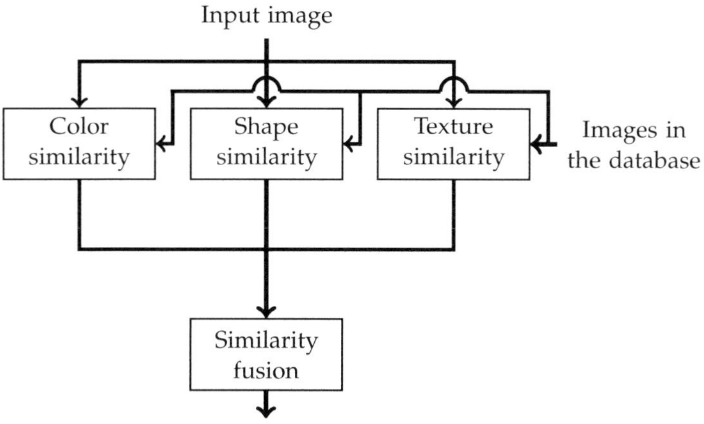

Figure 7.2 Sketch of the proposed sorting method fusing the detection of regions in images, the color, the shape, and the texture information.

7.2.2 Sorting method

An overview of the sorting method is shown in Fig. 7.2. The extracted significant patterned regions are actually the ones that are being sorted, as the sorting of the images according to the similarity of their content is transferred in this thesis to the sorting of these regions. If the input image consists of several significant patterned regions, then as many sorting results of the images will be given as number of extracted significant patterned regions, namely one per region. The sorting of the images is resolved in two stages.

First, the images in the database are sorted three times, one according to their color similarity with the input image, one according to their shape similarity, and one according to their texture similarity. The sorting of the images according to the different characteristics can be therefore done in parallel, which enables a higher performance. In case that an image in the database contains more than one significant patterned region, then the image will appear as many times in the sorting results as extracted significant patterned regions.

In the second step the information of the similarity sorting according to the color, shape, and texture is fused. All of these comparisons respectively yield per image in the database a value that expresses the dissimilarity distance (in case of the color and shape comparisons) or similarity (in case of the texture comparison) with the input image. However, these values cannot be compared between each other directly. On the one hand they have different magnitudes, on the other hand the total similarity does not always depend with the same strength on the different characteristics. To overcome the challenging task of finding a model that combines the three values directly, the direct consideration of the rank position achieved by each extracted significant patterned region is proposed. The median value of the three rank positions (color, shape, and texture similarity) is calculated per extracted significant patterned region. This permits an automatic adjustment of the strength of the color, shape, and texture similarity depending on the compared significant patterned regions. According to the median values of the rank positions of the extracted significant patterned regions, the images are sorted. Images in the database that contain more than one extracted patterned region are then retrieved only at their first achieved position.

8 Results

Several methods have been proposed in the previous chapters inspired by the content-based image retrieval problem. The detection of regions in images (Sec. 6), the analysis of the color (Sec. 3), shape (Sec. 4), and texture (Sec. 5) properties, and the fusion of all of these methods (Sec. 7) have been considered. The results of all of these methods are presented and discussed in this chapter. For this purpose, the methods have been implemented using *Matlab* [97] as software.

General evaluation concerns are addressed in Sec. 8.1 followed by the results considering color (Sec. 8.2), shape (Sec. 8.3), and texture properties (Sec. 8.4). The results yielded by the region detectors are presented in Sec. 8.5. The results achieved by the fusion of the previously independently considered characteristics are shown in Sec. 8.6, where the fusion of the different methods for a content-based image retrieval is considered.

8.1 General evaluation concerns

Adequate images and quality parameters are necessary to be able to evaluate new presented methods. Two self-made databases are presented in Sec. 8.1.1 that are used to test the presented methods. Furthermore, in Sec. 8.1.2 common criteria used to measure the quality of retrieval applications are discussed. A strategy to measure the quality of content-based image retrieval applications is also presented in Sec. 8.1.2.

8.1.1 Self-made databases

Adequate images are necessary to evaluate the proposed methods optimally. Several databases were created during this work that are presented next.

Figure 8.1 A selection of the images in the IIIT texture database.

The **IIIT texture database** consists of 1079 gray-level textured images and was developed to analyze and compare the different types of textures (see Sec. 5.1.1). All of the images in the database were digitally computed with a ray-tracing program [3]. Images containing regular, structural-statistical, and irregular textures form the database. As no clear boundary exists between the types of textures, a previous classification of the images is difficult. However, this is a necessary step to be able to evaluate the methods presented in Sec. 5.2. 698 images are classified in this database as regular textures, which may succumb small stochastic variations along the texels due to, e.g., lighting conditions or variations at their edges representation. 193 images form the structural-statistical textures of the database and allow a bigger deviation of the displacement vectors and the texel representation, not being able in some cases to group the displacement vectors. Finally, 188 images are classified as irregular textures in the database. These images consist of completely irregular textures, where not even a texel can be identified. One-dimensional and two-dimensional textures form part of the regular and the structural-statistical textures. An overview of some images of the database is shown in Fig. 8.1. This database was preliminarily used in [155].

The **IIIT patterned image database** consists of 50 colored images that contain both patterned objects and patterned backgrounds, whereas the patterns are textures of structural-statistical type. Some of the images even consist of a patterned object in front of a patterned background. This database was developed to test the different proposed methods with the challenges of ordinary images, where no high resolution can always be expected. Almost all of the images were taken with a mobile phone under different lighting conditions and perspectives of patterned objects and patterned backgrounds. Objects with similar patterns but different colors, as well as similar patterns over different objects, can be found in the database. Textiles, floor tiles, and lacquered metallic surfaces form the patterned regions. An example of some of the images is shown in Fig. 8.2.

8.1.2 Quality measurements for retrieval applications

Precision and recall are established methods in the literature to evaluate the quality of retrieval applications [4, 5, 10, 13, 43, 53, 77, 83, 85, 90, 91, 106, 118, 124, 128, 129, 138, 144, 146–148, 150, 152]. Precision q_k^{pre} depends on the number of considered retrievals and is calculated as the quotient of the number of good matches that are retrieved n_k^{GM} divided by the number of retrievals k [80]:

$$q_k^{\text{pre}} = \frac{n_k^{\text{GM}}}{k}. \tag{8.1}$$

The higher the precision values are, the better the results will be. However, no information about the completeness of the results can be deduced from the precision values as the total number of good matches is not considered. Recall q_k^{rec} completes in this sense the analysis of the quality of retrieval applications, as it compares the good matches that are retrieved to the total number of good matches in the database n^{GM} [80]:

$$q_k^{\text{rec}} = \frac{n_k^{\text{GM}}}{n^{\text{GM}}}. \tag{8.2}$$

8.1.2.1 Quality criterion used in this thesis

The evaluation of retrieval systems on a database consisting of different classes with different total number of good retrievals becomes complex and confusing when precision and recall are used. On the one hand two different functions have to be considered, and on the other hand precision and recall cannot be compared between classes containing different numbers of good matches, as no normalization exists. In this work the sole use of one quality value is aimed to overcome these issues. Because the fast retrieval of good matches is more important for the applications that motivate this thesis (see Sec. 1) than the completeness of the results, the quality value is extracted from the k-dependent precision. The higher the summation of the k-dependent precision over all retrievals is, the better and more complete the results will be. However, no conclusions can be obtained from the comparison of these values between classes containing different number of good matches. To overcome this issue, the summation of the k-dependent precision over all retrievals is compared to the summation of the precision that would be reached in the ideal case $q_k^{\text{pre,ideal}}$, where all good matches are retrieved first. The value reached by the tested method is expressed as percentage of the ideal one:

$$q^{\text{retr}} = \frac{\sum_k q_k^{\text{pre}}}{\sum_k q_k^{\text{pre,ideal}}} \cdot 100\,\%. \tag{8.3}$$

Figure 8.2 A selection of the images in the IIIT patterned image database.

8.2 Results of the color

The results of the color processing methods presented in Sec. 3 are shown in this section. The use of the compact color signature in CIELAB color space is considered in Sec. 8.2.1 and the representation of color information via humans' color categories in Sec. 8.2.2.

8.2.1 A compact color signature in CIELAB color space for images

In this section the compact color signature presented in Sec. 3.2 is compared to the signature obtained from two *k*-d trees [122] which inspired it. For this purpose, every pixel of the image is assigned to one of the final color regions obtained via the two *k*-d trees. The mean value along each color dimension releases the centroid of the regions. The weight of each color region is then the percentage of pixels in the image belonging to the appendant region. In both cases the CIELAB color space (see Sec. 3.1.1) is used and the maximal length along each dimension is set to 25 as in [122]. The signatures are evaluated at a database which consists of 700 images of natural scenes that is available in the Internet [2, 137].

The criteria used for the evaluation is presented in Sec. 8.2.1.1 and the results are shown in Sec. 8.2.1.2.

8.2.1.1 Evaluation criteria

Three criteria are considered to evaluate the results of the color signatures: the number of color representatives, the comparison of the color distributions, and the sorting of images according to the similarity to the input image.

The extraction of the color representatives and their weights is necessary in many applications for further processing. The smaller the number of clusters representing the color information of the image is, the faster and more efficient further processing may become.

However, a compact representation of the color distribution of the image may lead to bigger deviations compared to the color distribution of the input image due to the compression. The color distribution of the input image is therefore compared to the color distribution after the compression. For this purpose, a synthetic image is calculated from the assignment of every pixel in the input image to its next color representative of the color signature. The distance is calculated using the ℓ_2-norm (see Sec. 2.1). The mean image representation error derived from the color signatures is the mean color difference (calculated using the ℓ_2-norm) from the synthetic image to the input image over all pixels and color dimensions.

Table 8.1 Average numbers of color representatives and their standard deviations.

Method	Mean number of color representatives	Standard deviation of the number of color representatives
One k**-d tree**	61.57	48.85
Two k**-d trees**	28.49	22.10
Proposed method	23.69	14.87

Finally, the impact of the signatures for the content-based image retrieval is considered. Every image in the database is therefore pairwise compared using the earth mover's distance (see Sec. 2.1) with all of the images in the database. These ones are sorted according to their similarity with the input image, from more to less similar. As no ground truth is available about the similarity between the images according to humans' concerns, the ranking of the images depending on the number of retrievals is compared between the two considered color signatures. Per input image the percentage of retrievals matching in both signatures is obtained depending on the number of retrieved images.

8.2.1.2 Evaluation results

The results according to the evaluation criteria presented in Sec. 8.2.1.1 are presented next.

The **number of cluster representatives** needed on average by the considered methods to extract the color signatures and the standard deviations of the number of cluster representatives are shown in Table 8.1. The use of two k-d trees to obtain the color signature compared to the sole use of one k-d tree reduces on average the number of color representatives by 53.73 %. The standard deviation of the number of color representatives is also considerably reduced when two k-d trees are used to obtain the color signature instead of one. This implies less sensitivity to the input image. However, the lowest number of color representatives and the lowest standard deviation towards the number of color representatives are reached by the method presented in Sec. 3.2. 23.69 color representatives are needed on average by this method in contrast to the 28.49 of the two k-d trees and the 61.57 of the one k-d tree.

The standard deviation is about two thirds of the one obtained from the two *k*-d trees and almost a third part of the one obtained from the one *k*-d tree. By these means, the total number of color representatives obtained via the method presented in Sec. 3.2 is less sensitive towards the input image than the ones extracted via *k*-d trees.

Despite the lower number of color representatives needed on average by the method proposed in Sec. 3.2 compared to the two *k*-d trees, the actual number of representatives is compared per image over both methods. For each image in the database the number of color representatives extracted via the method presented in Sec. 3.2 is subtracted from the number of color representatives obtained from the use of two *k*-d trees. The histogram over all differences is shown in Fig. 8.3.

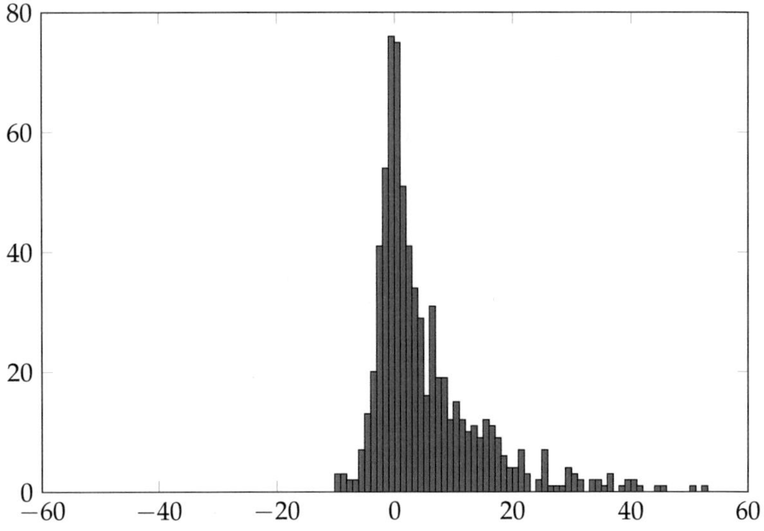

Figure 8.3 Histogram of the number of color representatives of the two *k*-d trees method minus the proposed method.

For most of the images in the database the number of color representatives is smaller if the method from Sec. 3.2 is used to extract them, with up to 52 numbers of color representatives less. Although the two *k*-d tree method provides in some cases less number of color representatives (31.57 %), the method from Sec. 3.2 only needs a few representatives more.

Table 8.2 Averages of the mean image representation errors and their standard deviations.

Method	Average of the mean image representation errors	Standard deviation of the mean image representation errors
Two *k*-d trees	$11.17 \cdot 10^{-3}$	$1.26 \cdot 10^{-3}$
Proposed method	$9.80 \cdot 10^{-3}$	$1.11 \cdot 10^{-3}$

At this point the conclusion can be drawn that the smallest number of color clusters together with less sensitivity to the input image is achieved by the method proposed in Sec. 3.2.

The averages and standard deviations over all images in the database from the **mean image representation error** created by the color signatures extracted from the two *k*-d trees and the method proposed in Sec. 3.2 are shown in Table 8.2. On average, the method presented in Sec. 3.2 not only possesses a smaller error of the color representation, its standard deviation is also smaller, which implies a more stable method towards the analyzed image. Figure 8.4 shows the histogram of the differences of the mean image representation errors by the color signatures, where per image in the database the error obtained from the method proposed in Sec. 3.2 is subtracted from the one obtained from the two *k*-d trees. For most of the images in the database (96.86 %) the error of the distribution of the color due to the compression is smaller if the method presented in Sec. 3.2 is used.

The **percentage of retrievals matching in both signatures** per input image is shown in Fig. 8.5 in case that all of the images in the database are considered as retrievals (top) and for the first 150 retrievals (bottom). Small deviations can be noticed by little number of retrievals, but a high compliance of retrievals exists between both signatures as the number of retrievals increases. As it can be recognized in Fig. 8.6, over 90 % of the retrieved images match on average between the two color signatures by 21 retrievals. On average 100 % of the retrievals match when one image is retrieved because the input image is always retrieved first for both color signatures.

Overall, the following conclusions can be drawn. The method proposed in Sec. 3.2 reduces for most of the images in the database the number of color representatives or needs a comparable number to the ones extracted by the two *k*-d trees. The error due to the color compression is for 96.86 % of the images in the database smaller if the method presented in Sec. 3.2 is used, although the number of color representatives decreases on average. The retrievals of images sorted by color similarity with an input image are comparable for both signatures.

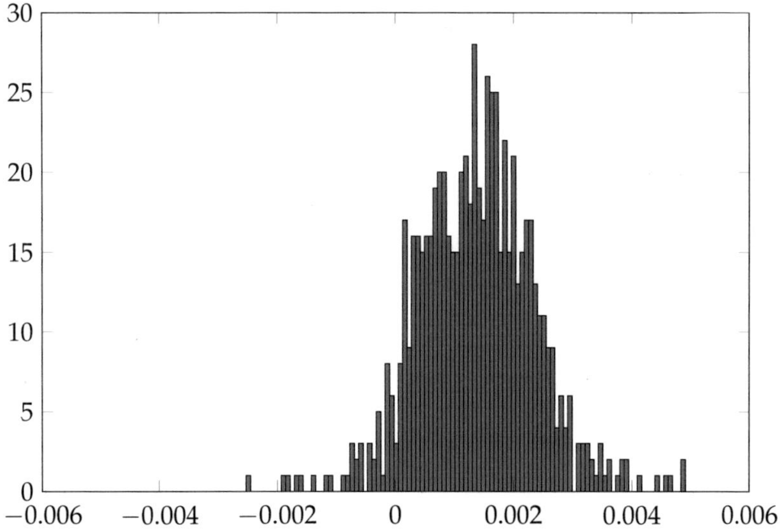

Figure 8.4 Histogram of the differences of the mean image representation errors achieved by the two *k*-d trees method minus the proposed one.

8.2.2 Humans' color categories

In this section the humans' color categories extracted according to Sec. 3.3 are presented. After the editing of the color names (Sec. 3.3.1.1) and the suppression of spam answers (Sec. 3.3.1.2), with τ^{C2} set to 10, only 8.73 % of the color names of the raw database remain and are therefore not considered as misspellings or spam answers.

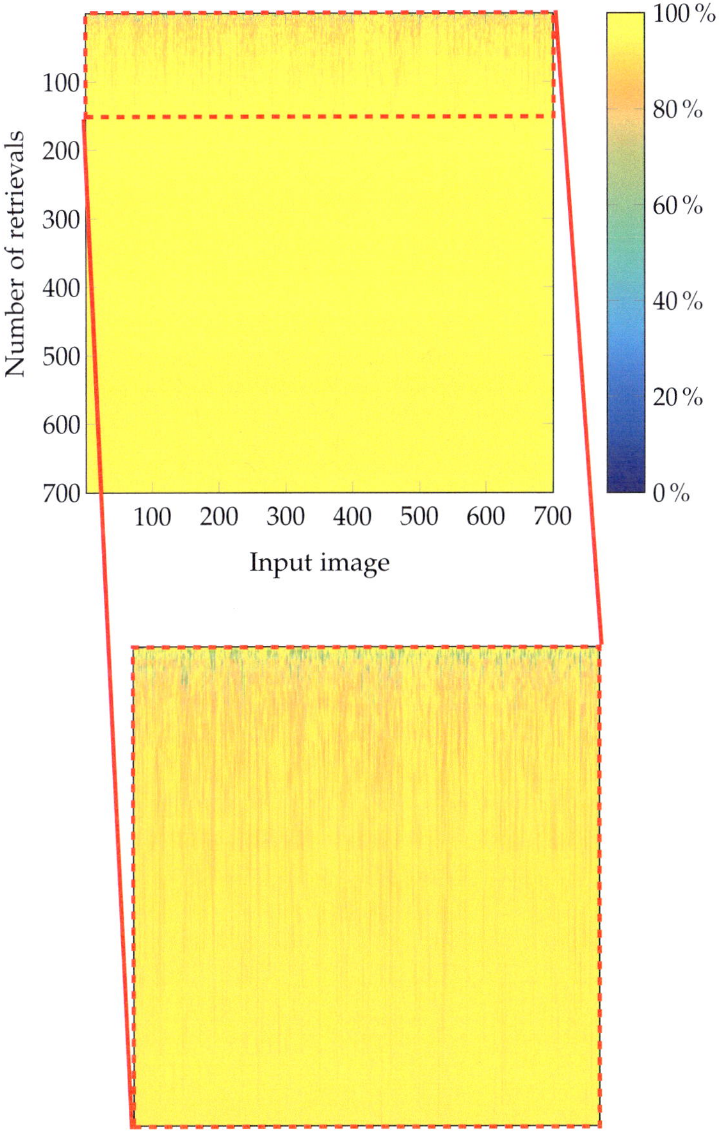

Figure 8.5 Percentage of retrievals matching for both signatures.

From the remaining valid answers the color categories were extracted as explained in Sec. 3.3.2. For this purpose, the CIELAB color space must be quantized. 25 bins are used for the channel that represents the brightness of the color and 64 bins for the other two channels. The extracted humans' color categories are then 145 color names that are shown in Table 8.3 together with their mean color value calculated in CIELAB color space.

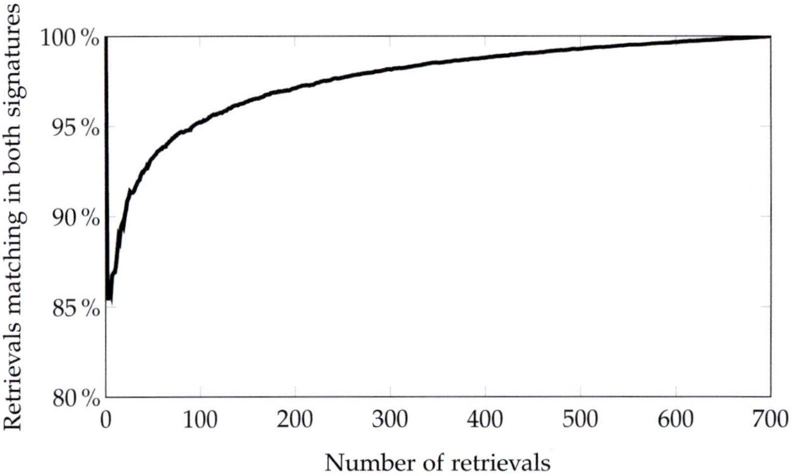

Figure 8.6 Average of the percentage of retrievals matching in both signatures per number of retrievals.

Table 8.3 Extracted humans' color categories.

1.	anthracite		74.	ligh green	
2.	aqua		75.	light blue	
3.	aqua marine		76.	light brown	
4.	aquamarine		77.	light green	
5.	army green		78.	light grey	
6.	azul		79.	light lavender	
7.	azure		80.	light light purple	
8.	baby blue		81.	light orange	
9.	baby puke		82.	light pink	
10.	baby shit brown		83.	light purple	
11.	baby yellow		84.	light tan	

12. beige
13. black
14. blackish
15. blood
16. blue
17. blue green
18. blue grey
19. bluegreen
20. bordeaux
21. brick
22. brick red
23. bright fuchsia
24. bright green
25. bright purple
26. brown
27. brown orange
28. burgundy
29. burnt orange
30. burnt umber
31. butter yellow
32. chartreuse
33. claret
34. coral
35. coral red
36. cream
37. custard
38. cyan
39. dark blue
40. dark blue green
41. dark brown
42. dark er pink
43. dark green
44. dark grey
45. dark magenta
46. dark maroon
47. dark olive
48. dark pink
49. dark purple
85. light yellow
86. lilac
87. lime
88. lime green
89. magenta
90. maroon
91. mauve
92. midnight blue
93. mud
94. mulberry
95. mustard
96. mustard yellow
97. navy
98. navy blue
99. nude
100. ocher
101. off white
102. olive
103. olive green
104. orange
105. orange tan
106. pale blue
107. pale green
108. pale lavender
109. pale orange
110. pale pink
111. pale rose
112. pale yellow
113. peach
114. pee yellow
115. periwinkle
116. pink
117. puce
118. puke green
119. purple
120. purple pink
121. red
122. red orange

50.	dark red		123.	red purple	
51.	dark salmon		124.	robin egg blue	
52.	dark teal		125.	rose	
53.	deep purple		126.	royal blue	
54.	dove grey		127.	salmon	
55.	eggplant		128.	sea foam green	
56.	eggshell		129.	shit brown	
57.	emerald green		130.	sky blue	
58.	flesh		131.	tan	
59.	forest green		132.	teal	
60.	fuchsia		133.	turquoise	
61.	gold		134.	vermillion	
62.	grapefruit		135.	very dark green	
63.	grass green		136.	very light blue	
64.	green		137.	very light green	
65.	green grey		138.	violet	
66.	green yellow		139.	viridian	
67.	grey		140.	vivid blue	
68.	grey blue		141.	white	
69.	grey green		142.	wine red	
70.	hot pink		143.	yellow	
71.	indigo		144.	yellow green	
72.	khaki		145.	yellowish brown	
73.	lavender				

Notice that some of the names of the color categories suggest misspellings (like, e.g., *aquamarine* and *aqua marine* or *ligh green* and *light green*). The fusion of color categories has been considered by the author, but it is outside the scope of this work. The 145 color categories represent 0.08 % of all color names used by the users.

Figure 8.7 shows the histogram of the color values named with the extracted color categories. The bins are represented by the mean color of each category. Notice that the number of colors assigned to each color category is different, from the 36 colors that form *ligh green* to the 315,933 colors that span *green*. This implies that different forms of subspaces in the CIELAB color space are spanned by the color categories. These ones may overlap or even contain each other.

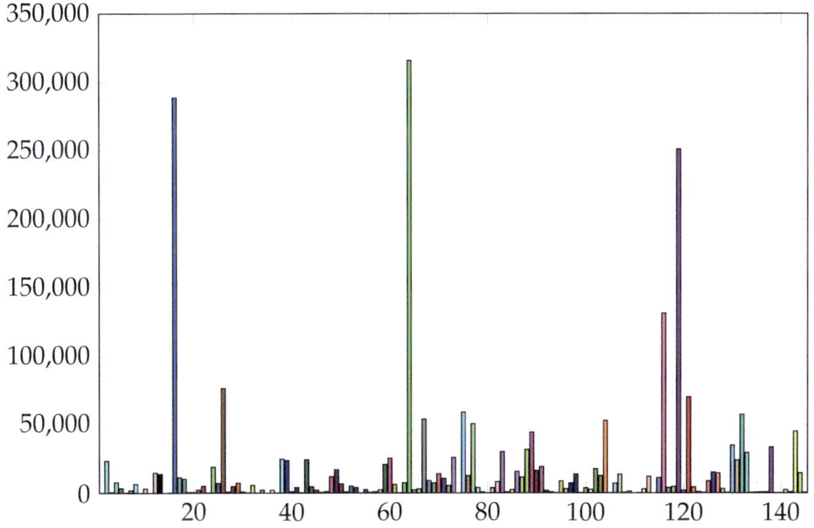

Figure 8.7 Histogram of the extracted color categories. The colors of the bins represent the average color of the respective categories.

The implications of processing the color information with humans' color categories instead of directly using the CIELAB color space is shown in Secs. 8.5.1 and 8.5.2, where these types of color processing are compared on applications.

8.3 Results of the shape

The suitability of the normal angular descriptors together with their similarity comparisons presented in Sec. 4.2 and the suitability of the Fourier descriptors presented in Sec. 4.3 for the content-based shape retrieval are considered in this section. An overview of the tested combinations between descriptors and similarity distances is shown in Table 8.4.

Three similarity distances are presented in Sec. 4.2.2 to compare shapes described by normal angular descriptors. Their consequences for shape retrieval purposes can be deduced from the comparison of the results achieved by the the combinations S1, S2, and S3. S1 is based on unwarped normal angular descriptors, whereas S2 and S3 consider warped normal angular descriptors (see Sec. 4.2.2.2). Furthermore, S1 and S2 use the correlation for circular data (see Sec. 2.1) while S3 uses the comparison method based on the Euclidean distance.

Table 8.4 Tested combinations for shape retrieval.

	Descriptors				Similarity distances			
Com.	η_k	$f_{1,f}^{\text{Fourier}}$	$f_{2,f}^{\text{Fourier}}$	$f_{3,f}^{\text{Fourier}}$	d_1^{NAD}	d_2^{NAD}	d_3^{NAD}	d_f^{Fourier}
S1	•				•			
S2	•					•		
S3	•						•	
S4		•						•
S5			•					•
S6				•				•
S7				•				•
S8				•				•

The combinations S4 to S8 are based on the Fourier descriptors, whose similarities between two objects are always calculated by the Euclidean distance (see Sec. 2.1). S4 uses scaling-invariant descriptors, S5 Fourier descriptors with normalized energy, and S6 to S8 the scaling- and rotation-invariant descriptors (with the desired rotation symmetry of the object s set to 1). S6 to S8 correspond with the three tested combinations of the parameter q presented in Sec. 4.3.3.

The methods are evaluated at the MPEG-7 CE-Shape database [1], which is commonly used to test such cases [13, 16, 67, 81, 146, 150]. This database consists of 1400 images of white objects on a black background. There are 70 object classes, each of them containing 20 images. For the evaluation of the proposed methods, the boundaries of the objects are extracted and described with 101 points as in [157] and [158]. The extracted boundaries consisting of more than 101 points are reduced to 101 using the Fourier descriptors by eliminating the higher frequency components.

The parameter q^{retr} is used to evaluate the retrieval quality of the combinations presented in Table 8.4. For this purpose, the images in the database are sorted 1400 times. Every image in the database is used as query and according to the sorted results q_k^{retr} is calculated per query object, where $1 \leq k \leq 1400$ represents the query object. Objects from the same object class as the query object are defined as its good matches. Notice that some objects belonging to other classes may be considered similar to the shape of the query object as similarity is a human dependent task. However, as established in literature, only objects that belong to the same class are defined as good matches.

Two parameters are used to compare the quality of the retrieval results between the different tested combinations. Per object class the mean value of q_k^{retr} from all objects that belong to the class is calculated $q_{k_1}^{\text{retr}}$, $1 \leq k_1 \leq 70$. The mean value $\mu(q_{k_1}^{\text{retr}})$ and standard deviation $\sigma(q_{k_1}^{\text{retr}})$ from this parameter over all object classes yield the two evaluation parameters.

8.3.1 Evaluation results

The evaluation results of the tested combinations are shown in Table 8.5. The methods based on the Fourier descriptors yield lower $\mu(q_{k_1}^{\text{retr}})$ values than those based on the normal angular descriptors. Among the methods based on the Fourier descriptors the highest $\mu(q_{k_1}^{\text{retr}})$ is reached by the Fourier descriptors with the normalized energies (S5). This combination also possesses under the Fourier descriptors based methods the lowest standard deviation $\sigma(q_{k_1}^{\text{retr}})$, which implies a higher robustness against the query object. Mixed quality results are reached by the scaling- and rotation-invariant descriptors (S6 to S8). On the one hand it yields the second highest $\mu(q_{k_1}^{\text{retr}})$ value under the Fourier descriptors based methods, but on the other hand it also yields the lowest one. Under these combinations, the highest values are reached by the third combination presented in Sec. 4.3.3 which allows $q \in \mathbb{Z}$ although $q \in \mathbb{N}_+$ is expected in [25]. However, this combination also reaches the highest standard deviation of all tested combinations.

The best $\mu(q_{k_1}^{\text{retr}})$ values are achieved by the combinations based on the normal angular descriptors. Whereas the use of the correlation for circular data (S1 and S2) yields higher $\mu(q_{k_1}^{\text{retr}})$ values than in case of the similarity distance based on the Euclidean distance (S3), the comparisons of warped angular descriptors (S2 and S3) possess the lowest standard deviations $\sigma(q_{k_1}^{\text{retr}})$ of all tested combinations. The use of warped angular descriptors with the correlation for circular data as similarity distance yields therefore the best trade-off between a high $\mu(q_{k_1}^{\text{retr}})$ and a low $\sigma(q_{k_1}^{\text{retr}})$.

Table 8.5 Evaluation parameters of the shape retrieval.

Com.	$\mu\left(q_{k_1}^{\text{retr}}\right)$	$\sigma\left(q_{k_1}^{\text{retr}}\right)$
S1	77.25 %	21.02 %
S2	77.06 %	18.63 %
S3	76.03 %	18.74 %
S4	68.85 %	23.75 %
S5	73.04 %	19.78 %
S6	50.63 %	20.51 %
S7	49.64 %	20.58 %
S8	72.10 %	25.09 %

Overall, the following conclusions can be drawn. The presented normal angular descriptors are a promising feature for the sorting of objects' shapes according to their similarity. Furthermore, the similarity between objects' shapes seems to be beyond scale and rotation variations, as the scaling- and rotation-invariant descriptors did not yield the best results. The results also show that the use of a warping method to the normal angular descriptors can improve the robustness against the different shapes of the input objects, and that the correlation for circular data yields better retrieval quotes than the use of the similarity distance based on the Euclidean distance.

8.4 Results of the texture

In this section the results of the methods dealing with texture from Sec. 5 are presented and discussed. The results of the methods focused on regular textures (see Sec. 5.2) are shown in Sec. 8.4.1 and the results of the methods focused on near-regular textures (see Sec. 5.3) in Sec. 8.4.2.

8.4.1 Regular textures

The results of the extraction of the displacement vectors and valid texels of regular textures is discussed in Sec. 8.4.1.1. These characteristics are necessary to be able to detect and sort regular textures as proposed in Sec. 5.2. The detection of regular textures is considered next. For this purpose, the detections in space and in frequency domain were considered in Sec. 5.2.2. The criteria used to evaluate the quality of the detection methods are presented in Sec. 8.4.1.2 followed by the evaluation results of the detection in space (Sec. 8.4.1.3) and in frequency domain (Sec. 8.4.1.4). Once the regular textures have been detected, their sorting according to their similarity was considered in Sec. 5.2.3. The sorting results achieved by this method are presented in Sec. 8.4.1.5. Finally, in Sec. 8.4.1.6 the perception map of regular textures derived from the results of the experiment presented in Sec. 5.2.4 is shown, discussed, and compared with the sorting results achieved by the proposed method.

8.4.1.1 Extraction of the texel and its displacement vectors in the real case

The extraction of the displacement vectors and texels of regular textures for an ideal case was presented in Sec. 5.2.1.1. However, as mentioned in Sec. 5.2.1.2, due to the discretization of the images in space domain and the lack of a clear boundary between regular and structural-statistical textures, the real case must be considered. 14 window functions, two types of interpolations, and the use of zero padding were proposed in Sec. 5.2.1.2 to overcome the issues related to the real case. Their appropriateness for the extraction of the characteristics are compared in this section. For this purpose, the textures classified as regular in the IIIT texture database (see Sec. 8.1.1) are considered.

The evaluation of the different methods for the extraction of the characteristics of regular textures is not trivial. On the one hand, many displacement vectors combined with different texels may describe the considered regular texture correctly (see Sec. 5.1.1), so no unique solution exists. On the other hand, the displacement vectors must not be of discrete nature in contrast to the input image, which makes their exact extraction from a given image difficult. Furthermore, an exact extraction of the displacement vectors is not even possible if the regular texture underlies small stochastic variations. The storage of all valid displacement vectors and texels that may describe the input images as ground truth data is not possible and alternative evaluation methods are necessary. The better the extraction of the displacement vectors is, the better the extraction of the texel in the image will be and therefore the better the original image may be represented. By these means, the absolute difference between an input image and its respective reconstructed image $d^{T,1}(g_{\mathbf{u}}, \tilde{g}_{\mathbf{u}})$ (as presented in Sec. 5.2.2.1) is a good indicator of the quality of the extracted displacement vectors and texel. The smaller $d^{T,1}(g_{\mathbf{u}}, \tilde{g}_{\mathbf{u}})$ is, the better the estimation of the texture characteristics will be. Furthemore, as images containing big areas spanned by their displacement vectors are directly classified as irregular and therefore not reconstructed, the number of regular textures in the database that are directly classified as irregular is also an important parameter to evalute the goodness of the analyzed combinations, as all of the textures considered in this section are regular.

Figure 8.8 shows the average of $d^{T,1}(g_{\mathbf{u}}, \tilde{g}_{\mathbf{u}})$ over all the regular textures in the database that were reconstructed depending on the window function, the kind of interpolation, and the type of zero padding used for the extraction. From now on the use of no zero padding and its use by increasing the size of the input image by a factor of two and three is also referred as a zero padding of zero, one, and two degree, respectively. The results show that the use of a bilinear interpolation (dashed and/or dotted curves) instead of the nearest neighbor interpolation (solid curves) reduces the average error $\mu(d^{T,1}(g_{\mathbf{u}}, \tilde{g}_{\mathbf{u}}))$ over all images in the database. This error also becomes smaller, the higher the degree of zero padding (coded by the color) is. Among the window functions the conclusions can be drawn that the quality of the extracted characteristics of the regular textures by the flat top window is on average worse than when the other window functions are used. Particularly at the rectangular and Kaiser windows, the improvements of the bilinear interpolation and the use of zero padding can be noticed. Whereas these windows deliver together with the flat top window the highest average errors over all images in the database $\mu(d^{T,1}(g_{\mathbf{u}}, \tilde{g}_{\mathbf{u}}))$ when the nearest neighbor interpolation and no zero padding is used, they reach on average the smallest errors $\mu(d^{T,1}(g_{\mathbf{u}}, \tilde{g}_{\mathbf{u}}))$ when zero padding and the bilinear interpolation is used. The modified Bartlett-Hann, Hamming, Taylor, and triangular windows together with a bilinear interpolation and zero padding yield similar good results to those achieved by the Kaiser and rectangular windows.

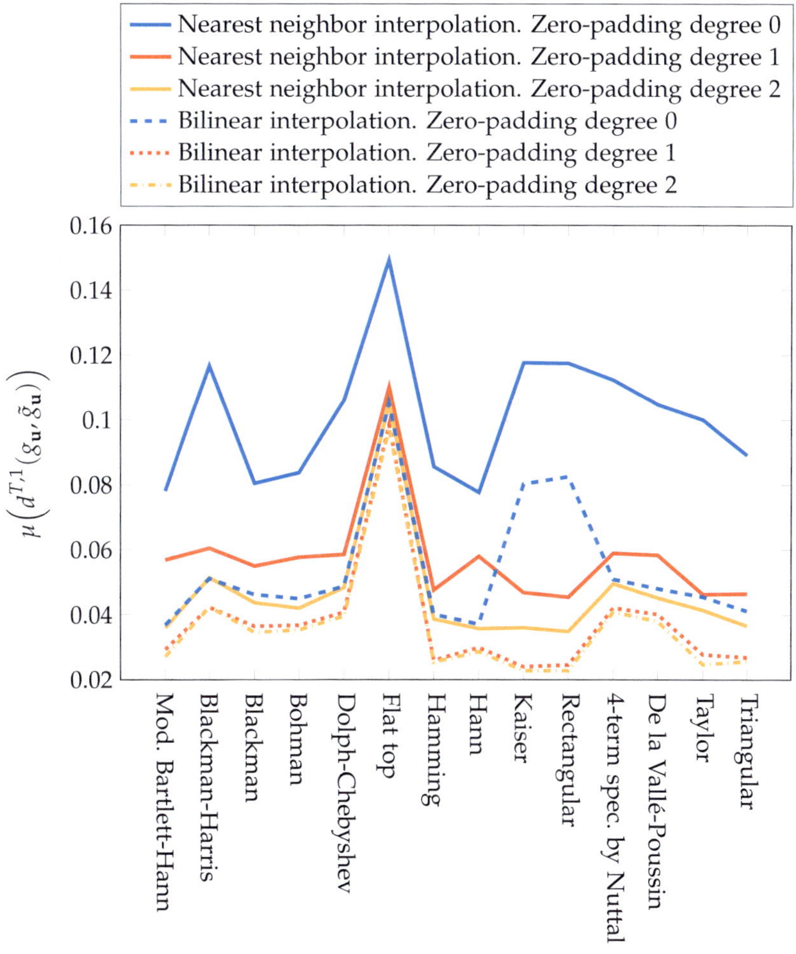

Figure 8.8 Average of the absolute differences between input images and their resconstructed ones using different window functions, interpolation methods, and degrees of zero padding.

Table 8.6 Number of images whose displacement vectors have been estimated too long.

Window function	Nearest neighbor interpolation			Bilinear interpolation		
	Degree of zero padding			Degree of zero padding		
	0	1	2	0	1	2
Mod. Bartlett-Hann	3	2	3	2	2	2
Blackman-Harris	4	3	3	3	3	3
Blackman	2	3	3	3	3	2
Bohman	3	3	3	3	2	2
Dolph-Chebyshev	5	3	3	3	3	3
Flat top	7	7	8	6	6	6
Hamming	3	1	1	2	0	0
Hann	3	2	3	2	2	2
Kaiser	4	2	1	0	2	2
Rectangular	4	2	1	0	1	2
4-term spec. by Nuttal	4	3	3	3	2	2
De la Vallé-Poussin	5	3	3	3	2	3
Taylor	0	1	0	0	0	0
Triangular	1	1	0	1	0	0

Table 8.6 shows over all analyzed combinations the number of images that were directly classified as irregular, because the area spanned by their extracted displacement vectors was too big. Ideally, none of the analyzed images should be classified as irregular, as only the regular textures were analyzed from the database. The results show that over all combinations only a small number of textures are directly considered of irregular type (up to 1.15 % for the flat top window). The Hamming, Kaiser, rectangular, Taylor, and triangular windows are the only windows that manage not to classify input textures directly as irregular. In case of the Kaiser and rectangular windows this only happens with a bilinear interpolation and no zero padding. However, these two combinations yielded a high average error $\mu(d^{T,1}(g_{\mathbf{u}}, \tilde{g}_{\mathbf{u}}))$. The Hamming window achieves it in combination with the bilinear interpolation and zero padding, and the triangular window together with bilinear interpolation and zero padding and also in case of the

nearest neighbor interpolation if a zero padding degree of two is applied. The stablest window towards the interpolation methods and the usage of zero padding to avoid an assignment of the analyzed images as irregular is the Taylor window. When it is applied together with the nearest neighbor interpolation and a zero padding degree of one, only one image is directly classified as irregular, otherwise the characteristics of regular textures were extracted for all considered images in the database.

Overall, the following conclusions can be drawn. The higher the degree of zero padding together with a bilinear interpolaton, the better the extraction of the characteristics of regular textures is. Furthermore, for these combinations the Hamming, Taylor, and triangular windows extract for all considered images in the database their displacement vectors and texel. The best trade-off between a small average error $\mu(d^{T,1}(g_{\mathbf{u}}, \tilde{g}_{\mathbf{u}}))$ and a good extraction of the characteristics of regular textures over all considered images in the database is reached by the Taylor window together with the bilinear interpolation and a zero padding degree of two.

8.4.1.2 Evaluation criteria for the detection of regular textures

In Sec. 5.2.2 the detection of regular textures in space and frequency domain is respectively considered. The modus operandi in both cases is to assume first that the analyzed input texture is of regular type and to extract therefore its displacement vectors. If the area spanned by its displacement vectors in space domain is too big, then the analyzed texture is directly classified as not regular. If the area is small, then the analyzed texture is further processed until a final value is extracted, according to which the input texture is classified as regular or not. For the detection in space domain (see Sec. 5.2.2.1) this value is the result of the similarity distance function defined in Eq. 5.8, for the detection in frequency domain (see Sec. 5.2.2.2) two different features are proposed in Eq. 5.11 and Eq. 5.12. In order to evaluate the appropriateness of the different methods, the suitability of the extracted values is considered together with the classification results of the analyzed images, which are the textured images from the IIIT texture database (see Sec. 8.1.1). Since the Taylor window together with the bilinear interpolation and a degree of two for the zero padding yielded the best results in Sec. 8.4.1.1, this combination is also used in the following Secs. 8.4.1.3 and 8.4.1.4.

The **suitability of the extracted parameters** for the detection of regular textures is measured considering their similarity within textures of the same type together with the similarity between the two classified groups. This way of proceeding is the basis of the Fisher linear discriminant analysis [45] to reduce the dimension of data taking into consideration a good separability between the different groups. The higher

$$q^{\mathrm{S1}} = \frac{(\mu_1 - \mu_2)^2}{\sigma_1^2 + \sigma_2^2}, \tag{8.4}$$

where

$$\mu_k = \frac{1}{|\mathcal{M}_k|} \sum_{m \in \mathcal{M}_k} m, \tag{8.5}$$

$$\sigma_k^2 = \sum_{m \in \mathcal{M}_k} (m - \mu_k)^2, \tag{8.6}$$

$k \in \{1,2\}$ for the two groups, and $\mathcal{M}_k$ is the set of all features m belonging to the cluster k, the better the separability between the two groups.

The goal of the approaches presented in Sec. 5.2.2 is the detection of regular textures and thus the classification into regular or not regular. The appropriateness of the approaches can be compared by their achieved quotient q^{S1}. Furthermore, it is also interesting to analyze the limits of the extracted classification features if a further classification into the three types of textures (regular, structural-statistical, and irregular) is considered. However, as the number of representatives per texture type in the IIIT texture database is different, this may distort q^{S1}. To overcome this issue, the within class variations σ_k^2 are normalized by their number of representatives in the database:

$$\tilde{q}^{\mathrm{sep}} = \frac{(\mu_1 - \mu_2)^2}{\tilde{\sigma}_1^2 + \tilde{\sigma}_2^2}, \tag{8.7}$$

where

$$\tilde{\sigma}_k^2 = \frac{\sum_{m \in \mathcal{M}_k} (m - \mu_k)^2}{|\mathcal{M}_k|}, \tag{8.8}$$

$k \in \{1,2\}$. $\tilde{q}^{\mathrm{sep}}$ is named from now on as separability quotient.

The **confusion matrix** [130] of the classification of the images in the database into regular and not regular is the second evaluation criterion. 18.90 % of the textures in the database that are not of regular type (72 images) are directly classified as not regular, because the area spanned by their extracted displacement vectors in space domain is too big. 10.03 % (31 images) are randomly chosen from the remaining irregular and structural-statistical textures in the database that have not been directly classified as not regular. Together with 31 randomly chosen regular textures from the database they form the training data [80, 130], which is used to obtain the threshold value according to which the input images are classified. The confusion matrix is evaluated for the remaining images in the database that were not part of the training procedure to avoid overfitting [45].

8.4.1.3 Evaluation results for the detection in space domain

The quality of the similarity distance $d^{T,1}(g_{\mathbf{u}}, \tilde{g}_{\mathbf{u}})$ for the detection and classification according to the type of textures is presented and discussed next.

The **similarity distances** between an input image and its reconstructed one $d^{T,1}(g_{\mathbf{u}}, \tilde{g}_{\mathbf{u}})$ for all images in the database whose area spanned by their displacement vectors is small enough to not be directly classified as an irregular texture are presented in form of a histogram in Fig. 8.9. We can recognize that the distance values are much smaller for textures of regular type. There is even a gap between the distance values obtained from the regular textures and the other ones. Furthermore, within the textures that are not regular, the structural-statistical textures tend to have smaller distance values than the irregular textures, which corresponds to the fact that no clear boundary exists between the different types of textures. The gap between the regular textures and the structural-statistical ones should be therefore reduced if more textures are considered with a finer transition from their regularity to structural-statistical ones. According to these results the similarity distance between an input image and its reconstructed one is a valid feature for a successful detection of regular textures. Moreover, this feature can also be used as an orientation for the type of irregularity.

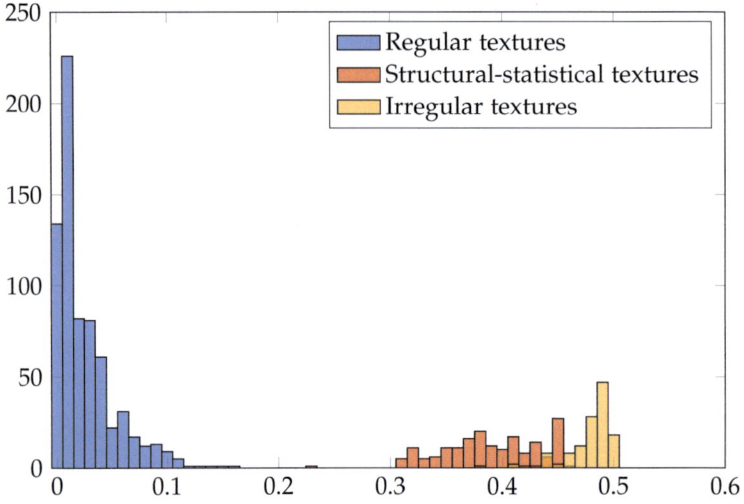

Figure 8.9 Histogram of the similarity distance $d^{T,1}(g_{\mathbf{u}}, \tilde{g}_{\mathbf{u}})$ of the reconstructed images.

The good detection of regular textures is also shown by the high separability quotient $\tilde{q}^{\mathrm{sep}}$ of 42.91. Table 8.7 contains the separability quotients between the different types of textures. The best separability is reached between regular textures and irregular ones. Nevertheless the separability between regular textures and structural-statistical ones is also high. The fact that structural-statistical textures cannot be always separated by $d^{T,1}(g_{\mathbf{u}}, \tilde{g}_{\mathbf{u}})$ is shown at the lower separability quotient between them.

The **confusion matrix** over the tested images is shown in Table 8.8. The threshold for the detection of regular textures is obtained from the similarity distances of the images in the training set. For this purpose, the mean value between the highest similarity distance of the regular textures and the lowest one of the not regular textures is calculated. The results show that all of the regular textures are correctly detected. Apart from one two-dimensional texture that was detected as a one-dimensional one, the dimensions of all of the other images in the database are correctly detected. The wrong detection of the dimension of the image is due to an issue related with the extraction of the textures' characteristics, and it can be solved by reducing the threshold from which peaks are considered prominent.

Table 8.7 Separability quotients $\tilde{q}^{\mathrm{sep}}$ between different types of textures.

	Regular	Structural-statistical	Irregular
Regular	-	52.27	188.35
Structural-statistical	52.27	-	3.43
Irregular	188.35	3.43	-

Table 8.8 Confusion matrix over the tested images.

	1-D regular	2-D regular	Not regular
1-D regular	100 %	0 %	0 %
2-D regular	0.76 %	99.24 %	0 %
Not regular	0 %	0 %	100 %

Overall, the following conclusions can be drawn. The method proposed in Sec. 5.2.2.1 to detect regular textures in space domain reaches its goal, as all of the images in the database were successfully classified. Furthermore, the recognition of the tendency of the type of irregularity for not regular textures is even possible.

8.4.1.4 Evaluation results for the detection in frequency domain

Seven templates, eight regions in frequency domain, and two features are presented in Sec. 5.2.2.2 to detect if a texture is of regular type or not. This implies 112 possible methods. Their suitability for the detection of regular textures is discussed in this section.

The **separability coefficients** between regular and not regular textures for all methods presented in Sec. 5.2.2.2 are shown in Fig. 8.10. m^{T1} is used as feature for the two upper diagrams and m^{T2} for the bottom one. The consequence of the proposed templates is coded along the x-axis and the colors contain the information about the size considered in frequency domain. The diagram in the middle shows the results in case that the energies immediately close to the origin are suppressed.

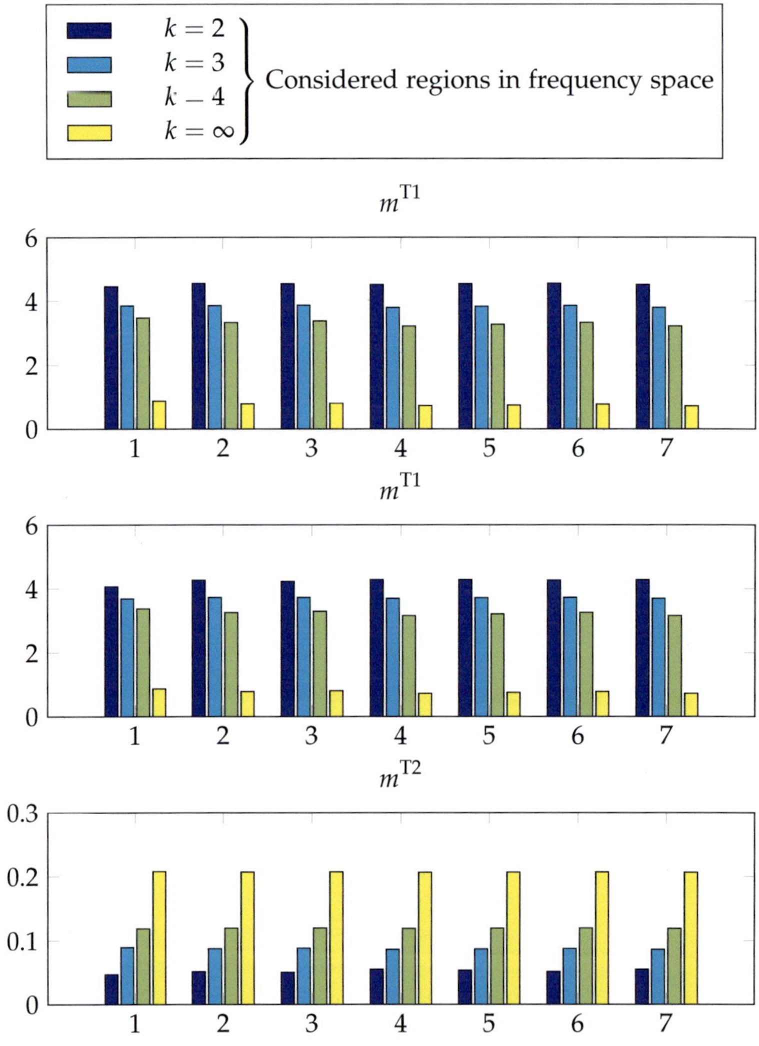

Figure 8.10 Separability coefficients achieved by the tested methods.

The separability values (y-axis) are much smaller than in case of the detection in space domain (42.91, see Sec. 8.4.1.3). Within the detectors in frequency domain, the extraction of the features via m^{T1} yields a better separability than in case of m^{T2}. Furthermore, a tendency between the sizes of the considered regions in frequency domain can be observed. For m^{T1}, the smaller the size of the regions in frequency domain, the better the detection of regular textures is. On the other hand, the bigger the size of the regions in frequency domain, the better the detection of regular textures if m^{T2} is used as feature. The type of template used for the detection plays a less important role in comparison to the other degrees of freedom.

The feature values m^{T1} (top) and m^{T2} (middle and bottom) are shown in Fig. 8.11 as histograms of their respective combinations that reached the best separability coefficient. No matter if m^{T1} or m^{T2} is used, the regular textures tend to have higher features than the not regular ones. However, in contrast to the detection in space domain, the features in the histogram are not clearly grouped depending on their type of texture, which explains the lower separability coefficients.

Table 8.9 Confusion matrices over the tested images.

m^{T1}	**1-D regular**	**2-D regular**	**Not regular**
1-D regular	75.37 %	0 %	24.63 %
2-D regular	0.76 %	97.71 %	1.53 %
Not regular	0 %	1.44 %	98.56 %
m^{T2}	**1-D regular**	**2-D regular**	**Not regular**
1-D regular	5.97 %	0 %	94.03 %
2-D regular	0 %	0 %	100 %
Not regular	0.89 %	0 %	99.11 %

The **confusion matrices** over all tested images per best combinations of m^{T1} and m^{T2} are shown in Table 8.9. The thresholds for the detection of regular textures were calculated per considered feature m^{T1} and m^{T2} from the feature values of the textures that form the training set. For this purpose, the mean values between the lowest value of the regular textures and the highest one of the not regular ones were respectively calculated. The majority of the regular textures and their dimensions are correctly detected by the method using m^{T1} as feature. Almost all two-dimensional regular textures are correctly detected in this case (97.71 %). Like in the case of the detection in space domain, one of the two-dimensional textures is detected as a one-dimensional one. The percentage of one-dimensional textures that are detected is also high (75.37 %) but not as high as in the case of two-dimensional textures. Furthermore, almost all not regular textures are also correctly identified, apart from 1.44 % which are detected as two-dimensional regular textures.

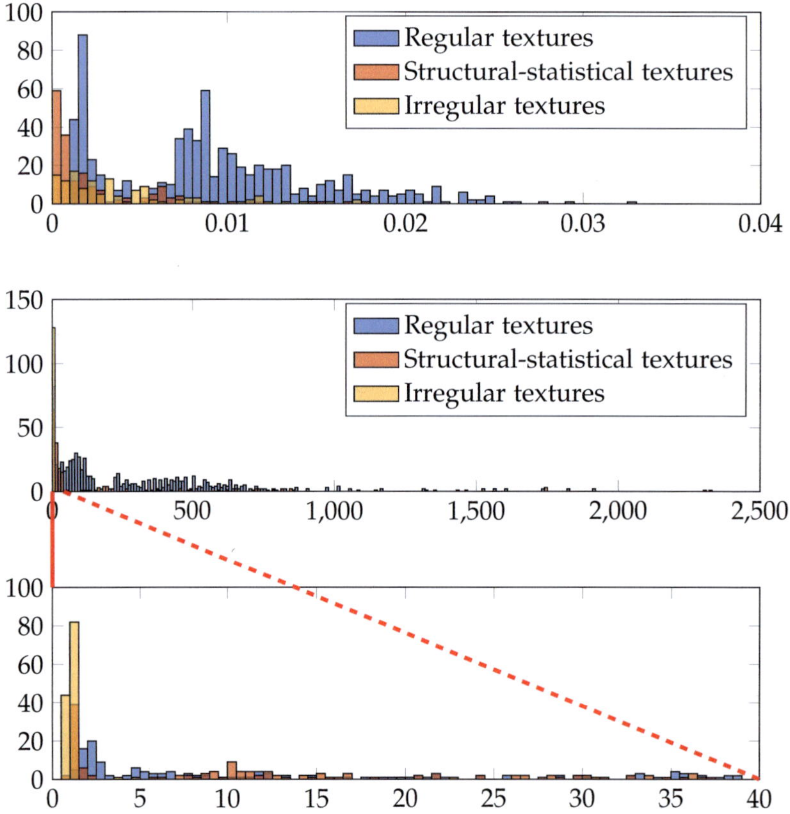

Figure 8.11 Histogram of the best separability results reached by the features m^{T1} (top) and m^{T2} (middle and bottom).

The detections rates are different if m^{T2} is used as feature. In this case almost all textures are detected as not regular ones independently of their real types.

8.4.1.5 Sorting of regular textures

The suitability of the sorting method for regular textures presented in Sec. 5.2.3 is discussed in this section. For this purpose, the textures of the IIIT texture database detected as regular in space domain using a Taylor window, bilinear interpolation, and a zero padding degree of two are considered. Eight different similarity features whose strength can be independently selected were presented in Sec. 5.2.3 to compare pairs of regular textures. This implies many possible ways to combine the similarity features, which makes possible to focus on different characteristics of the textures like their size or rotation. However, as the similarity perception is a human dependent task and no ground truth data is established in the literature or known to the author so far, the evaluation of the results and especially the optimization of the selection of the strengths of the different similarity parameters is a challenging task. Following the procedure established in literature to evaluate image retrieval systems, the regular textures of the IIIT texture database are grouped for the evaluation into classes, so that quality measurements like the precision and recall functions can be calculated (see Sec. 8.1.2). In Sec. 8.4.1.6 the results achieved by this sorting method are compared to the perception map extracted according to Sec. 5.2.4.

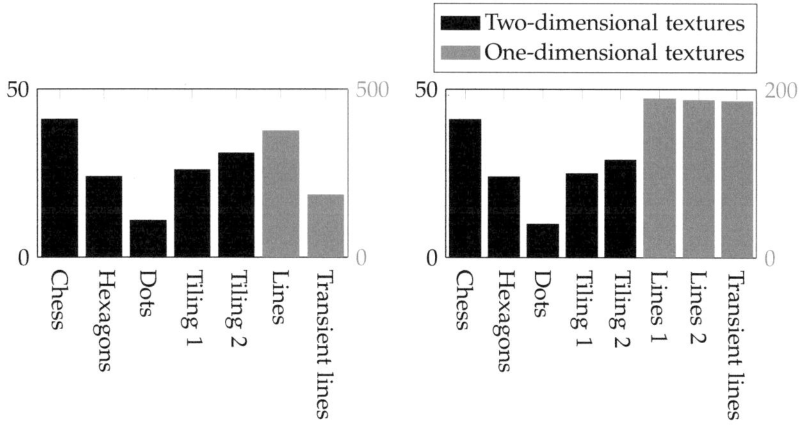

Figure 8.12 Histogram of the images in the database belonging to the bigger classes. A total of 10 classes is permitted if a higher stochastic variation is permitted (left) or 11 classes for a small stochastic variation (right).

For the evaluation of the results, in this section, a class consists of images containing the same pattern which may be rotated, scaled, contain different gray values, or small stochastic variations of the texels. Two different allocations of the regular textures into classes are considered depending on the permitted amount of stochastic variation. 10 and 11 bigger classes respectively appear in the database (see Fig. 8.12, which shows the amount of images per class, where two-dimensional textures are represented in black and one-dimensional ones in gray), whereas more smaller classes exist. Whilst the number of images in the classes slightly decreases for most of the types of patterns, the *Lines* class is split into two classes (*Lines 1*, *Lines 2*) when a smaller stochastic variation of the texels is permitted. Together with the two considered allocations of the images into classes two different strength configurations of the similarity distances are considered for the evaluation results. In the first case all of the similarity distances are considered equally strong; in the second case all of the similarity distances contribute to the total similarity between pairs of textures except the one considering the orientation ($w_7 = 0$).

The value q^{retr}, presented in Sec. 8.1.2.1 to evaluate the quality of retrieval applications, is shown for every image that belongs to one of the bigger classes in Fig. 8.13 for a bigger permitted stochastic variation and in Fig. 8.14 in case of a smaller permitted variation. The blue color represents the results when all similarity distances are considered equally strong and the red color when the orientation information is not considered, whereas the dashed lines represent the average results at the considered class. The results show that for both allocations of the images into classes and for both strength configurations, the retrieval of the images are very close to the ideal one. Only at the *Transient Lines* class some of the input images did not achieve as good retrievals as the other input images. This happened mainly at horizontal and vertical oriented transient lines, where the displacement features predominated over the texels' features. Nevertheless, very good retrieval results are obtained on average for each class (see Table 8.10) and over all classes (see Table 8.11). This happens although the strengths for the different similarity distances were not adjusted to detect textures of same classes.

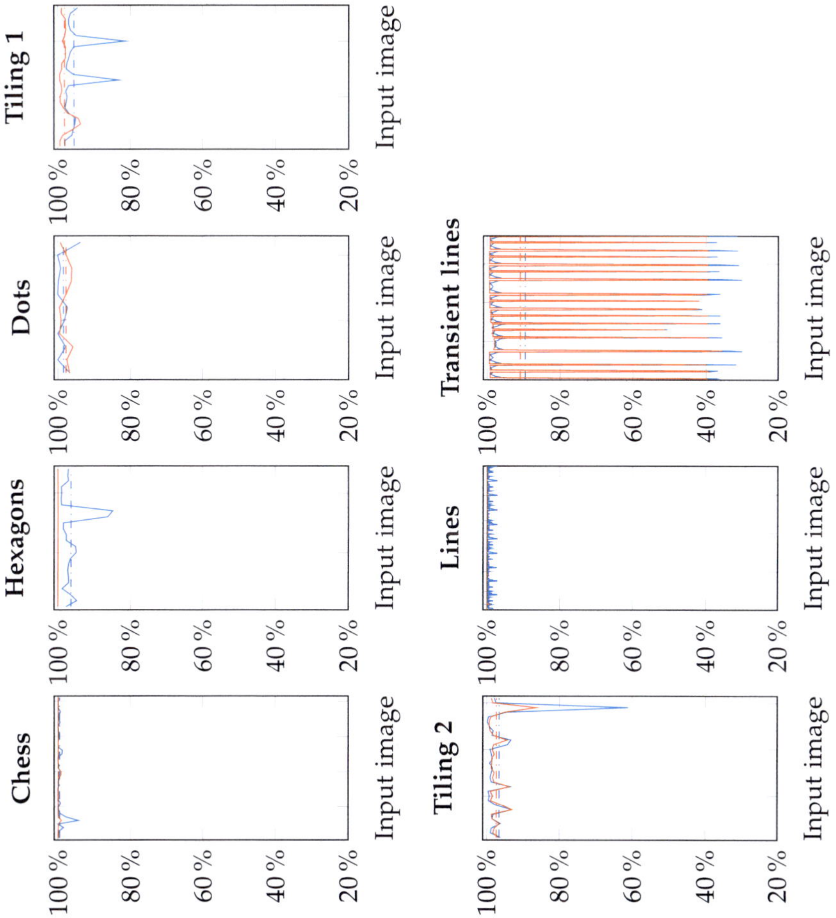

Figure 8.13 q^{retr} per texture class and features' strength in case of bigger accepted stochastic variations.

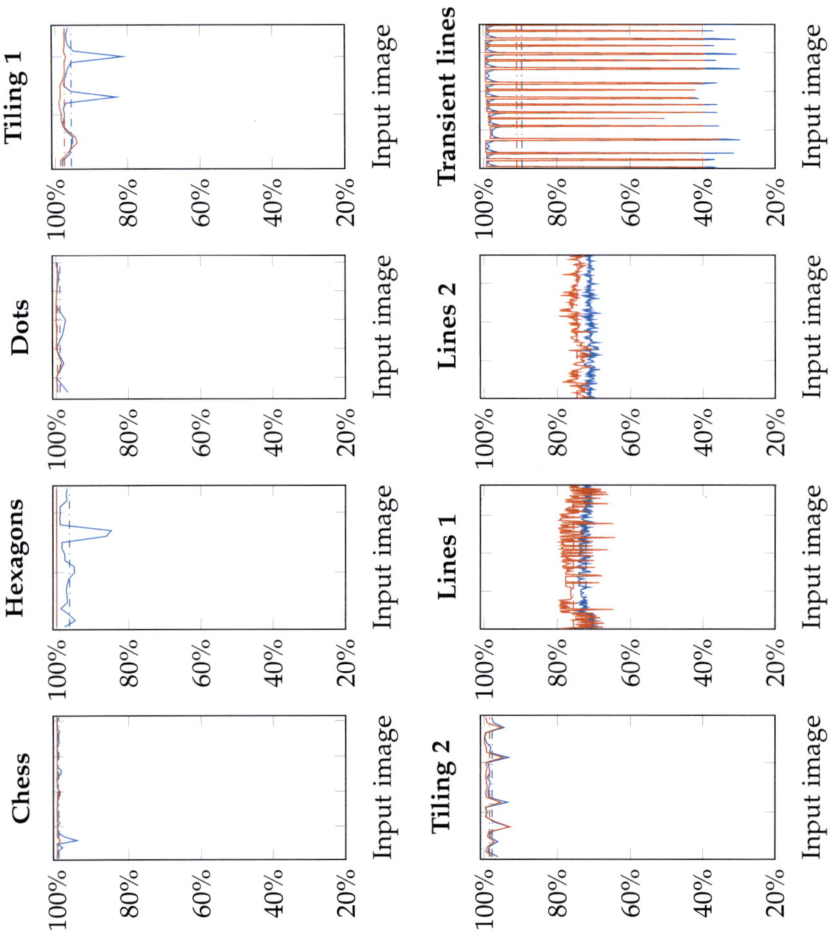

Figure 8.14 q^{retr} per texture class and features' strength in case of smaller accepted stochastic variations.

Table 8.10 Average q^{retr} per texture class and features' strength.

Pattern class	Bigger stochastic variations: $w_k = 1, \forall k$	Bigger stochastic variations: $w_7 = 0$, $w_k = 1, \forall_{k \neq 7} k$	Smaller stochastic variations: $w_k = 1, \forall k$	Smaller stochastic variations: $w_7 = 0$, $w_k = 1, \forall_{k \neq 7} k$
Chess	99.52 %	99.90 %	99.52 %	99.90 %
Hexagons	96.42 %	100 %	96.42 %	100 %
Dots	98.45 %	97.82 %	98.92 %	99.69 %
Tiling 1	95.55 %	98.17 %	95.59 %	97.49 %
Tiling 2	96.53 %	97.35 %	97.83 %	98.54 %
Lines	99.41 %	100 %	-	-
Lines 1	-	-	72.13 %	75.61 %
Lines 2	-	-	70.94 %	74.59 %
Transient lines	89.46 %	90.87 %	89.46 %	90.87 %

Table 8.11 Average q^{retr} per features' strength over all textures.

	$w_k = 1, \forall k$	$w_7 = 0$, $w_k = 1, \forall_{k \neq 7} k$
Bigger stochastic variations	96.48 %	97.73 %
Smaller stochastic variations	90.10 %	92.09 %

8.4.1.6 Perception map of regular textures

In this section the details of the experimental procedure to extract a perception map according to Sec. 5.2.4 are presented first, followed by the analysis of the experimental data. A comparison between the conclusions drawn from the perception map and the sorting of regular textures according to their similarity as presented in Sec. 5.2.3 is available at the end of this section.

Figure 8.15 Selected images for the experiment.

For the **experimental procedure** the IIIT texture database is selected. As the number of pairs of textures increases enormously with the number of considered textures and a variety of texture characteristics and repetitions is necessary to be able to draw relationships between the textures, in this experiment the focus is set on regular textures. From the 698 regular textures in the database 34 are selected, 9 one-dimensional textures and 25 two-dimensional ones (see Fig. 8.15). This implies 595 pairs of textures, whose similarity must be evaluated by the subjects. The one-dimensional textures are variations (rotation, scale, small stochastic variations) from two texture types (the classes *Lines* and *Transient Lines* or *Lines 1*, *Lines 2*, and *Transient Lines* from Sec. 8.4.1.5). The two-dimensional textures are made up from 22 textures belonging to the five bigger classes that appear in the database (the classes *Chess*, *Hexagons*, *Dots*, *Tiling 1* and *Tiling 2* from Sec. 8.4.1.5). The remaining three textures used in the experiment contain each a new pattern. The software *OpenSesame* [111] was used to create and run the experiment.

The **analysis of the experiment** is presented next. According to the judgments of the subjects, the similarity criterion *shape* is the most mentioned one, followed by *color*, *orientation*, *color gradient*, and *size*.

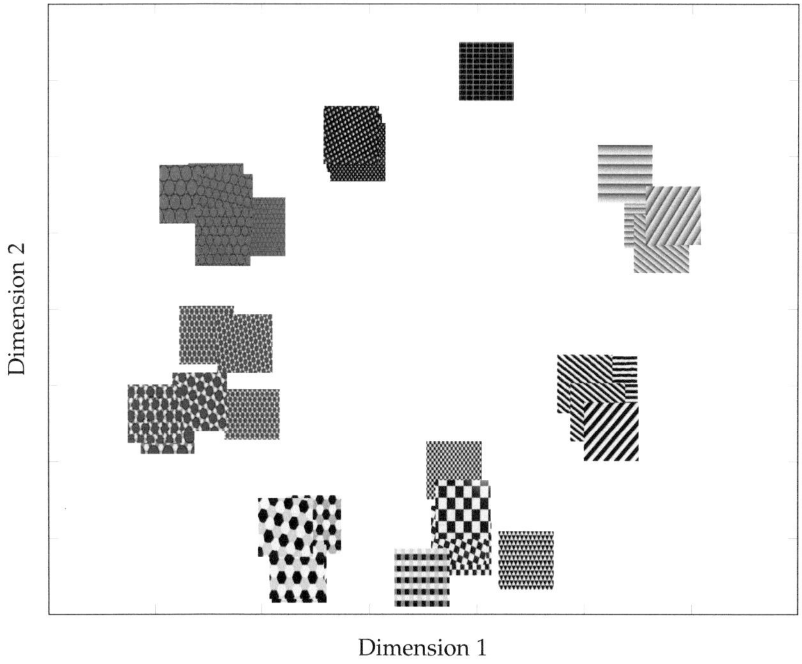

Figure 8.16 Two-dimensional perception map obtained via non-metric multidimensional scaling.

The two-dimensional perception map obtained via non-metric multidimensional scaling is shown in Fig. 8.16. It is noticeable that all of the considered textures are grouped according to their type of pattern independently of rotation, scaling, or small stochastic variations of the texels. This indicates the importance of the texels forming the textures over the characteristic of the displacement vectors that span the textures' lattices. The clusters of the textures are approximately placed along an ellipse. The one-dimensional textures are on the right side of the plot and placed in the ellipse opposite to textures whose texels contain circular forms. Although no clear arrangement of the textures inside the groups can be noticed, it seems that the textures with very small displacement vectors (and thus a smaller size of the texels) are closer to the center of the ellipse.

The **conclusions drawn from the perception map** validate the potential of the sorting method presented in Sec. 5.2.3 for regular textures. The sorting results achieved by it (see Sec. 8.4.1.5) showed that the method is capable of sorting regular textures. Furthermore, many of the proposed similarity features reflect the similarity criteria that the subjects stated to use.

8.4.2 Near-regular textures

The results of the methods presented in Sec. 5.3 to detect and extract near-regular textures from images are discussed in this section. Several options were presented in Sec. 5.3 for the three global blocks (see Fig. 5.13) that form the modus operandi, which lead to a total of 3072 possible combinations for the detection and extraction of near-regular textures. However, not every single combination needs to be evaluated to determine the influence of the presented methods. A total of 13 combinations are evaluated. Table 8.12 shows which options are evaluated for the detection and grouping of the characteristic points and for the extraction of the texels. Table 8.13 shows which kind of post-processing is tested at the combinations once the texels have been extracted. N1 is the closest combination to the one presented in [66]. For the resolution of the goal of the first block, the detection and grouping of the characteristic texel points, the SURF detector is used together with the mean-shift approach and their results are not post-processed. For the extraction of the texels, which is the aim of the second block, the lattice is started from three characteristic points that are neighbors, span an L-shaped pair of vectors (option **I** under **Start lat.**), and do not need to have similar gray values (option **I** under **Neigh.**). For the expansion of the lattice from the starting lattice the maximum number of outneighbors per node is not considered (option **I** under **Exp.**).

Table 8.12 Tested combinations for the detection and grouping of the characteristic texel points (up) and for the extraction of the texels (down).

	Detec. PoI		Clustering		Post-
Com.	**SURF**	**MSER**	**Mean-shift**	**Graph**	**processing**
N1	•		•		
N2	•			•	
N3	•			•	
N4	•			•	
N5	•			•	
N6	•			•	
N7	•			•	
N8	•			•	•
N9	•			•	•
N10	•			•	•
N11	•			•	•
N12		•		•	•
N13	•			•	•

	Neigh.		Start lat.			Exp.		Weig.	Lim.	Extr.	
Com.	**I**	**II**	**I**	**II**	**III**	**I**	**II**			**I**	**II**
N1	•		•			•				•	
N2	•		•			•				•	
N3	•			•		•				•	
N4		•		•		•				•	
N5		•			•	•				•	
N6		•			•		•			•	
N7		•			•	•					•
N8		•			•	•					•
N9		•			•	•					•
N10		•			•	•		•			•
N11		•			•	•			•		•
N12		•			•	•					•
N13		•			•	•					•

The suitability of all projected texels is considered by suppressing all transformed texels with no repeatability at the contours before the median one is calculated (option **I** under **Extr.**). No limitation of the number of transformed texels (option **Lim.**) is imposed together with no weights to the transformed texels (option **Weig.**). Furthermore, no additional post-processing of the extracted texels is considered (see Table 8.13). Differences to the detection and extraction of near-regular textures due to the clustering method can be determined by comparing the results of the methods N1 and N2 as the only difference between them is the clustering method used to group the detected characteristic texel points. While N1 uses the mean-shift approach, N2 uses the graph based method presented in Sec. 5.3.1.2. The consequences of starting from a local regular texture (option **II** under **Start lat.**) instead of starting from three neighboring points can be deduced from the comparison of the results achieved by N2 and N3. N4, in contrast to N3, requires neighboring points of the local regular starting lattice to have a similar gray value. The consequences of considering the similarity of the vectors between neighboring points when the starting lattice is created (option **III** under **Start lat.**) can be deduced from the comparison of the results of N4 and N5. N6, in contrast to N5, considers the maximum number of outneighbors per node when the starting lattice is expanded (option **II** under **Exp.**). From the comparison of the results of N5 and N7 deductions can be made about the influence of the occlusion of outliers and the grouping of the texels according to their similarity. For this purpose, in N7 the repeatability of the contours of the texels is proved from the median filtered extracted texels (option **II** under **Extr.**). Furthermore, the comparison of the results from N7 and N8 yields an information about the post-processing of the extracted and grouped characteristic points before the extraction of the texels. N9 fuses all of the proposed methods for the detection and extraction of regular textures. It extends N8 with the methods proposed to reach the goal of the third block, the post-processing. N10 to N13 are very similar to N9. N10 incorporates the option to weight the texels that are transformed to the quadrangles that are robust to affine transformations and lighting variations (option **Weig.**), N11 limitates the number of texels that are transformed to the quadrangles (option **Lim.**), N12 uses the MSER detector to detect the characteristic points instead of the SURF detector, and N13 uses the color information of the input image when the extracted texels are post-processed (option **Color**).

Table 8.13 Tested options for the post-processing of already extracted texels.

Com.	Gray-levels	Color
N1		
N2		
N3		
N4		
N5		
N6		
N7		
N8		
N9	•	
N10	•	
N11	•	
N12	•	
N13		•

The criteria used to evaluate the quality of the different combinations are explained in Sec. 8.4.2.1, whereas the results are presented in Sec. 8.4.2.2.

8.4.2.1 Evaluation criteria

The precision of the detection of near-regular textures and the quality of the extraction of the detected near-regular textures are considered at the evaluation of the results. Different evaluation criteria are presented next to evaluate the results of the combinations presented in Tables 8.12 and 8.13. The combinations are all tested at the IIIT patterned image database.

Figure 8.17 Two black and white images are shown on the top containing each two textured surfaces. As the texels of the textures of each object per image are very similar, only one kind of texture type is expected per image. If the color of the images is considered, then two kind of texture types are expected per image (lower images).

The **quality of the detection** is measured using three values per analyzed image. The first one is the number of near-regular textures that are correctly detected in an input image (without repetitions). If the color of the image is considered during the detection and extraction, then a distinction is made between the number of near-regular textures that should be detected. For example, in Fig. 8.17 one texture type is expected per gray-level image but two texture types per color image. The second value contains the number of times that a near-regular texture is repeated in the detections, and the third value is the number of wrong detections. In order to become an overview of the potential of the tested combinations, these three quality values are added over all images in the database. The higher the number of correctly detected textures and the smaller the number of both wrong detections and correctly detected but repeated textures are, the better the considered method will be.

To measure the **quality of the extraction,** a synthetic image $g_{\mathbf{u}}^{\mathrm{Synth}}$ is created per extracted near-regular texture. For this purpose, the extracted median texel of the texture is projected back onto the image plane (see Fig. 8.18). The affine transformation used for the transformation into the quadrangles is inverted. The texels in the quadrangles were also normalized towards their gray values to overcome lighting variations along the image. Because of this, the input image must also be modified before it can be compared with the synthetic one (see Fig. 8.18). For this purpose, the gray values of the detected texels in the input image are respectively normalized as

$$t_{\mathbf{u}}^{\mathrm{Mod}} = \frac{t_{\mathbf{u}} - \min\limits_{\mathbf{u}}(t_{\mathbf{u}})}{\max\limits_{\mathbf{u}}(t_{\mathbf{u}}) - \min\limits_{\mathbf{u}}(t_{\mathbf{u}})}, \tag{8.9}$$

and all other pixels that do not belong to the detected texels are suppressed. The addition of the respective gray-level offset $\min\limits_{\mathbf{u}}(t_{\mathbf{u}})$ to $t_{\mathbf{u}}^{Mod}$ across the whole modified input image $g_{\mathbf{u}}^{\mathrm{Mod}}$ yields an impression of the variation of the brightness.

Two characteristics are defined to measure the quality of the extraction of the textures. The bigger the area of the expanded lattice over the near-regular textures is, the better the detections of the surfaces will be. This implies a better extraction. The percentage of the area covered by the expanded lattice over the patterned surface in the image $q^{\mathrm{T1}}(\mathbf{g}_{\mathbf{u}})$ is therefore the first quality characteristic, where $\mathbf{g}_{\mathbf{u}}$ denotes the analyzed image. For this purpose ground truth data was generated from the IIIT patterned image database. The patterned surfaces in the image were manually labeled. The achievement of a 100 % overlap between the area spanned by any expanded lattice and a patterned surface in an image is almost impossible. On the one hand the surfaces can have any shape at the contour, whereas the lattice is limited by the parallelograms of the cells (see Fig. 8.18 middle), on the other hand the labeled surfaces may contain areas where no characteristic points may be detected or possess similar characteristics due to strong scale variations, limitations of the resolution, or reflections on the surfaces (see Fig. 8.19).

If detected texels overlap more than τ^{T4} (normalized to the area of the texels and set here to 0.20), then only the one with the smallest difference between its projection onto the synthetic image and the normalized input image is further considered. Small overlaps between texels (e.g., at edges) become their average gray value in the synthetic image, as well as in the modified input image $g_{\mathbf{u}}^{\mathrm{Mod}}$.

The second characteristic used to measure the quality of the extracted textures considers the error between the synthetic image and the modified input image:

$$q^{\mathrm{T2}}(\mathbf{g_u}) = \frac{\sqrt{\sum_{\mathbf{u}\in\mathcal{V}^{\mathrm{N}}} \left(g_{\mathbf{u}}^{\mathrm{Mod}} - g_{\mathbf{u}}^{\mathrm{Synth}}\right)^2}}{\left|\mathcal{V}^{\mathrm{N}}\right|} \cdot 100\,\%. \tag{8.10}$$

For this purpose, only the pixels that belong to at least one of the extracted texels $\mathcal{V}^{\mathrm{N}}$ are considered.

Similar to the criteria used to evaluate the quality of the detection, both evaluation characteristics for the quality of the extracted textures are obtained from all images in the database. The mean values $\mu(q^{\mathrm{T1}}(\mathbf{g_u}))$, $\mu(q^{\mathrm{T2}}(\mathbf{g_u}))$ and standard deviations $\sigma(q^{\mathrm{T1}}(\mathbf{g_u}))$, $\sigma(q^{\mathrm{T2}}(\mathbf{g_u})$ are considered in this case. The higher mean value of the covered percentage and the lower the mean value of the error representations are, the better the results will be. Furthermore, the smaller the standard deviations are, the more stable the methods towards the input image will be. Notice that even if the color information of the input image is used to detect and extract the near-regular textures, the quality of the extraction is always evaluated at the gray-level images, as the detection and extraction take place at the gray-level images and the color information is only used to decide if detected and extracted texels should be merged.

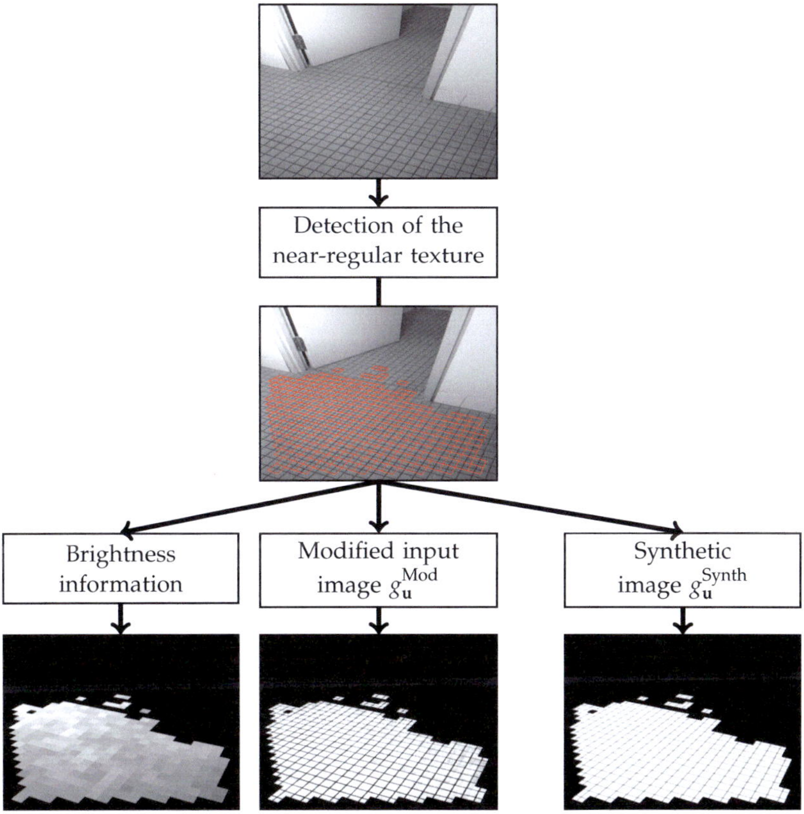

Figure 8.18 Once the lattice has been expanded over the near-regular texture and the texels detected, a synthetic image is created from the median texel and the input image is modified to separate the information given by the brightness.

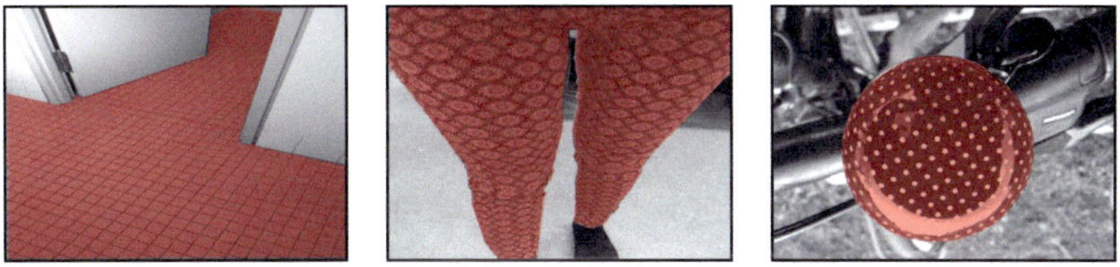

Figure 8.19 Example images from the database displayed with gray values. The area manually marked as ground truth data is highlighted in red.

Table 8.14 Evaluation of the quality of the detected near-regular textures. The percentage of the correctly detected textures is shown together with the percentage of correctly extracted but repeated textures from the total number of correctly detected textures.

Com.	To detect	True		Repeat		False
N1	52	36	69.23 %	19	52.78 %	14
N2	52	36	69.23 %	16	44.44 %	5
N3	52	44	84.62 %	24	54.55 %	7
N4	52	48	92.31 %	25	52.08 %	5
N5	52	48	92.31 %	25	52.08 %	2
N6	52	45	86.54 %	26	57.78 %	10
N7	52	49	94.23 %	25	51.02 %	2
N8	52	50	96.15 %	36	72.00 %	1
N9	52	50	96.15 %	2	4.00 %	0
N10	52	51	98.08 %	6	11.76 %	2
N11	52	50	96.15 %	2	4.00 %	0
N12	52	47	90.38 %	1	2.13 %	1
N13	57	55	96.49 %	2	3.64 %	0

8.4.2.2 Evaluation results

The evaluation results of the quality of the near-regular texture detection are presented next followed by the evaluation results of the quality of the extraction.

The **parameters used to measure the quality of the detection** for the different evaluated combinations are shown in Table 8.14, whereas **True** is the number of detected textures (without repetitions), **Repeat** the number of correctly extracted but repeated textures, and **False** the number of wrong detections. A total of 52 textures should be detected (**To detect**) at the gray-level images, 57 if the color information is considered. The closest combination to the one presented in [66] (N1) yields the highest number of wrong detections (14) together with the lowest number of correctly detected textures (69.23 %). The number of correctly extracted but repeated textures is also quite high (52.78 % of the correctly detected textures).

The use of the sorting method proposed in Sec. 5.3.1.2 instead of the mean-shift approach (N2 vs. N1) did not increment the number of correctly detected textures (69.23 %), but it reduced the number of wrong detections by 64.29 % and also the number of correctly extracted but repeated textures by 15.79 %. The use of the presented sorting method from Sec. 5.3.1.2 instead of the mean-shift approach is therefore promising.

Starting from a local regular texture instead of a single cell (N3 vs. N2) clearly increments the number of correctly detected textures (84.62 % vs. 69.23 %), but it also implies a higher number of both correctly extracted but repeated textures and wrong detections. Nevertheless, due to the higher number of correctly detected textures, the start with a local regular texture is worth the mild increment of correctly extracted but repeated textures and wrong detections.

Furthermore, if similar gray values are required between valid neighbors in the local regular texture (N4 vs. N3), then the number of correctly detected textures is incremented (92.31 % vs. 84.62 %) and the number of wrong detections decreases. The total number of correctly extracted but repeated textures is incremented by one when similar gray values are required, but compared to the total number of correctly detected textures it implies a decrease of 2.45 %.

A further reduction of the number of wrong detections (2 vs. 5) with no worsen of both the detection rate (92.31 %) and the percentage of correctly extracted but repeated textures (52.08 %) is achieved if the similarity between the vectors of neighboring characteristic points is considered when the starting lattice is created (N5 vs. N4).

The comparison of the results yielded by N6 and N5 shows that the consideration of the maximum number of outneighbors per node at the expansion of the local regular texture does not improve the results. The number of detected and extracted regular textures is decreased in N6 compared to N5 (86.54 % vs. 92.31 %). The number of wrong detections and the number of correctly extracted but repeated textures achieved by N6 is also worsen than those achieved by N5.

As N5 has reached the best trade-off so far between many good detected textures and little number of wrong detections, it is widened to occlude outliers and group similar extracted texels in the combination N7. This permits the correct detection and extraction of one more texture (94.23 %) with no additional costs of more correctly extracted but repeated textures or wrong detections. Furthermore, the percentage of correctly extracted but repeated textures is decreased (51.02 %) due to the higher number of correctly detected textures.

The expansion of N7 to N8 considers the post-processing of the clustered points of interest. The number of correctly extracted textures is incremented by one (96.15 %), and the number of wrong detections is also decreased by one. The number of correctly extracted but repeated textures increases in a remarkable way. This can be explained because in the post-processing step the spatial localization of the clustered points is taken into consideration. If an image consists of more than one surface with a similar near-regular texture, then only one texture should be detected. However, when the spatial information is considered, these spatially separated surfaces will be independently extracted.

The post-processing step from Sec. 5.3.3 is proposed to reduce the number of correctly extracted but repeated textures and the number of wrong detections. N9 adds to N8 the post-processing step without considering the color information of the input image. The best detection results so far are achieved by N9. 96.15 % of the textures are correctly detected and there are no wrong detections. Furthermore, only 4.00 % of the correctly detected textures are repeatedly extracted.

The weighting of the extracted texels (N10) reaches a correct detection of the textures of 98.08 %, but it also increments the percentage of correctly extracted but repeated textures (11.76 %) and the number of wrong detections.

From the comparison of N9 and N11 no consequences towards the quality of the detection can be noticed for the case that the number of texels projected onto the quadrangles are limited.

The use of the MSER detector instead of the SURF detector (N12 vs. N9) reduces the number of correctly detected textures (90.38 %), and it increments the number of wrong detections by one. However, the percentage of correctly extracted but repeated textures depending on the number of correctly detected textures is the lowest one of all combinations (2.13 %).

Finally, the color information is considered in the combination N13. All other methods are selected as in N9, as it has yielded the best results so far. 57 textures should be detected if the color information is considered. N13 yields a detection rate of 96.49 % by a repetition rate of 3.64 % and no wrong detections.

The **parameters used to measure the quality of the extraction** are shown in Table 8.15 for the different tested combinations. N1, which is the closest version to [66], yields the highest mean error between the synthetic image and the normalized input image (11.78) and the highest standard deviation (8.16) across the mean errors of all extracted patterns. Furthermore, the covered percentage of the near-regular textures is quite low (20.00 %) in comparison with the other tested combinations.

Table 8.15 Evaluation of the near-regular texture extraction quality.

	$q^{T1}(\mathbf{g_u})$		$q^{T2}(\mathbf{g_u})$	
Com.	μ	σ	μ	σ
N1	20.00 %	14.04 %	11.78	8.16
N2	20.36 %	12.57 %	9.51	7.63
N3	23.37 %	18.26 %	9.26	5.18
N4	22.88 %	16.72 %	9.48	5.74
N5	21.98 %	16.00 %	9.08	5.14
N6	25.08 %	17.65 %	10.68	7.90
N7	18.07 %	14.38 %	7.18	2.83
N8	17.09 %	14.60 %	6.99	2.45
N9	24.12 %	16.03 %	7.07	2.41
N10	23.18 %	17.15 %	6.90	2.84
N11	21.23 %	11.05 %	7.07	2.39
N12	38.40 %	18.24 %	7.57	2.74
N13	24.18 %	16.30 %	7.03	2.40

The use of the proposed sorting method from Sec. 5.3.1.2 instead of the mean-shift approach (N2 vs. N1) improves the results towards the quality of the extraction, as the mean error is reduced (9.51) and the covered percentage of the surfaces is, on average (20.36 %), slightly incremented.

The quality of the extractions achieved by N2 is further improved if the lattice is expanded from a local regular texture (N3) instead of a single cell. This option reduces the mean error more (9.26), and it increments the covered percentage of the near-regular textures in the input image (23.37 %).

Whereas the imposition of similar gray values between neighboring characteristic points at the starting lattice (N4) slightly reduces the covered percentage of the near-regular textures and slightly increments the mean error, its combination with the consideration of similar vectors of neighboring characteristic points (N5) reduces the mean error over all extracted patterns (9.08). However, N5 does not increment the common area of the extracted textures and the textured surfaces in the real images (21.98 %).

Although the covered percentage is higher if the maximum number of outneighbors is considered when the starting lattice is expanded (N6 vs. N5, 25.08 % vs. 21.98 %), the mean error reaches in this case the second highest value of all combinations (10.68).

The mean error parameter is clearly reduced if outliers are occluded and similar extracted texels grouped before the median texel is calculated (N7 vs. N5, 7.18 vs. 9.08). The standard deviation is almost reduced to its half (2.83 vs. 5.14), which implies a higher robustness towards the kind of input image. However, the covered percentage of the near-regular textures is reduced (18.07 % vs. 21.98 %), which is explained by the occlusion of outliers.

N8 further reduces the mean extraction error (6.99) of N7 by adding the post-processing step to the clustered points of interest. Because of this, the mean covered percentage of the images is also slightly reduced, which is explained by the creation of more spatially separated detected textures that become smaller.

The addition of the post-processing step without considering the color information to the combination N8 (N9) slightly increments the mean error (7.07), but it reduces its standard deviation implying a higher robustness towards the input image and it also increments considerably on average the covered percentage of the textured surfaces (24.12 %).

Similar good results to N9 are reached if the projected texels into the quadrangles are weighted (N10) or limited (N11). Notice that the limitation of the number of projected texels must imply a smaller percentage of the covered area of the near-regular textures in the input image, which is reflected in the results.

The best trade-off between a high covered percentage of the near-regular textures (38.40 %) and a small mean extraction error (7.57) is reached by N12, which uses the MSER detector instead of the SURF detector.

If the color information of the input image is considered (N13), similar good results are achieved to the case when the color information is suppressed (N9).

Whereas the mean extraction error is reduced by the different detection and extraction methods proposed in Sec. 5.3, its standard deviation is also reduced, which has also the advantage of more robust methods towards the analyzed input image.

Overall, the following conclusions can be drawn. The method closer to [66] possesses the worse detection and extraction quality, as it delivers both the lowest number of correctly detected textures and the highest mean extraction error. On the other hand, the methods proposed in Sec. 5.3 improve the results. A good trade-off between a good detection quality and a good extraction quality is reached by the combination N9, which searches for a local regular texture first that is expanded along the near-regular part of the surface and post-processes the detected and clustered characteristic points and the extracted median texels. N9 also occludes outliers and groups similar texels before the median texel is calculated. The limitation of the number of projected texels into the quadrangles (N11) is a good alternative to N9 if a faster detection and extraction is desired, as the quality of the detection and the extraction error are comparable, at the cost of lower covered areas between the extracted textures and the surfaces of the near-regular textures in the input image.

Both detectors, MSER and SURF, are valid for this task. While for this tested database the SURF detector achieved better detection results, the MSER detector yielded better extraction results. The selection of the kind of detector depends on the images that are analyzed, as the SURF detector searches for characteristic points, whereas the MSER detector searches for areas with an almost stable gray value.

Furthermore, if the color is taken into consideration, N13 yields comparable results to those from N9, where only the gray-level information of the input image is considered.

8.5 Results of the detection of regions

Two region detectors with similar modus operandi were presented in Sec. 6. Their results are shown and discussed in this section. The results of the detection of color regions in images are shown and discussed in Sec. 8.5.1, whereas the results of the pattern extraction are presented in Sec. 8.5.2.

8.5.1 Color regions in images

In this section the results of the methods proposed in Sec. 6.3 to detect color regions in images are analyzed. One method was presented in Sec. 6.3.1 if the color is directly processed in CIELAB color space. This method is represented from now on as C0. On the other hand, if the processing of the color is inspired by the humans' color categories, then two forms of measuring the color relationship between pixels and three optional post-processing methods were proposed which imply 24 variations of the detector (see Sec. 6.3.2). However, not every combination must be processed to determine which variations are more promising. Table 8.16 shows the combinations of the tested detectors. The comparison of the results of the combinations C2 and C3 shows the consequences of the different distance functions ($d_{\mathbf{u}}^{\mathrm{CC},1}$,$d_{\mathbf{u}}^{\mathrm{CC},2}$) to obtain the color relationship between pixels. Furthermore, C5 and C6 compared to C2 and C3 incorporate the post-processing step to expand the areas of the color regions (option **Exp.** in Table 8.16). For the sake of completeness C1 and C4 follow the same combinations as C2 and C5 with the exception that the color is directly processed in CIELAB color space and not with the humans' color categories. The detectors of the combinations C7 and C8 incorporate the post-processing method to reduce the number of color regions via a 8- and 4-neighborhood, respectively (option **Red.** in Table 8.16). C9 incorporates the division of color regions containing a color gradient (option **Div.** in Table 8.16) to C6. Finally, C10 possesses all of the post-processing methods.

The criteria used to evaluate the quality of the different combinations is explained in Sec. 8.5.1.1 and the results are presented in Sec. 8.5.1.2.

8.5.1.1 Evaluation criteria

Three criteria are considered to evaluate the quality of the detection and extraction of color regions.

The smaller the number of detected color regions is, the faster future post-processing may become. The first evaluation criterion considers therefore the number of detected color regions per input image $q^{\mathrm{P1}}(\mathbf{g_u})$. Over all images in the tested database the mean value $\mu(q^{\mathrm{P1}}(\mathbf{g_u}))$ and standard deviation $\sigma(q^{\mathrm{P1}}(\mathbf{g_u}))$ of the extracted number of color regions is calculated. The higher the standard deviation is, the bigger the difference according to the number of color regions between the input images will be.

Table 8.16 Tested combinations for the detection and extraction of color regions in images.

	Color representation		Color relationship		Post-processing		
Com.	**CIELAB**	**Catego.**	$d_{\mathbf{u}}^{CC,2}$	$d_{\mathbf{u}}^{CC,1}$	**Exp.**	**Div.**	**Red.**
C1	•		•				
C2		•	•				
C3		•		•			
C4	•		•		•		
C5		•	•		•		
C6		•		•	•		
C7		•		•	•		•
C8		•		•	•		•
C9		•		•	•	•	
C10		•		•	•	•	•

However, not enough color regions may lead to a faulty or even an incomplete representation of the content of the image. The goal of the color region detectors presented in Sec. 6.3 is to group neighboring pixels with similar colors into color regions. Neighboring pixels with different colors, like, e.g., at edges or overlaid with noise, may not belong to a color region. Because of this, the detected color regions will not contain all of the pixels in the image. The higher the percentage of the image that is included in a color region $q^{P2}(\mathbf{g_u})$, the more information of the image can be processed in the future. For this purpose, the mean value over the covered percentage of the images in the tested database $\mu(q^{P2}(\mathbf{g_u}))$ together with the standard deviation of the covered percentage of the images $\sigma(q^{P2}(\mathbf{g_u}))$ is used as second evaluation criterion.

The third evaluation criterion considers how good the analyzed image can be represented by the detected color regions. Let $\mathbf{g_u^R}$ be the reconstructed image in CIELAB color space of the analyzed image, whereas the detected color regions are represented by the mean color of their respective pixels. Pixels that were not assigned to a color region are represented in $\mathbf{g}_{\mathbf{u}}^{\mathrm{R}}$ by black pixels for representation purposes. The mean image representation error per image is calculated as

$$q^{\mathrm{P3}}(\mathbf{g}_{\mathbf{u}}) = \frac{\sum_{\mathbf{u} \in \mathcal{V}^{\mathrm{C}}} \left\| \mathbf{g}_{\mathbf{u}} - \mathbf{g}_{\mathbf{u}}^{\mathrm{R}} \right\|_2}{\left| \mathcal{V}^{\mathrm{C}} \right|}, \tag{8.11}$$

where $|\mathcal{V}^{\mathrm{C}}|$ is the set of all pixels that belong to a color region and $\mathbf{g}_{\mathbf{u}}$ the analyzed image in CIELAB color space. The mean value over all mean image representation errors of the images in the tested database $\mu(q^{\mathrm{P3}}(\mathbf{g}_{\mathbf{u}}))$ and the standard deviation of the mean image representation errors of the images $\sigma(q^{\mathrm{P3}}(\mathbf{g}_{\mathbf{u}}))$ are the parameters used for the evaluation.

Table 8.17 Evaluation of the detected and extracted color regions.

Com.	$q^{\mathrm{P1}}(\mathbf{g}_{\mathbf{u}})$		$q^{\mathrm{P2}}(\mathbf{g}_{\mathbf{u}})$		$q^{\mathrm{P3}}(\mathbf{g}_{\mathbf{u}})$	
	μ	σ	μ	σ	μ	σ
C0	401.7	366.29	73.99 %	25.89 %	7.55	5.36
C1	2795.3	3179.4	74.87 %	14.61 %	6.26	4.79
C2	1378.5	1305.1	76.96 %	13.14 %	6.09	2.63
C3	1404.8	1317.9	76.45 %	13.18 %	5.97	2.59
C4	2795.3	3179.4	93.01 %	6.43 %	7.02	4.50
C5	1378.5	1305.1	92.07 %	5.97 %	6.91	2.38
C6	1404.8	1317.9	91.68 %	6.01 %	6.79	2.35
C7	694.7	570.6	91.68 %	6.01 %	7.06	2.32
C8	761.1	653.2	91.68 %	6.01 %	7.04	2.32
C9	1519.7	1362.6	91.68 %	6.01 %	6.19	1.78
C10	927.9	814.7	91.68 %	6.01 %	6.33	1.78

8.5.1.2 Evaluation results

The evaluation results for the images of the IIIT patterned image database are shown in Table 8.17. Δ was set to two for the detectors C1 to C10 and their analyzed image was the input image filtered with a median filter. The method presented in Sec. 6.3.1, which processes the color information directly in CIELAB color space (C0), yields on average the smallest number of detected color regions, but their covered portion of the image, as well as the mean image representation error, are on average worse than when the other detectors are used. The standard deviations concerning the covered percentage of the image and the mean image representation errors are also higher than in case of the other detectors, which implies that the color region detector is more sensitive to the type of analyzed image.

When the color is directly processed in CIELAB color space but the color regions are detected following the modus operandi presented in Sec. 6.3.2, then the number of detected color regions is higher than in case of processing the color with the humans' color categories (2795.3 from C1 vs. 1378.5 from C2 and 2795.3 from C4 vs. 1378.5 from C5). A higher sensitiveness to the input image can also be appreciated for the number of color regions (3179.4 vs. 1305.1) but also towards the covered portion of the image (14.61 % vs. 13.14 % and 6.43 % vs. 5.97 %) and the mean image representation error (4.79 vs. 2.63 and 4.50 vs. 2.38). The higher average mean image representation error also shows worse results than when the color is processed over the humans' color categories (6.26 vs. 6.09 and 7.02 vs. 6.91). Overall, the conclusion can be drawn that the processing of color with humans' color categories, instead of directly using the CIELAB color space, improves the detection of color regions.

Among the two distance functions proposed in Sec. 6.3.2.1 to extract the color relationship between pixels (C2 vs. C3 and C5 vs. C6), the one based on the ℓ_2-norm reduces indeed on average the number of color regions (1378.5 vs. 1404.8), but its mean image representation error is on average also higher than in case of the distance function based on the correlation coefficient (6.09 vs. 5.97 and 6.91 vs. 6.79). As a distortion of the input image will also distort further post-processing steps, the color relationship based on the correlation function should be preferred to obtain the color relationship between pixels.

The expansion of the color regions (C6 vs. C3) slightly increases on average the mean image representation error (6.79 vs. 5.97), as expected. However, this approach also implies a significant increment of the covered portion of the image (91.68 % vs. 76.45 %), which justifies the small increment of the mean image representation error. Furthermore, the mean image representation error and the covered percentage of the image are on average more stable when the color regions are expanded. This can be deduced from the respective smaller standard deviations (2.35 vs. 2.59 and 6.01 vs. 13.18).

The average number of detected color regions is decreased by the method proposed in Sec. 6.3.2.3 for the reduction of the total number of extracted color regions to 49.45 % if a 4-neighborhood is used (761.1 from C8 vs. 1404.8 from C6) and to 54.18 % in case of a 8-neighborhood (694.7 from C7 vs. 1404.8 from C6). The mean image representation error slightly increases by the reduction of the number of color regions (7.04 and 7.06 vs. 6.79), but it also becomes more robust towards the input image, as indicated by the lower standard deviations (2.32 and 2.32 vs. 2.35). On the other hand, the division of color regions containing a color gradient increments on average the number of color regions by 8.18 % (1519.7 from C9 vs. 1404.8 from C6), but it reduces the mean image representation error over the input images in the database (6.19 vs. 6.79) and its dependence on the type of analyzed image (1.78 vs. 2.35).

Finally, the color region detector based on processing color using the humans' color categories, the determination of the color relationship between pixels via the correlation function, and all of the proposed post-processing methods (C10) yields the best trade-off between a low number of color regions (927.9), a high coverage of the analyzed images (91.68 %), and a small image representation error over the input images (6.33), plus a smaller dependence on the analyzed image.

Overall, the following conclusions can be drawn. The processing of the color information via the humans' color categories yields better detections and extractions of the color regions in the images. The use of the correlation function to determine the color relationship between neighboring pixels and the incorporation of all of the proposed post-processing methods yield the best quality towards the detection and extraction of the color regions.

8.5.2 Pattern extraction

One global modus operandi (see Fig. 6.6) is presented in Sec. 6.4 to detect and extract patterns. However, several methods are proposed for the resolution of each block. In this section the results achieved by the methods of Sec. 6.4 are presented and discussed. An overview of the tested combinations is shown in Table 8.18 and is clarified next.

Table 8.18 Tested combinations for the pattern extraction.

	Color regions		Pattern detection										
			CIELAB			Color categories							
						2-D expansion					P-p	
Com.	C0	C10	**I**	**II**	**III**	**I**	**II**	**III**	**IV**	**V**	**I**	**II**
P1	•		•									
P2	•		•	•								
P3	•		•	•	•							
P4		•	•	•	•							
P5		•				•						
P6		•				•					•	
P7		•				•					•	•
P8		•					•				•	•
P9		•						•			•	•
P10		•							•		•	•
P11		•							•	•	•	

The detected color regions of the input image are the starting point for the detection of the patterns. From the eleven tested methods for the detection of color regions (see Sec. 8.5.1), the results from C0 and C10 are further considered for the pattern detection as representatives of the processing of the color information in CIELAB color space and with the extracted humans' color categories, respectively.

On the one hand, the direct processing of the color information in CIELAB color space is considered in Sec. 6.4.1. For this purpose, P1 starts from the color regions detected by C0 (option **I** under **CIELAB**) and detects and extracts the patterns without any of both proposed optional methods at the post-processing step. The consequences of merging spatially overlapping patterns can be deduced from the comparison of the results of P1 and P2, as P2 widens P1 by merging spatially overlapping patterns as proposed in the post-processing step in Sec. 6.4.1.4 (option **II** under **CIELAB**). Furthermore, P3 widens P2 by also merging nested patterns as proposed in Sec. 6.4.1.4 (option **III** under **CIELAB**). The consequences of this additional and optional approach can therefore be concluded from the comparison of their respective results. The last tested combination considering the processing of color directly in the CIELAB color space for the pattern detection is P4, which also includes both optional post-processing methods. However, in contrast to P3, the color regions used for the pattern detection are the ones detected by the color categories via the combination C10 (see Table 8.16) instead of C0.

On the other hand, humans' color categories are considered for color representation and processing for the pattern detection and extraction in Sec. 6.4.2. A total of seven different combinations are tested to prove their suitability for pattern extraction. The color regions extracted via C10 are used as starting point for the pattern extraction, as this combination reached the best trade-off. Due to this fact, the color information is presented from now on via the normalized likelihood functions and compared via the distance function based on the correlation function. Four different similarity comparisons are proposed in Sec. 6.4.2.3 to expand the one-dimensional detected pattern to a two-dimensional one. P5 uses the approximation of the colors in the pattern as similarity criterion (option **I** under **2-D expansion**) with no post-processing after the expansion of the one-dimensional pattern to a two-dimensional one. P6 widens P5 by including the post-processing approach of merging patterns with a high percentage of area in common once the one-dimensional pattern has been expanded to a two-dimensional one as presented in Sec. 6.4.2.4 (option **I** under **P-p**). The inclusion of all proposed approaches at the post-processing step (see Sec. 6.4.2.4), the merger of patterns with a high percentage of area in common and also with highly overlapping areas spanned by their convex hulls (option **II** under **P-p**) are done at the combination P7 as an expansion of P5 and P6.

The three remaining similarity comparisons used to expand the one-dimensional pattern to a two-dimensional one (presented in Sec. 6.4.2.3) are tested in P8, which considers the approximation of the colors and sizes of the color regions belonging to the pattern (option **II** under **2-D expansion**), P9, which uses an exact color comparison (option **III** under **2-D expansion**), and P10, which considers an exact comparison of the color and size of the color regions (option **IV** under **2-D expansion**). For these combinations both optional approaches from the post-processing step are also implemented. The consequences of the different similarity comparisons can be therefore deduced from the comparisons between each other and with P7.

Finally, P10 is widened to P11 by incorporating the optional processing approach proposed at the expansion of the one-dimensional pattern to the two-dimensional one in Sec. 6.4.2.3, where patterns with convex hulls that highly overlap are merged directly, without waiting to the post-processing step (option **V** under **2-D expansion**).

Across the results of the eleven presented combinations the consequences of the different methods presented in Sec. 6.4 can be deduced without the need of implementing the 396 possible combinations, 36 if only the pattern extraction is considered.

The evaluation criteria used to compare the results of the different methods to detect and extract patterns are presented in Sec. 8.5.2.1 and the evaluation results are then shown and discussed in Sec. 8.5.2.2.

8.5.2.1 Evaluation criteria

The goodness of the detection of the patterns and the quality of the extracted patterns are considered for the evaluation of the results. For this purpose, the tested combinations presented in Table 8.18 are evaluated at the IIIT patterned image database.

The **goodness of the detection** is measured using three parameters. The first one is the total number of patterns that has been detected and extracted. Many valid patterns may be detected at the real images. However, if further knowledge is incorporated, patterns that form surfaces of objects or textiles will be more significant than patterns that appear between the color regions of different objects. As the IIIT patterned image database consists of 57 patterned objects and backgrounds of near-regular texture types, the number of near-regular textures at detected and extracted patterns is used as second evaluation parameter. The higher this parameter is, the better the detection of patterns will be. The third parameter is the number of repeatedly extracted patterns containing one of the already detected near-regular textures. The smaller it is, the less overhead indicating better detection results.

The **quality of the extracted patterns** is measured at the extracted patterns that contain some part of one of the near-regular textures. As in Sec. 8.4.2.1 ground truth data has been manually generated first from the images in the database, highlighting the surfaces of objects or backgrounds that contain a valid near-regular texture. While the ground truth data from Sec. 8.4.2.1 is orientated towards near-regularly textured surfaces, the whole surface of the object is considered here (see Fig. 8.20). Two characteristics are obtained from the comparison of the areas spanned by the extracted patterns and the surfaces of the objects and backgrounds stored as ground truth data.

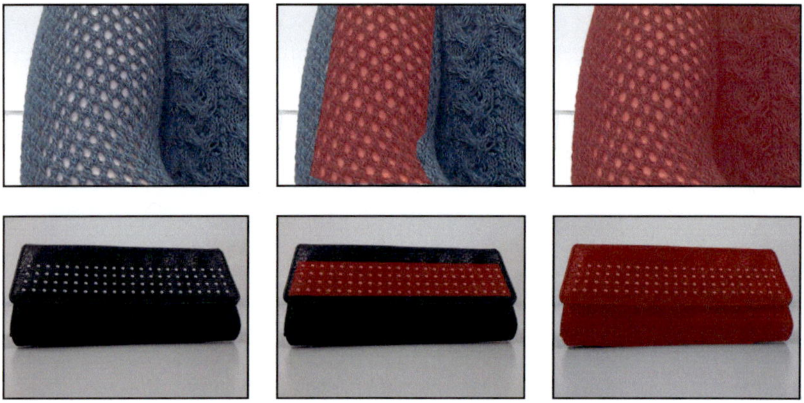

Figure 8.20 Examples of manually labeled ground truth data, highlighted in red, for the input images shown on the left. Whereas in Sec. 8.4.2.1 the ground truth is orientated towards near-regular textures (middle), the whole surface of the object is considered here (right).

On the one hand, the higher the overlap of the areas stored as ground truth data with the areas of the extracted patterns, the better the near-regular textures are detected and extracted as a single pattern (see Fig. 8.21). The first characteristic $q^{\mathrm{P4}}(\mathbf{g_u})$ is therefore the common area normalized by the real area of the surface. The mean value $\mu(q^{\mathrm{P4}}(\mathbf{g_u}))$ and standard deviation $\sigma(q^{\mathrm{P4}}(\mathbf{g_u}))$ of $q^{\mathrm{P4}}(\mathbf{g_u})$ over all detected patterns are the first quality parameters.

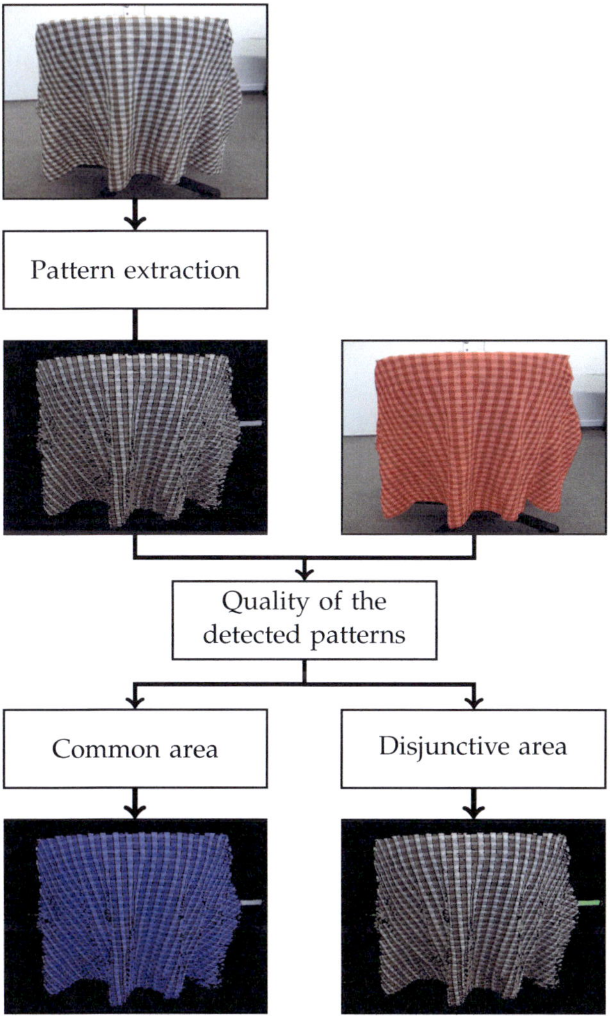

Figure 8.21 Overview of the characteristics used to measure the quality of the extracion. The ground truth data is highlighted in the input image in red, whereas the common area of the ground truth and the extracted pattern in blue, and their respective disjunctive area in green over the extracted pattern.

On the other hand, the bigger the amount of area of the extracted patterns that overlap with the areas stored as ground truth data, the better the quality of the extraction will be. The second characteristic is therefore the common area normalized by the total area of the extracted pattern $q^{P5}(\mathbf{g_u})$. This characteristic considers the disjunctive area between the extracted pattern and the ground truth area of the patterned surface (see Fig. 8.21). The bigger $q^{P5}(\mathbf{g_u})$ is, the better the quality of the pattern extraction will be, as less color regions are added to the extracted pattern that do not belong to the textured surface of the object or background. The mean value $\mu(q^{P5}(\mathbf{g_u}))$ and standard deviation $\sigma(q^{P5}(\mathbf{g_u}))$ of $q^{P5}(\mathbf{g_u})$ over all considered patterns are also used as quality criteria of the pattern extraction.

The higher $q^{P4}(\mathbf{g_u})$ and $q^{P5}(\mathbf{g_u})$ are, the better the quality of the extraction will be. However, a smaller $q^{P4}(\mathbf{g_u})$ combined with a higher $q^{P5}(\mathbf{g_u})$ is better than the other way around as it means an incomplete extraction of the whole surface but no wrongly incorporated regions to the pattern. This information about the relation between $q^{P4}(\mathbf{g_u})$ and $q^{P5}(\mathbf{g_u})$ gets lost when the mean values and standard deviations are calculated over all extracted patterns. To overcome this, $q^{P6}(\mathbf{g_u})$ is defined as

$$q^{P6}(\mathbf{g_u}) = \frac{100\,\% - q^{P5}(\mathbf{g_u})}{q^{P4}(\mathbf{g_u})} \tag{8.12}$$

per extracted pattern. The smaller $q^{P6}(\mathbf{g_u})$ is, the better the pattern extraction will be. The mean value of $\mu(q^{P6}(\mathbf{g_u}))$ over all considered extracted patterns is the last parameter used to measure the quality of the pattern extraction.

Finally, $q^{P4}(\mathbf{g_u})$ is plotted over $q^{P5}(\mathbf{g_u})$ for every extracted pattern per tested combination. The higher the density of the points on the right hand side of the plot is, the better the quality of the extraction will be, as less color regions have been added to the pattern that do not belong to any near-regular texture. In the ideal case all of the plotted points will lie on the upper right corner of the plot. This implies a high coverage of the near-regular textures by the extracted patterns with no inclusion of foreign color regions to the surfaces of the extracted patterns.

8.5.2.2 Evaluation results

The extracted parameters to measure the goodness of the pattern detection and extraction are shown in Table 8.19. **All** is the total number of extracted patterns, **Tex** the total number of near-regular textures that are part of an extracted pattern, and **Rep** the total number of repeatedly extracted patterns that contain a near-regular texture that is already part of another extracted pattern. The total number of near-regular textures that should be represented in the extracted patterns is 57.

The **parameters used to measure the goodness of the detection** can be divided into two groups, which correspond with the two paths to process the color information during the pattern detection and extraction. The direct processing of the color information in CIELAB color space (P1 to P4) yields in total a lower number of extracted patterns together with a lower number of extracted patterns containing a near-regular texture and repetitions from it.

72 patterns are extracted from the whole database when the color information is directly processed in the CIELAB color space and none of the optional methods at the post-processing step are used (P1). From the 57 near-regular textures 89.47 % can be recognized in at least one of the extracted patterns and 4 of the extracted patterns repeat an already recognized near-regular texture.

The merger of spatially overlapping patterns as an additional post-processing step (P2 vs. P1) does not increment the total number of extracted patterns, but it increments the near-regular textures that are part of an extracted pattern to 91.23 % and the number of extracted patterns that contain a near-regular texture that is already part of another extracted pattern to 6.

If nested patterns are also merged as a further additional post-processing step (P3), then the percentage of near-regular textures being part of an extracted pattern remains by 91.23 %, but the number of extracted patterns repeating a near-regular texture placed already at another extracted pattern is reduced to 2, which may imply less overhead. Also the number of total extracted patterns is decreased in this case to 66. The conclusion can therefore be drawn that the inclusion of both additional post-processing steps proposed in Sec. 6.4.1.4 to merge spatially overlapping and nested patterns improves the goodness of the pattern detection as more of the near-regular textures are part of the extracted patterns at a decrease of extracted patterns repeating near-regular textures.

Table 8.19 Evaluation of the pattern detection and extraction quality.

Com.	Goodness of the detections			Quality of the extracted patterns				
	All	Tex	Rep	$q^{P4}(\mathbf{g_u})$		$q^{P5}(\mathbf{g_u})$		$q^{P5}(\mathbf{g_u})$
				μ	σ	μ	σ	μ
P1	72	51	4	81.34 %	26.14 %	90.41 %	20.62 %	0.10
P2	72	52	6	74.84 %	29.34 %	91.01 %	20.00 %	0.10
P3	66	52	2	85.04 %	22.50 %	89.47 %	21.09 %	0.11
P4	62	49	2	91.35 %	19.07 %	72.77 %	26.76 %	0.54
P5	1143	57	1002	52.68 %	30.72 %	88.81 %	21.21 %	0.41
P6	165	57	69	39.17 %	36.52 %	96.06 %	10.96 %	0.21
P7	165	57	60	39.84 %	38.23 %	95.78 %	1.33 %	0.22
P8	327	56	255	13.63 %	25.21 %	99.40 %	4.27 %	0.17
P9	94	56	9	70.41 %	29.18 %	91.34 %	17.02 %	0.13
P10	101	57	16	62.67 %	30.90 %	98.24 %	4.69 %	0.02
P11	122	57	21	58.63 %	33.82 %	97.35 %	8.06 %	0.06

The combination of extracted color regions with color categories and pattern extraction processing the color information directly in CIELAB color space (P4) reduces the quality of the detected patterns. In contrast to a full processing of the color in CIELAB color space, only 85.96 % of the near-regular textures are part of an extracted pattern vs. the 91.23 % achieved by the tested combination P3.

On the other hand, the processing of the color information with the color categories (P5 to P11) increments the number of patterns containing a near-regular texture and the total number of extracted patterns.

A 100 % inclusion of the types of near-regular textures in the extracted patterns is already achieved by the combination P5, which uses the approximation of the colors in the pattern as similarity criterion to expand the one-dimensional pattern to a two-dimensional one and no post-processing. However, this combination also yields the highest number of extracted patterns with near-regular textures already included in other extracted patterns, which implies a high overhead.

The expansion of P5 by the merger of patterns with a high percentage of area in common once the one-dimensional pattern has been expanded to the two-dimensional one (P6) also reaches the 100 % inclusion of the types of near-regular textures in the extracted patterns. Furthermore, P6 reduces in comparison with P5 the number of extracted patterns that repeat an already detected near-regular texture by 93.11 %. The total number of extracted patterns is also reduced, in this case by 85.56 %. These big reductions imply an improvement of the goodness of the detection towards the combination P5, as less overhead is created.

If extracted patterns whose convex hulls highly overlap are also merged (P7), then the total number of extracted patterns repeating an already extracted near-regular texture is further reduced by 13.04 %, with no deterioration of the 100 % recognition of the near-regular textures in the extracted patterns and no increment of the total number of extracted patterns. By these means, the incorporation of both optional methods presented in Sec. 6.4.2.4 for the post-processing step is highly encouraged as it improves all of the parameters used to measure the goodness of the detection.

The similarity comparisons used to expand the one-dimensional pattern to a two-dimensional one influence the goodness of the detection. Whereas the similarity comparisons based on the approximation of the colors and sizes of the color regions belonging to the pattern (P8), as well as the exact color comparison (P9), do not contain over the extracted patterns any part of one of the near-regular textures (retrieval quote of 98.25 %), the similarity comparison based on the exact comparison of the color and size of the color regions (P10) achieves a 100 % retrieval quote. What is more, the combination P10 achieves under all combinations with a 100 % retrieval quote of the near-regular textures the lowest number of extracted patterns that contain a near-regular texture that is already part of another extracted pattern and the lowest number of extracted patterns. It possesses therefore the best trade-off between extracting as many patterns with near-regular textures as possible and as less number of repeated extracted patterns as possible.

Comparable good detection results are yielded by the combination P11, which merges patterns whose convex hulls highly overlap directly at the expansion of the one-dimensional patterns to the two-dimensional ones, without waiting to the post-processing step. While this combination produces some overhead of the results compared to P10, it accelerates the time needed for the pattern extraction.

The **quality of the pattern extraction** is discussed next. The methods based on the direct processing of the color in the CIELAB color space (P1 to P4) yield a better coverage of the area of the near-regular textures $q^{\mathrm{P4}}(\mathbf{g_u})$ than the methods that process the color information with the color categories. The highest coverage is reached on average (91.35 %) by P4, which uses the extracted color regions via the color categories for the pattern extraction. However, this combination also possesses the lowest $\mu(q^{\mathrm{P5}}(\mathbf{g_u}))$. Together with the high $\mu(q^{\mathrm{P6}}(\mathbf{g_u}))$, it indicates that many color regions were added by P4 to the extracted patterns that do not belong to the surfaces of the near-regularly textured objects and backgrounds. Among the other three tested combinations processing the color information directly in the CIELAB color space for the pattern extraction, comparable quality parameters are achieved. While the incorporation of all proposed optional post-processing steps (P3) yields the second highest $\mu(q^{\mathrm{P4}}(\mathbf{g_u}))$, it also yields the second lowest $\sigma(q^{\mathrm{P4}}(\mathbf{g_u}))$. The highest $\mu(q^{\mathrm{P5}}(\mathbf{g_u}))$ is reached by the combination that merges spatially overlapping patterns (P2), which achieves otherwise the lowest $\mu(q^{\mathrm{P4}}(\mathbf{g_u}))$. If $\mu(q^{\mathrm{P6}}(\mathbf{g_u}))$ is considered, then the combinations P1 and P2 are slightly better than P3. These impressions of the quality of the extractions are confirmed at the plots of $q^{\mathrm{P4}}(\mathbf{g_u})$ over $q^{\mathrm{P5}}(\mathbf{g_u})$ (see Fig. 8.22 upper row and second row left). P1 to P3 yield comparable results. Many of their points possess an $q^{\mathrm{P4}}(\mathbf{g_u})$ value close to 100 %, but some points also have a low $q^{\mathrm{P5}}(\mathbf{g_u})$ value. The worse results are yielded by the combination P4. The incorporation of many color regions that do not belong to the near-regular textures to the extracted patterns explains the high number of extracted regions with a lower $q^{\mathrm{P5}}(\mathbf{g_u})$ combined with a high $q^{\mathrm{P4}}(\mathbf{g_u})$.

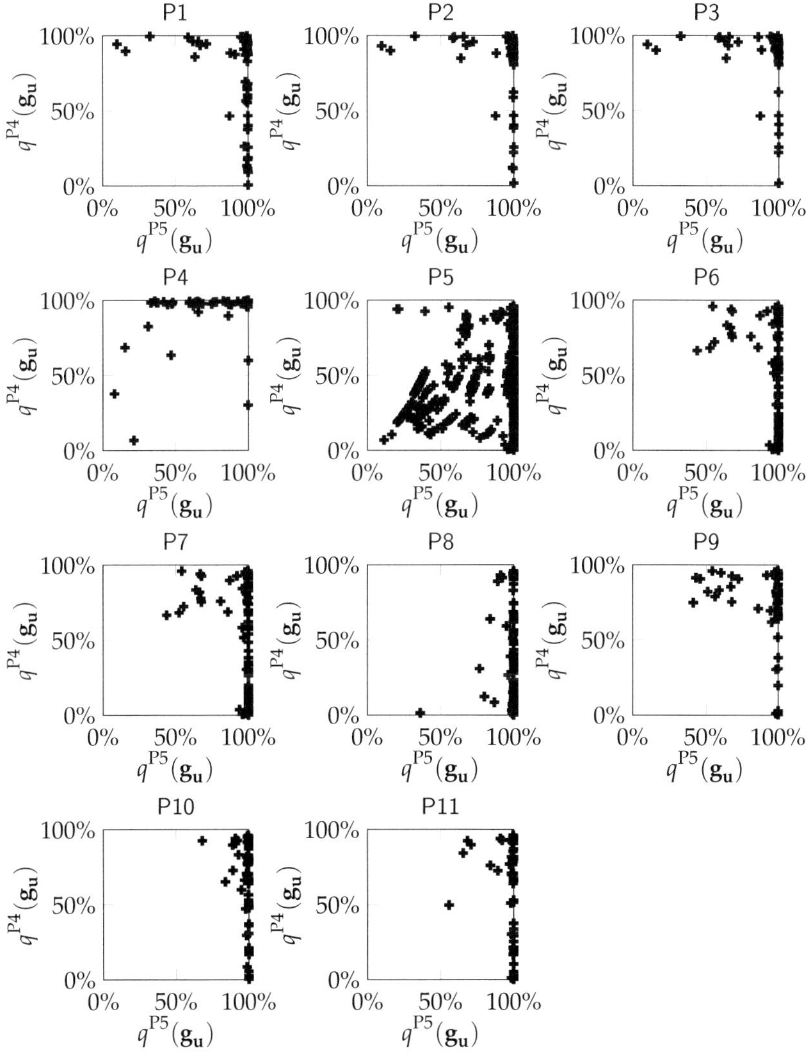

Figure 8.22 $q^{P4}(\mathbf{g_u})$ over $q^{P5}(\mathbf{g_u})$ for all tested combinations.

On the other hand, the combinations based on the processing of the color information by the color categories (P5 to P11) achieve on average the highest q^{P5} rates. This implies that less color regions are added to the extracted patterns that do not form part of the near-regular textures.

Along the $\mu(q^{\mathrm{P6}}(\mathbf{g_u}))$ values the consequences of the different proposed methods for the pattern extraction considering the color information by color categories can be recognized. The merger of patterns with a high percentage of area in common (P6), as well as the the merger of patterns whose convex hulls highly overlap once the one-dimensional pattern has been extracted to a two-dimensional one (P7), reduces $\mu(q^{\mathrm{P6}}(\mathbf{g_u}))$ in comparison with no implementation of the post-processing steps (P5) almost by a half. This implies a clear improvement of the quality of the pattern extraction.

Furthermore, the use of different similarity comparisons to expand the one-dimensional patterns to two-dimensional ones also has implications on $\mu(q^{\mathrm{P6}}(\mathbf{g_u}))$. The consideration of the approximation of the colors and sizes of the color regions appearing in the pattern (P8) as well as an exact color comparison (P9) reduces $\mu(q^{\mathrm{P6}}(\mathbf{g_u}))$ in contrast to the consideration of the similarity comparison by an approximation of the colors (P7). However, the best $\mu(q^{\mathrm{P6}}(\mathbf{g_u}))$ among all of the tested combinations for the pattern extraction is reached by the combination P10, which considers an exact comparison of the color and size of the color regions belonging to the patterns when the one-dimensional patterns are expanded to two-dimensional ones plus the merger of patterns with a high percentage of area in common. The $\mu(q^{\mathrm{P4}}(\mathbf{g_u}))$ over $\mu(q^{\mathrm{P5}}(\mathbf{g_u}))$ plots from P5 to P10 ratify this knowledge. The use of the post-processing steps (P6 and P7 vs. P5) increments the density of the points on the right hand side of the plots. This is also achieved by the incorporation of the size information of the color regions belonging to the patterns when the one-dimensional patterns are expanded to two-dimensional ones (P8). These points are further concentrated on the right hand side of the plot if exact similarity comparisons (P9 and P10) are used instead of approximated ones (P7 and P8).

The direct merger of patterns whose convex hulls highly overlap at the expansion of the one-dimensional patterns to two-dimensional ones (P11) reaches the second best $\mu(q^{\mathrm{P6}}(\mathbf{g_u}))$ value.

Overall, the following conclusions can be drawn. The pattern extraction processing the color information with color categories yields better results than the direct processing of the color in the CIELAB color space. The combination P10 reaches the best results as it incorporates parts from all of the near-regular textures in extracted patterns and it possesses the highest quality of the extracted patterns. The high $\mu(q^{\mathrm{P5}}(\mathbf{g_u}))$ values confirm that P10 did not add extra color regions to the patterns that describe parts of the near-regular textures. Although $\mu(q^{\mathrm{P4}}(\mathbf{g_u}))$ values are not concentrated around 100 %, 71.23 % of the extracted patterns that contain a part of a near-regular texture cover these ones by more than 50 % (see Fig. 8.23).

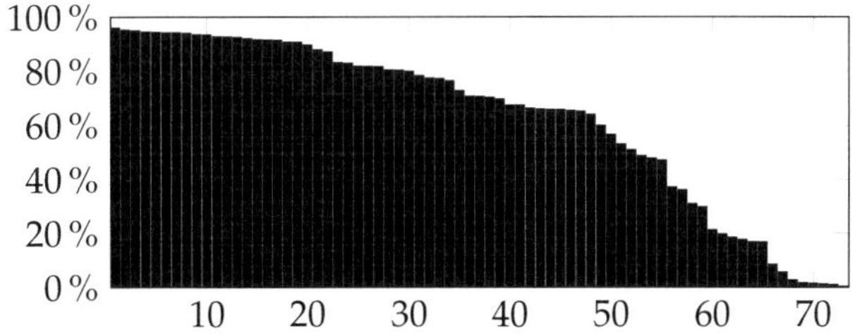

Figure 8.23 $q^{\mathrm{P4}}(\mathbf{g_u})$ over all extracted patterns using the combination P10 that contain part of a near-regular texture.

8.6 Results of the fusion of the methods

In this section the results achieved by the fusion of the proposed methods according to Sec. 7 are presented. The extracted significant patterned regions are presented and evaluated in Sec. 8.6.1, whereas the results of the sorting of the images fusing their color, shape, and texture information are shown in Sec. 8.6.2 together with their evaluation method.

8.6.1 Significant patterned regions

The consequences of the fusion of the near-regular textures from Sec. 5.3 and the extracted patterned regions from Sec. 6 to extract significant patterned regions as presented in Sec. 7.1 are considered in this section. For this purpose, the detected and extracted near-regular textures from combination N13 (see Tables 8.12 and 8.13) are combined with the extracted patterned regions from the combination P10 (see Table 8.18), as they reached the best trade-off between a high detection and extraction quality.

Like in Sec. 8.5.2, the quality of the detected significant patterns and their extraction quality are important. Because of this, the quality criteria presented in Sec. 8.5.2.1 to evaluate the results are also used in this section to evaluate the significant patterned regions. The results are presented in Sec. 8.6.1.1.

8.6.1.1 Evaluation results

The evaluation results are shown in Table 8.20. P10 are the results achieved by the region detector before its fusion with the information from the near-regular textures. SP1 are the results yielded before the significant patterned regions are extracted, at the stage where the detected and extracted patterns are fused with the help of the mask of the near-regular textures. SP2 are the results achieved by the extracted significant patterned regions.

Table 8.20 Evaluation of the pattern detection and extraction quality.

	Goodness of the detections			Quality of the extracted patterns				
	All	Tex	Rep	$q^{P4}(\mathbf{g_u})$		$q^{P5}(\mathbf{g_u})$		$q^{P6}(\mathbf{g_u})$
Com.				μ	σ	μ	σ	μ
P10	101	57	16	62.67 %	30.90 %	98.24 %	4.69 %	0.02
SP1	84	57	2	77.73 %	17.46 %	97.83 %	5.27 %	0.03
SP2	61	57	2	75.61 %	19.84 %	98.03 %	5.02 %	0.03

The fusion of the extracted patterned regions with the mask of the near-regular textures reduces the extracted patterns to 16.83 % and the patterned regions that contain a near-regular texture that is already part of another pattern by 87.50 %. As all of the near-regular textures are still detected, the quality of the detected patterns is improved compared to the results achieved by the region detector. Furthermore, the goodness of the detections is also better than the one achieved by the method to detect the near-regular textures, which detects 55 from the 57 surfaces.

With respect to the quality of the extracted patterns, the percentage of ground truth area covered by the patterns $\mu(q^{P4}(\mathbf{g_u}))$ of the combination SP1 (77.73 %) is higher than the one reached by P10 (62.67 %). Furthermore, the standard deviation $\sigma(q^{P4}(\mathbf{g_u}))$ reached by SP1 is almost the half of the one reached by P10, which implies a higher robustness of the combination SP1 towards the analyzed image. $\mu(q^{P5}(\mathbf{g_u}))$ and $\mu(q^{P6}(\mathbf{g_u}))$ achieved by SP1 are slightly worse than those achieved by P10, but due to the considerable increment of $\mu(q^{P4}(\mathbf{g_u}))$ and decrease of $\sigma(q^{P4}(\mathbf{g_u}))$ the quality of the patterns extracted via the combination SP1 is higher than the one extracted via P10.

The quality results of the detected significant patterns (SP2) show an improvement compared to the patterned regions detected by P10. The reduction of the detected regions by a 39.60 % implies that redundant extracted patterned regions are suppressed, without having worsened the number of patterns that contain part of a near-regular texture (100 % detection rate). Furthermore, the number of extracted patterned regions that contain a near-regular texture that is already part of another extracted region is clearly reduced by SP2 in comparison with P10 (87.50 %).

The quality of the extracted patterns achieved by SP2 is comparable to the results achieved by SP1 and therefore better than the ones achieved by P10. In this case SP2 yields a slightly better $q^{P5}(\mathbf{g_u})$ than SP1 but a slightly worsen $q^{P4}(\mathbf{g_u})$. However, both combinations reach a similar good $q^{P6}(\mathbf{g_u})$.

Overall, the following conclusions can be drawn. The fusion of the extracted patterns from Sec. 8.5.2 with the extracted near-regular textures from Sec. 8.4.2 to extract significant regions as presented in Sec. 7.1 improves the results. On the one hand, the goodness of the detections is higher, as no representative patterns are suppressed and redundant ones are clearly reduced. On the other hand, the quality of the extracted patterns is also improved. Although the percentage of the patterns that lie on a ground-truth pattern is slightly worsen, the covered area of the ground truth data is clearly higher and more robust towards the input image.

8.6.2 Image sorting according to their similarity fusing color, shape, and texture information

In this section the results of the fusion of the extracted patterned regions with their color, shape, and texture information in a content-based image retrieval environment are presented. As introduced in Sec. 7.2.2, the images in the database are sorted in a first step three times according to their color, shape, and texture information, respectively. The features describing these properties are extracted as described in Sec. 7.2.1. The earth mover's distance is then used to compare the extracted compact color signatures between the images as in Sec. 8.2.1, whereas the normal angular descriptors are warped first and compared next using the correlation for circular data d_2^{NAD}, which yielded the best results in Sec. 8.3. Furthermore, at the sorting of regular textures according to Sec. 5.2.3, the strength of the different properties that are compared can be differently selected. In Sec. 8.4.1.5 results were presented for regular textures for two strength combinations of the parameters: considering all similarity comparisons as equally important $w_k = 1,\ k \in \{1,2,3,4,5,6,7\}$, and considering all similarity comparisons except for the one considering the orientation $w_k = 1,\ k \in \{1,2,3,4,5,6\},\ w_7 = 0$. At this point, the use of all similarity comparisons apart from those comparing the orientation of the textures and the regions in their texels $w_k = 1,\ k \in \{1,2,3,4,6\},\ w_5 = 0,\ w_7 = 0$, is also considered. This is motivated from the suspicion that due to the projection of the texels from the image plane to the quadrangles of equal shape using the affine transformation and the nearest neighbor interpolation, clear boundaries between the regions may be difficult to find, hindering the detection of the regions in the image via the watershed filling method (see Sec. 5.2.3).

Furthermore, to evaluate the consequences of the fusion of the color, shape, and texture information for the sorting of the images, the performance will be compared to those achieved if only the color, the shape, or the texture information is used. The evaluation criteria are explained in Sec. 8.6.2.1 followed by the results in Sec. 8.6.2.2.

8.6.2.1 Evaluation criteria

The retrieval quality according to the content of the images is evaluated via the IIIT patterned image database and the parameter q^{retr} presented in Sec. 8.1.2.1. For this purpose, good matches of the images have to be defined. Within the content of the images in the database, eight characteristic classes can be found that are repeated over the images in the database, showing color, shape, or texture variations. Two images per class are shown in Fig. 8.24. The images are considered similar because they possess at least one region with high similarity in color, shape, or texture, but at least two of the characteristics (e.g., color and shape, or shape and texture) must be similar. For evaluation purposes every extracted significant patterned region is assigned to one of these eight classes, or a ninth class *Other* in case that the considered region is not similar to the regions that belong to the eight first classes. The number of representatives per class is shown in Fig. 8.25. Notice that the classes do not have the same sizes.

Per image in the database that contains a significant patterned region belonging to one of the eight classes, the quality of their retrievals is calculated via q^{retr}. Every significant patterned region that belongs to its class is considered as a good match. Per class the mean value $\mu(q^{\text{retr}})$ and standard deviation $\sigma(q^{\text{retr}})$ are calculated over the q^{retr} values achieved by the sorting results of every significant patterned region belonging to the class.

Finally, the mean value is also calculated from the q^{retr} values achieved by all extracted significant patterned regions that belong to one of the eight characteristic classes and also over the mean q^{retr} achieved per class, to weight all classes as equally important. This avoids that a class consisting of more objects than others distorts the results if it yields very good or very bad results.

8.6.2.2 Evaluation results

The evaluation results according to the criteria presented in Sec. 8.6.2.1 are shown next.

The sorting of the images **using only the texture** information is considered first. The retrieval results for the three tested strength combinations of the similarity distances are shown in Table 8.21. The results show that depending on the characteristic class different strength combinations of the similarity distances yield better results. However, if the average over all images and the average over all classes are considered, then the combination that does not consider the comparisons of the orientations and regions in the texels yields the best results. Furthermore, apart from the characteristic class *Bell*, this combination never yields over the other characteristic classes the worst average of q^{retr}. All in all, this combination yields therefore the best trade-off over all retrievals.

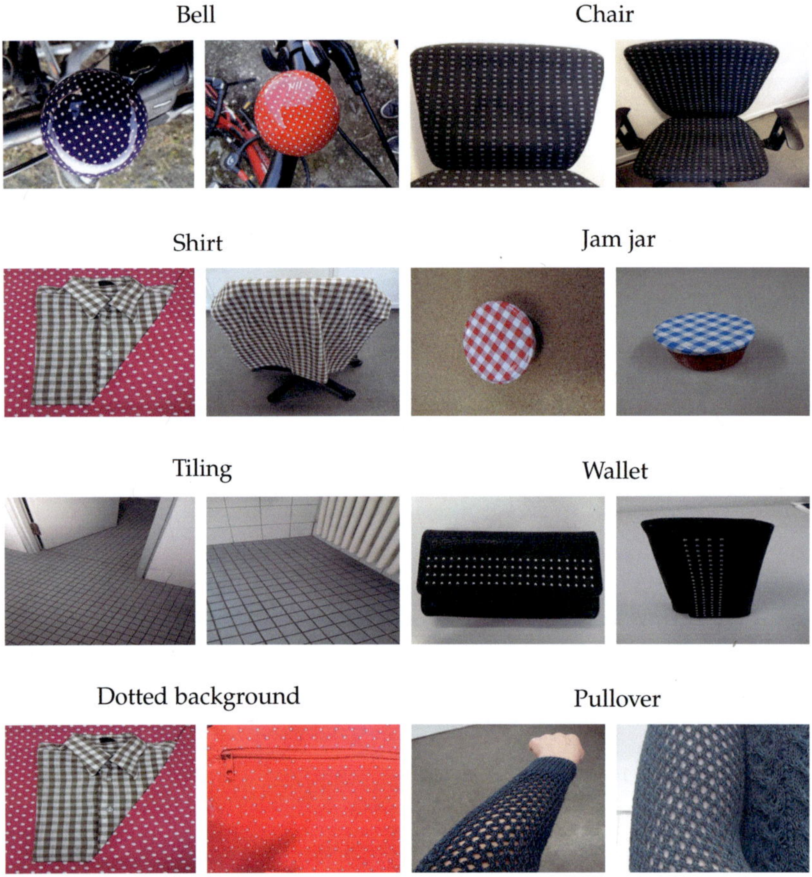

Figure 8.24 Example of images that contain at least one region of the considered class. Observe that one image may contain regions of different characteristic classes.

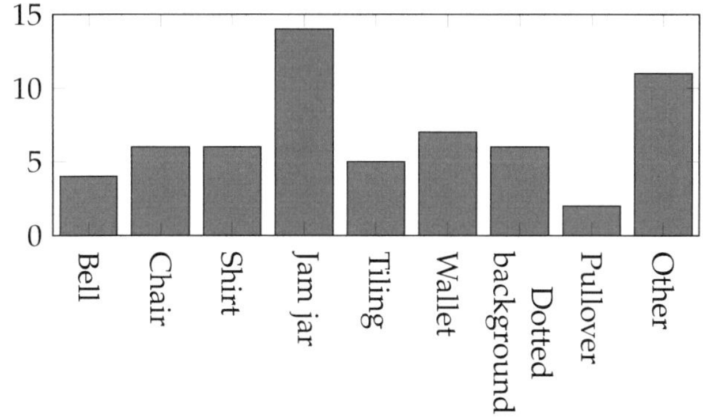

Figure 8.25 Histogram of the characteristic classes.

The performance of the method **considering the color, texture, and shape information** is considered next. The evaluated parameters are shown in Table 8.22 for the cases when only the color information (**Color**), the shape information (**Shape**), the texture information (**Texture**), and the fusion of all of the methods (**Fusion**) is used. The evaluated parameters considering only the texture information are the ones from the combination that consider all similarity distances except those considering the rotation of the textures and the regions in their texels $w_k = 1,\ k \in \{1,2,3,4,6\}$, $w_5 = 0,\ w_7 = 0$, as this yielded the best trade-off over all considered images and classes from the three tested combinations.

Let us concentrate first on the results achieved when only one characteristic is used to sort the images. Depending on the considered characteristic class the color, the shape, or the texture information yields better results. This strengths the statement from Sec. 7.2.2: *the total similarity does not always depend with the same strength on the different characteristics*. This is reasonable as significant patterned regions that belong to a characteristic class have similar color, shape, or texture properties in common but always at least two of the properties. However, the sorting of the images according to the shape similarities of their extracted significant patterned regions yields on average over all images in the database and over the classes the worst results, whereas the texture information yields the second best results and the color information achieves the best ones.

Table 8.21 Retrieval results of the images using only the texture information with the three considered strength combinations.

	q^{retr}					
	$w_k = 1,\ \forall k$		$w_7 = 0$ $w_k = 1,\ \forall_{k \neq 7}\ k$		$w_5 = w_7 = 0$ $w_k = 1,\ \forall_{k \neq 5,7}\ k$	
Class	μ	σ	μ	σ	μ	σ
Bell	86.19 %	13.64 %	89.97 %	14.72 %	82.84 %	12.87 %
Chair	75.52 %	17.95 %	69.51 %	18.97 %	71.79 %	18.47 %
Shirt	94.72 %	4.23 %	87.85 %	5.70 %	92.90 %	5.75 %
Jam jar	85.64 %	11.14 %	87.53 %	4.25 %	94.32 %	3.40 %
Tiling	77.21 %	7.57 %	89.09 %	6.48 %	94.40 %	3.50 %
Wallet	79.61 %	3.63 %	87.06 %	8.90 %	85.11 %	3.88 %
Dotted background	81.74 %	17.08 %	72.64 %	17.23 %	76.66 %	8.49 %
Pullover	72.14 %	20.24 %	82.38 %	16.07 %	94.79 %	7.37 %
Average over all images	82.87 %		83.70 %		87.15 %	
Average over the classes	81.60 %		83.25 %		86.60 %	

The fusion of all of the compared properties for the sorting of the images is considered next. The results from Table 8.22 show that over the different characteristic classes the fusion process always yields the best or second best result. This shows a clear improvement over the sorting of the images according to only one of its properties, as the results show that no property is capable of sorting all of the images optimally. The fusion of the color, shape, and texture information even improves for some classes on average the retrieval results achieved by the sorting methods using only one of the properties. This indicates that the method proposed in Sec. 7.2.2 to fuse the color, shape, and texture information is capable of automatically adjusting the strength with which the similarity sortings of the different properties weight the total similarity. An impression of the strength of the sorting method that fuses all of the informations can be gained at Fig. 8.26 and Fig. 8.27, where the first eight retrievals are shown for images from the characteristic classes *Jam jar*, *Wallet*, *Chair*, and *Tiling*.

Overall, the following conclusions can be drawn. The fusion of the extracted significant patterned regions with their sorting according to their color, shape, and texture information shows promising results for a retrieval of images according to the similarity of their content. The results show that a method capable of adjusting the strength of the color, shape, and texture similarity depending on the images compared for the estimation of the total similarity between images is advantageous.

Table 8.22 Retrieval results of the images using only color, shape, or texture information, and fusing all of them.

	q^{retr}							
	Color		**Shape**		**Texture**		**Fusion**	
Class	μ	σ	μ	σ	μ	σ	μ	σ
Bell	56.54 %	8.08 %	54.40 %	5.43 %	82.84 %	12.87 %	69.21 %	14.20 %
Chair	100 %	0 %	67.80 %	17.70 %	71.79 %	18.47 %	87.23 %	16.13 %
Shirt	85.88 %	12.01 %	52.01 %	10.40 %	92.90 %	5.75 %	89.68 %	9.73 %
Jam jar	81.44 %	7.90 %	94.96 %	4.20 %	94.32 %	3.40 %	96.60 %	3.21 %
Tiling	94.65 %	4.43 %	50.16 %	13.56 %	94.40 %	3.50 %	96.18 %	2.31 %
Wallet	98.97 %	2.03 %	75.19 %	14.85 %	85.11 %	3.88 %	95.19 %	4.16 %
Dotted background	97.13 %	3.97 %	68.50 %	21.79 %	76.66 %	8.49 %	89.42 %	8.76 %
Pullover	100 %	0 %	61.29 %	5.66 %	94.79 %	7.37 %	100 %	0 %
Average over all images	88.61 %		71.53 %		87.15 %		91.49 %	
Average over the classes	89.33 %		65.54 %		86.60 %		90.44 %	

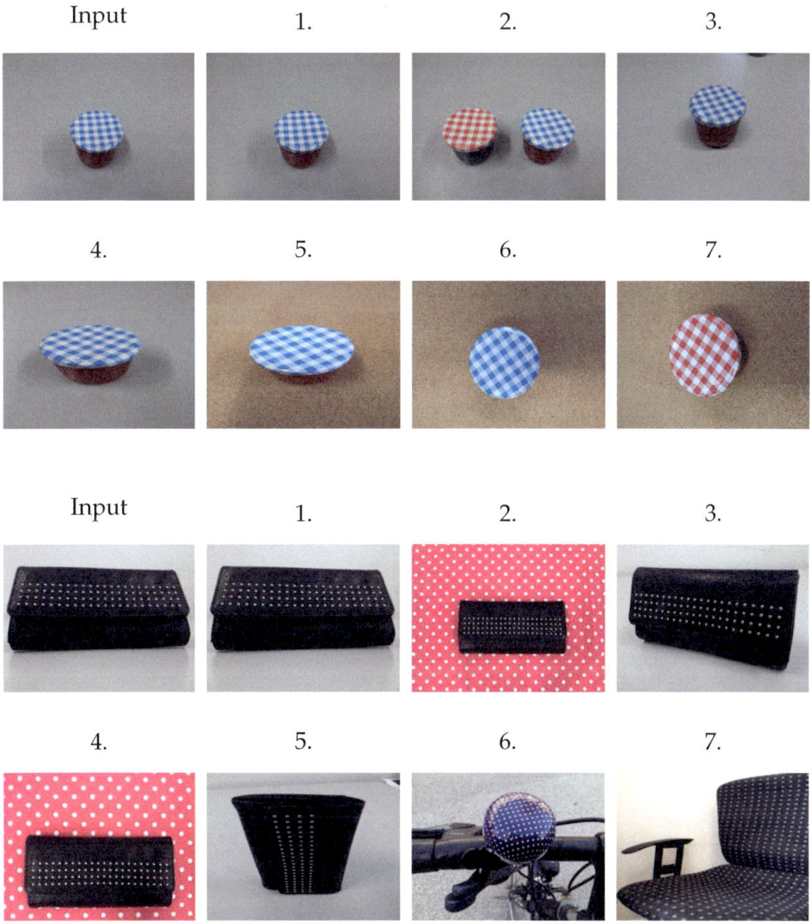

Figure 8.26 First seven retrieved images for an image of the class *jam jar* (top) and an image of the class *Wallet* (bottom). The number indicates the retrieval position.

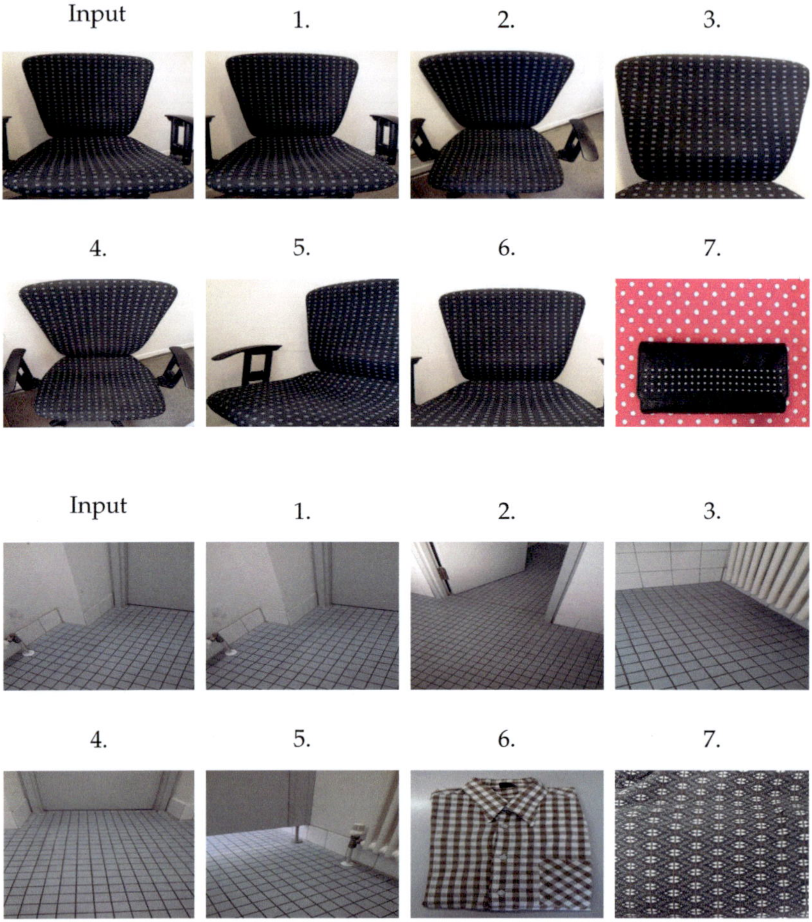

Figure 8.27 First seven retrieved images for an image of the class *Chair* (top) and an image of the class *Tiling* (bottom). The number indicates the retrieval position.

9 Conclusions

In this work the content-based image retrieval problem is considered. The extraction of color, shape, and texture features together with the detection of significant regions in the image are selected as modus operandi.

Every block forming part of the image retrieval approach is investigated. Solutions are proposed for all of them and conscientiously tested: a compact color signature (see Sec. 3.2), the color representation with the help of the humans' color categories (see Sec. 3.3), the normal angular descriptors (see Sec. 4.2), the detection of regular textures (see Sec. 5.2.2), features and similarity distances to compare textures of regular type (see Sec. 5.2.3), the detection of near-regular textures and the extraction of their regular textures (see Sec. 5.3), and the detection and extraction of meaningful regions in images (see Sec. 6).

With the help of psychologists, an experiment with subjects has also been performed. Its data is used to extract a perception map of regular textures (see Secs. 5.2.4). This one (see Sec. 8.4.1.6) indicates the similarity distances proposed in Sec. 5.2.3 for regular textures and their extracted features.

Furthermore, the fusion of the detected and extracted regions with the detected near-regular textures (see Sec. 7.1) improves the extraction of the near-regularly textured surfaces in the images, which results in a better extraction of their properties as they are less adulterated by the neighboring regions. The sorting of the images according to the automatic adjustment of their color, shape, and texture features (see Sec. 7.2) show promising results. This combination always yields the best or second best retrieval result. It even outperforms in many cases the best sorting result of images according to only one feature.

The decomposition of the problem to the detection of significant patterned regions and the independent extraction and comparison of the features of the images with a final fusion via an automatically adjustable weight of the features is thus a powerful approach. Whereas the comparison of the color, the shape, or the texture properties of the image can be independently analyzed and enhanced in the proposed approach, all of the properties are important and necessary to improve the quality of the retrievals.

The proposed approach for the content-based image retrieval can be further widened in the future. As the color representation with the help of the extracted humans' color categories improves the results in comparison with the direct representation of the color in the CIELAB color space, the analysis of the relationship between the extracted color categories is worthy. The spatial relation between significant patterned regions appearing in the same image is not considered for retrieval purposes. However, this reveals information about the spatial distribution of the content of the image and it could be therefore incorporated in the future to compare the similarity between images. Finally, the verification of the ideas and concepts proposed in this thesis shall be tested with more images.

Bibliography

[1] http://www.cis.temple.edu/~latecki/. Visited on 07.10.2014.

[2] https://www.mpi-inf.mpg.de/departments/computer-vision-and-multimodal-computing/software-and-datasets/. Visited on 14.03.2013.

[3] http://www.povray.org/. Visited on 22.01.2014.

[4] **Afifi, A. J.** and **Ashour, W. M.** *Content-Based Image Retrieval Using Invariant Color and Texture Features.* In: *2012 International Conference on Digital Image Computing Techniques and Applications (DICTA).* IEEE, 2012.

[5] **Afifi, A. J.** and **Ashour, W. M.** *Image Retrieval Based on Content Using Color Feature.* In: *ISRN Computer Graphics* 2012 (2012).

[6] **Ahonen, T.**, **Matas, J.**, **He, C.**, and **Pietikäinen, M.** *Rotation Invariant Image Description with Local Binary Pattern Histogram Fourier Features.* In: *Image Analysis: 16th Scandinavian Conference, SCIA 2009, Oslo, Norway, June 2009. Proceedings.* Ed. by **Salberg, A.-B.**, **Hardeberg, J. Y.**, and **Jenssen, R.** Berlin, Heidelberg: Springer, 2009, pp. 61–70.

[7] **Alabiso, C.** and **Weiss, I.** *A Primer on Hilbert Space Theory: Linear Spaces, Topological Spaces, Metric Spaces, Normed Spaces, and Topological Groups.* UNITEXT for Physics. Cham i.a.: Springer, 2015.

[8] **Alessio, S. M.** *Digital Signal Processing and Spectral Analysis for Scientists: Concepts and Applications.* Signals and Communication Technology. Cham, i.a.: Springer, 2016.

[9] **Arkin, E. M.**, **Chew, L. P.**, **Huttenlocher, D. P.**, **Kedem, K.**, and **Mitchell, J. S. B.** *An Efficiently Computable Metric for Comparing Polygonal Shapes.* In: *IEEE Transactions on Pattern Analysis and Machine Intelligence* 13.3 (1991), pp. 209–216.

[10] **Babu Rao, M.**, **Prabhakara Rao, B.**, and **Govardhan, A.** *CTDCIRS: Content Based Image Retrieval System Based on Dominant Color and Texture Features.* In: *International Journal of Computer Applications (0975-8887)* Volume 18-No.6 (2011).

[11] **Backhaus, K.**, **Erichson, B.**, and **Weiber, R.** *Fortgeschrittene multivariate Analysemethoden: Eine anwendungsorientierte Einführung.* 2. ed. Springer-Lehrbuch. Berlin Heidelberg: Springer Gabler, 2013.

[12] **Balakrishnan, R.** and **Ranganathan, K.** *A Textbook of Graph Theory*. 2. ed. Universitext. New York, NY: Springer, 2012.

[13] **Bartolini, I., Ciaccia, P.**, and **Patella, M.** *Warp: Accurate Retrieval of Shapes Using Phase of Fourier Descriptors and Time Warping Distance*. In: *IEEE Transactions on Pattern Analysis and Machine Intelligence* 27.1 (2005), pp. 142–147.

[14] **Bay, H., Tuytelaars, T.**, and **Van Gool, L.** *SURF: Speeded Up Robust Features*. In: *Computer Vision–ECCV 2006: 9th European Conference on Computer Vision, Graz, Austria, May 2006. Proceedings, Part I*. Berlin Heidelberg: Springer, 2006, pp. 404–417.

[15] **Bay, H., Ess, A., Tuytelaars, T.**, and **Van Gool, L.** *Speeded-Up Robust Features (SURF)*. In: *Computer Vision and Image Understanding* 110.3 (2008), pp. 346–359.

[16] **Belongie, S., Malik, J.**, and **Puzicha, J.** *Shape Matching and Object Recognition Using Shape Contexts*. In: *IEEE Transactions on Pattern Analysis and Machine Intelligence* 24.4 (2002), pp. 509–522.

[17] **Bentley, J. L.** *Multidimensional Binary Search Trees Used for Associative Searching*. In: *Communications of the ACM* 18.9 (1975), pp. 509–517.

[18] **Berlin, B.** and **Kay, P.** *Basic Color Terms: Their Universality and Evolution*. Berkeley: Univ. of California Press, 1969.

[19] **Beyerer, J., Puente León, F.**, and **Frese, C.** *Automatische Sichtprüfung: Grundlagen, Methoden und Praxis der Bildgewinnung und Bildauswertung*. 2 ed. Berlin Heidelberg: Springer Vieweg, 2016.

[20] **Beyerer, J., Puente León, F.**, and **Frese, C.** *Machine Vision – Automated Visual Inspection: Theory, Practice and Applications*. Berlin Heidelberg: Springer, 2016.

[21] **Blackman, R. B.** and **Tukey, J. W.** *The Measurement of Power Spectra: From the Point of View of Communications Engineering*. New York: Dover Publications Inc., 1958.

[22] **Bohman, H.** *Approximate Fourier Analysis of Distribution Functions*. In: *Arkiv för Matematik* 4.2 (1961), pp. 99–157.

[23] **Broek, E. L. van den, Kisters, P. M. F.**, and **Vuurpijl, L. G.** *The Utilization of Human Color Categorization for Content-Based Image Retrieval*. In: *Human Vision and Electronic Imaging IX*. Vol. 5292. Proc. SPIE. SPIE, 2004, pp. 351–362.

[24] **Broek, E. L. van den, Vuurpijl, L. G., Kisters, P. M. F.**, and **Schmid, J. C. M. von**. *Content-Based Image Retrieval: Color-selection exploited.* In: *Proceedings of the Third Dutch-Belgian Information Retrieval Workshop (DIR-2002).* Ed. by **Moens, M.-F., Brusser, R. de, Hiemstra, D.**, and **Kraaij, W.** Leuven, Belgium, 2002.

[25] **Burkhardt, H.** *Transformationen zur lageinvarianten Merkmalgewinnung.* Düsseldorf: VDI-Verlag, 1979.

[26] **Burkhardt, H., Fenske, A.**, and **Schulz-Mirbach, H.** *Invariants for the Recognition of Planar Contour and Gray-Scale Images.* In: *tm - Technisches Messen* 59.10 (1992), pp. 398–407.

[27] **Candès, E. J.** and **Donoho, D. L.** *Ridgelets: A Key to Higher-Dimensional Intermittency?* In: *Philosophical Transactions of the Royal Society of London A: Mathematical, Physical and Engineering Sciences* 357.1760 (1999), pp. 2495–2509.

[28] **Canny, J.** *A Computational Approach to Edge Detection.* In: *IEEE Transactions on Pattern Analysis and Machine Intelligence* PAMI-8.6 (1986), pp. 679–698.

[29] **Carrara, W. G., Goodman, R. S.**, and **Majewski, R. M.** *Spotlight Synthetic Aperture Radar: Signal Processing Algorithms.* The Artech House Remote Sensing Library. Boston London: Artech House, 1995.

[30] **Carson, C., Belongie, S., Greenspan, H.**, and **Malik, J.** *Blobworld: Image Segmentation Using Expectation-Maximization and Its Application to Image Querying.* In: *IEEE Transactions on Pattern Analysis and Machine Intelligence* 24.8 (2002), pp. 1026–1038.

[31] **Chalom, E., Asa, E.**, and **Biton, E.** *Measuring Image Similarity: An Overview of Some Useful Applications.* In: *IEEE Instrumentation & Measurement Magazine* 16.1 (2013), pp. 24–28.

[32] **Chavez, A.** and **Gustafson, D.** *Color-Based Extensions to MSERs.* In: *Advances in Visual Computing: 7th International Symposium, ISVC 2011, Las Vegas, NV, USA, September 2011. Proceedings, Part II.* Berlin Heidelberg: Springer, 2011, pp. 358–366.

[33] **Cheng, Y.** *Mean Shift, Mode Seeking, and Clustering.* In: *IEEE Transactions on Pattern Analysis and Machine Intelligence* 17.8 (1995), pp. 790–799.

[34] **Clausi, D. A.** and **Jernigan, M. E.** *Designing Gabor Filters for Optimal Texture Separability.* In: *Pattern Recognition* 33.11 (2000), pp. 1835–1849.

[35] **Comaniciu, D.** and **Meer, P.** *Mean Shift: A Robust Approach Toward Feature Space Analysis.* In: *IEEE Transactions on Pattern Analysis and Machine Intelligence* 24.5 (2002), pp. 603–619.

[36] **Crow, F. C.** *Summed-Area Tables for Texture Mapping*. In: *ACM SIGGRAPH Computer Graphics* 18.3 (1984), pp. 207–212.

[37] **D'Antona, G.** and **Ferrero, A.** *Digital Signal Processing for Measurement Systems: Theory and Applications*. Information Technology: Transmission, Processing, and Storage. New York, NY: Springer, 2006.

[38] **Datta, R.**, **Li, J.**, and **Wang, J. Z.** *Content-Based Image Retrieval – Approaches and Trends of the New Age*. In: *Proceedings of the 7th ACM SIGMM International Workshop on Multimedia Information Retrieval*. MIR '05. ACM, 2005, pp. 253–262.

[39] **Datta, R.**, **Joshi, D.**, **Li, J.**, and **Wang, J. Z.** *Image Retrieval: Ideas, Influences, and Trends of the New Age*. In: *ACM Computing Surveys* 40.2 (2008), 5:1–5:60.

[40] **Daubechies, I.** *Ten Lectures on Wavelets*. Philadelphia, Pa.: Society for Industrial and Applied Mathematics, 1992.

[41] **Davies, E. R.** *Machine Vision: Theory, Algorithms, Practicalities*. 3. ed. Amsterdam [i.a.]: Morgan Kaufmann, 2005.

[42] **Deng, Y.** and **Manjunath, B. S.** *Unsupervised Segmentation of Color-Texture Regions in Images and Video*. In: *IEEE Transactions on Pattern Analysis and Machine Intelligence* 23.8 (2001), pp. 800–810.

[43] **Deng, Y.**, **Manjunath, B. S.**, **Kenney, C.**, **Moore, M. S.**, and **Shin, H.** *An Efficient Color Representation for Image Retrieval*. In: *IEEE Transactions on Image Processing* 10.1 (2001), pp. 140–147.

[44] **Do, M. N.** and **Vetterli, M.** *The Finite Ridgelet Transform for Image Representation*. In: *IEEE Transactions on Image Processing* 12.1 (2003), pp. 16–28.

[45] **Duda, R. O.**, **Hart, P. E.**, and **Stork, D. G.** *Pattern Classification*. 2. ed. New York [i.a.]: Wiley, 2001.

[46] **Edelsbrunner, H.**, **Kirkpatrick, D. G.**, and **Seidel, R.** *On the Shape of a Set of Points in the Plane*. In: *IEEE Transactions on Information Theory* 29.4 (1983), pp. 551–559.

[47] **Ester, M.**, **Kriegel, H.-P.**, **Sander, J.**, and **Xu, X.** *A Density-Based Algorithm for Discovering Clusters in Large Spatial Databases with Noise*. In: *Proceedings of the Second International Conference on Knowledge Discovery and Data Mining (KDD-96)*. 1996, pp. 226–231.

[48] **Everitt, B.** and **Hothorn, T.** *An Introduction to Applied Multivariate Analysis with R*. Use R! New York, NY: Springer, 2011.

[49] **Fisher, N. I.** and **Lee, A. J.** *A Correlation Coefficient for Circular Data*. In: *Biometrika* 70.2 (1983), pp. 327–332.

[50] **Forssén, P.-E.** *Maximally Stable Colour Regions for Recognition and Matching.* In: *IEEE Conference on Computer Vision and Pattern Recognition.* 2007.

[51] **Forsyth, D. A.** and **Ponce, J.** *Computer Vision: A Modern Approach.* Prentice Hall Series in Artificial Intelligence. Upper Saddle River, NJ: Pearson Education, 2003.

[52] **Fukunaga, K.** and **Hostetler, L. D.** *The Estimation of the Gradient of a Density Function, with Applications in Pattern Recognition.* In: *IEEE Transactions on Information Theory* 21.1 (1975), pp. 32–40.

[53] **Gonde, A. B., Maheshwari, R. P.**, and **Balasubramanian, R.** *Multiscale Ridgelet Transform for Content Based Image Retrieval.* In: *Advance Computing Conference (IACC), 2010 IEEE 2nd International.* IEEE. 2010, pp. 139–144.

[54] **Gonzalez, R. C.** and **Woods, R. E.** *Digital Image Processing.* 3. ed. Upper Saddle River, NJ: Pearson Education, 2008.

[55] *Google.* https://search.googleblog.com/2011/06/search-by-text-voice-or-image.html. Visited on 25.08.2016.

[56] *Google.* https://support.google.com/websearch/answer/1325808?p=searchbyimagepage&hl=en. Visited on 25.08.2016.

[57] *Google Images.* https://images.google.com/. Visited on 25.08.2016.

[58] **Gopi, E. S.** *Digital Speech Processing Using Matlab.* Signals and Communication Technology. New Delhi, i.a.: Springer, 2014.

[59] **Grewal, M. S.** and **Andrews, A. P.** *Kalman Filtering: Theory and Practice Using MATLAB.* 2. ed. New York [i.a.]: Wiley, 2001.

[60] **Gupta, L.** and **Srinath, M. D.** *Contour Sequence Moments for the Classification of Closed Planar Shapes.* In: *Pattern Recognition* 20.3 (1987), pp. 267–272.

[61] **Ha, Y. H.** and **Pearce, J. A.** *A New Window and Comparison to Standard Windows.* In: *IEEE Transactions on Acoustics, Speech, and Signal Processing* 37.2 (1989), pp. 298–301.

[62] **Harris, C.** and **Stephens, M.** *A Combined Corner and Edge Detector.* In: *In Proc. of Fourth Alvey Vision Conference.* 1988, pp. 147–151.

[63] **Harris, F. J.** *On the Use of Windows for Harmonic Analysis with the Discrete Fourier Transform.* In: *Proceedings of the IEEE* 66.1 (1978), pp. 51–83.

[64] **Hays, J., Leordeanu, M., Efros, A. A.**, and **Liu, Y.** *Discovering Texture Regularity as a Higher-Order Correspondence Problem.* In: *Computer Vision–ECCV 2006: 9th European Conference on Computer Vision, Graz, Austria, May 2006. Proceedings, Part II.* Berlin Heidelberg: Springer, 2006, pp. 522–535.

[65] **Heer, J.** and **Stone, M.** *Color Naming Models for Color Selection, Image Editing and Palette Design.* In: *Proceedings of the SIGCHI Conference on Human Factors in Computing Systems.* ACM. 2012, pp. 1007–1016.

[66] **Hilsmann, A.**, **Schneider, D. C.**, and **Eisert, P.** *Warp-Based Near-Regular Texture Analysis for Image-Based Texture Overlay.* In: *Proc. International Workshop on Vision, Modeling and Visualization (VMV).* Ed. by **Eisert, P.**, **Polthier, K.**, and **Hornegger, J.** Eurographics Association, 2011, pp. 73–80.

[67] **Hu, R.-X.**, **Jia, W.**, **Ling, H.**, **Zhao, Y.**, and **Gui, J.** *Angular Pattern and Binary Angular Pattern for Shape Retrieval.* In: *IEEE Transactions on Image Processing* 23.3 (2014), pp. 1118–1127.

[68] **Huang, J.**, **Kumar, S. R.**, **Mitra, M.**, **Zhu, W.-J.**, and **Zabih, R.** *Image Indexing Using Color Correlograms.* In: *Proceedings., 1997 IEEE Computer Society Conference on Computer Vision and Pattern Recognition.* IEEE. 1997, pp. 762–768.

[69] **Huang, W.**, **Gao, Y.**, and **Chan, K. L.** *A Review of Region-Based Image Retrieval.* In: *Journal of Signal Processing Systems* 59.2 (2010), pp. 143–161.

[70] **Jafari-Khouzani, K.** and **Soltanian-Zadeh, H.** *Radon Transform Orientation Estimation for Rotation Invariant Texture Analysis.* In: *IEEE Transactions on Pattern Analysis and Machine Intelligence* 27.6 (2005), pp. 1004–1008.

[71] **Jafari-Khouzani, K.** and **Soltanian-Zadeh, H.** *Rotation-Invariant Multiresolution Texture Analysis Using Radon and Wavelet Transforms.* In: *IEEE Transactions on Image Processing* 14.6 (2005), pp. 783–795.

[72] **Jhanwar, N.**, **Chaudhuri, S.**, **Seetharaman, G.**, and **Zavidovique, B.** *Content Based Image Retrieval Using Motif Cooccurrence Matrix.* In: *Image and Vision Computing* 22.14 (2004), pp. 1211–1220.

[73] **Julesz, B.** *Experiments in the Visual Perception of Texture.* In: *Scientific American* 232.4 (1975), pp. 34–43.

[74] **Kaiser, J. F.** *Nonrecursive Digital Filter Design Using the I_0-sinh Window Function.* In: *Proceedings 1974 IEEE International Symposium on Circuits and Systems.* 1974.

[75] **Kay, P.** and **Regier, T.** *Resolving the Question of Color Naming Universals.* In: *Proceedings of the National Academy of Sciences of the United States of America* 100.15 (2003), pp. 9085–9089.

[76] **Kiencke, U.**, **Schwarz, M.**, and **Weickert, T.** *Signalverarbeitung: Zeit-Frequenz-Analyse und Schätzverfahren.* München: Oldenbourg, 2008.

[77] **Konstantinidis, K., Gasteratos, A.,** and **Andreadis, I.** *Image Retrieval Based on Fuzzy Color Histogram Processing*. In: *Optics Communications* 248.4-6 (2005), pp. 375–386.

[78] **Kruskal, J. B.** *Multidimensional Scaling by Optimizing Goodness of Fit to a Nonmetric Hypothesis*. In: *Psychometrika* 29.1 (1964), pp. 1–27.

[79] **Kruskal, J. B.** *Nonmetric Multidimensional Scaling: A Numerical Method*. In: *Psychometrika* 29.2 (1964), pp. 115–129.

[80] **Kubat, M.** *An Introduction to Machine Learning*. Cham i.a.: Springer, 2015.

[81] **Latecki, L. J.** and **Lakämper, R.** *Shape Similarity Measure Based on Correspondence of Visual Parts*. In: *IEEE Transactions on Pattern Analysis and Machine Intelligence* 22.10 (2000), pp. 1185–1190.

[82] **Lilien, G. L., Rangaswamy, A.,** and **De Bruyn, A.** *Principles of Marketing Engineering*. 2. ed. State College, Pa.: DecisionPro, 2013.

[83] **Lin, C.-H., Chen, R.-T.,** and **Chan, Y.-K.** *A Smart Content-Based Image Retrieval System Based on Color and Texture Feature*. In: *Image and Vision Computing* 27.6 (2009), pp. 658–665.

[84] **Lin, H.-C., Wang, L.-L.,** and **Yang, S.-N.** *Regular-Texture Image Retrieval Based on Texture-Primitive Extraction*. In: *Image and Vision Computing* 17.1 (1999), pp. 51–63.

[85] **Liu, G.-H., Zhang, L., Hou, Y.-K., Li, Z.-Y.,** and **Yang, J.-Y.** *Image Retrieval Based on Multi-Texton Histogram*. In: *Pattern Recognition* 43.7 (2010), pp. 2380–2389.

[86] **Liu, Y., Lin, W.-C.,** and **Hays, J.** *Near-Regular Texture Analysis and Manipulation*. In: *ACM Transactions on Graphics (TOG) – Proceedings of ACM SIGGRAPH 2004* 23.3 (2004), pp. 368–376.

[87] **Liu, Y., Zhang, D., Lu, G.,** and **Ma, W.-Y.** *A Survey of Content-Based Image Retrieval with High-Level Semantics*. In: *Pattern Recognition* 40.1 (2007), pp. 262–282.

[88] **Lowe, D. G.** *Object Recognition from Local Scale-Invariant Features*. In: *The Proceedings of the Seventh IEEE International Conference on Computer Vision*. IEEE. 1999.

[89] **Lowe, D. G.** *Distinctive Image Features from Scale-Invariant Keypoints*. In: *International Journal of Computer Vision* 60.2 (2004), pp. 91–110.

[90] **Mahmoudi, F., Shanbehzadeh, J., Eftekhari-Moghadam, A.-M.,** and **Soltanian-Zadeh, H.** *Image Retrieval Based on Shape Similarity by Edge Orientation Autocorrelogram*. In: *Pattern Recognition* 36.8 (2003), pp. 1725–1736.

[91] **Mangijao Singh, S.** and **Hemachandran, K.** *Content-Based Image Retrieval Using Color Moment and Gabor Texture Feature*. In: *International Journal of Computer Science Issues* 9.5 (2012), pp. 299–309.

[92] **Manjunath, B. S.** and **Ma, W. Y.** *Texture Features for Browsing and Retrieval of Image Data*. In: *IEEE Transactions on Pattern Analysis and Machine Intelligence* 18.8 (1996), pp. 837–842.

[93] **Marques, O., Mayron, L. M., Borba, G. B.,** and **Gamba, H. R.** *Using Visual Attention to Extract Regions of Interest in the Context of Image Retrieval*. In: *Proceedings of the 44th Annual Southeast Regional Conference*. ACM. 2006, pp. 638–643.

[94] **Marques, O., Mayron, L. M., Borba, G. B.,** and **Gamba, H. R.** *An Attention-Driven Model for Grouping Similar Images with Image Retrieval Applications*. In: *EURASIP Journal on Advances in Signal Processing* 2007 (2007), pp. 1–17.

[95] **Masotti, M.** and **Campanini, R.** *Texture Classification Using Invariant Ranklet Features*. In: *Pattern Recognition Letters* 29.14 (2008), pp. 1980–1986.

[96] **Matas, J., Chum, O., Urban, M.,** and **Pajdla, T.** *Robust Wide-Baseline Stereo from Maximally Stable Extremal Regions*. In: *Image and Vision Computing* 22.10 (2004), pp. 761–767.

[97] *Matlab*. https://www.mathworks.com/. Last visit on 19.02.2017.

[98] **Mikolajczyk, K.** and **Schmid, C.** *Indexing Based on Scale Invariant Interest Points*. In: *Proceedings. Eighth IEEE International Conference on Computer Vision*. IEEE. 2001, pp. 525–531.

[99] **Mikolajczyk, K.** and **Schmid, C.** *An Affine Invariant Interest Point Detector*. In: *Computer Vision - ECCV 2002: 7th European Conference on Computer Vision, Copenhagen, Denmark, May 2002. Proceedings, Part I*. Springer. Berlin Heidelberg, 2002, pp. 128–142.

[100] **Mikolajczyk, K.** and **Schmid, C.** *Scale & Affine Invariant Interest Point Detectors*. In: *International Journal of Computer Vision* 60.1 (2004), pp. 63–86.

[101] **Mikolajczyk, K.** and **Schmid, C.** *A Performance Evaluation of Local Descriptors*. In: *IEEE Transactions on Pattern Analysis and Machine Intelligence* 27.10 (2005), pp. 1615–1630.

[102] **Mikolajczyk, K., Tuytelaars, T., Schmid, C., Zisserman, A., Matas, J., Schaffalitzky, F., Kadir, T.,** and **Van Gool, L.** *A Comparison of Affine Region Detectors*. In: *International Journal of Computer Vision* 65.1 (2005), pp. 43–72.

[103] **Mokhtarian, F., Abbasi, S.**, and **Kittler, J.** *Robust and Efficient Shape Indexing through Curvature Scale Space.* In: *Proceedings of British Machine Vision Conference.* 1996, pp. 53–62.

[104] **Mokhtarian, F., Abbasi, S.**, and **Kittler, J.** *Efficient and Robust Retrieval by Shape Content through Curvature Scale Space.* In: *Image Databases And Multi-Media Search.* Vol. 8. World Scientific, 1997, pp. 51–58.

[105] **Mokhtarian, F.** and **Mackworth, A. K.** *A Theory of Multiscale, Curvature-Based Shape Representation for Planar Curves.* In: *IEEE Transactions on Pattern Analysis and Machine Intelligence* 14.8 (1992), pp. 789–805.

[106] **Murala, S., Gonde, A. B.**, and **Maheshwari, R. P.** *Color and Texture Features for Image Indexing and Retrieval.* In: *2009 IEEE International Advance Computing Conference . IACC 2009.* IEEE. 2009, pp. 1411–1416.

[107] **Nadler, M.** and **Smith, E. P.** *Pattern Recognition Engineering.* A Wiley-Interscience Publication. New York [i.a.]: Wiley, 1993.

[108] **Niblack, W., Barber, R., Equitz, W., Flickner, M., Glasman, E., Petkovic, D., Yanker, P., Faloutsos, C.**, and **Taubin, G.** *The QBIC Project: Querying Images By Content Using Color, Texture, and Shape.* In: *Proc. SPIE 1908, Storage and Retrieval for Image and Video Databases.* 1993, pp. 173–187.

[109] **Nuttall, A. H.** *Some Windows with Very Good Sidelobe Behavior.* In: *IEEE Transactions on Acoustics, Speech, and Signal Processing* ASSP-29.1 (1981), pp. 84–91.

[110] **Ojala, T., Pietikäinen, M.**, and **Mäenpää, T.** *Multiresolution Gray-Scale and Rotation Invariant Texture Classification with Local Binary Patterns.* In: *IEEE Transactions on Pattern Analysis and Machine Intelligence* 24.7 (2002), pp. 971–987.

[111] *OpenSesame.* http://osdoc.cogsci.nl/. Visited on 17.06.2015.

[112] **Oppenheim, A. V.** and **Schafer, R. W.** *Discrete Time Signal Processing.* Prentice Hall Signal Processing Series. Englewoods Cliffs, NJ: Prentice-Hall International, 1989.

[113] **Oppenheim, A. V., Schafer, R. W.**, and **Buck, J. R.** *Zeitdiskrete Signalverarbeitung.* 2. ed. München [i.a.]: Pearson Studium, 2004.

[114] **Papoulis, A.** and **Unnikrishna Pillai, S.** *Probability, Random Variables and Stochastic Processes.* 4. ed. Boston, i.a.: McGraw-Hill, 2002.

[115] **Park, M., Brocklehurst, K., Collins, R. T.**, and **Liu, Y.** *Deformed Lattice Detection in Real-World Images Using Mean-Shift Belief Propagation.* In: *IEEE Transactions on Pattern Analysis and Machine Intelligence* 31.10 (2009), pp. 1804–1816.

[116] **Parzen, E.** *Mathematical Considerations in the Estimation of Spectra.* In: *Technometrics* 3.2 (1961), pp. 167–190.

[117] **Pass, G., Zabih, R.,** and **Miller, J.** *Comparing Images Using Color Coherence Vectors.* In: *Proceedings of the Fourth ACM International Conference on Multimedia.* MULTIMEDIA '96. New York, NY, USA: ACM, 1996, pp. 65–73.

[118] **Petrakis, E. G. M., Diplaros, A.,** and **Milios, E.** *Matching and Retrieval of Distorted and Occluded Shapes Using Dynamic Programming.* In: *IEEE Transactions on Pattern Analysis and Machine Intelligence* 24.11 (2002), pp. 1501–1516.

[119] **Puente León, F.** *Messtechnik: Systemtheorie für Ingenieure und Informatiker.* 10 ed. Berlin Heidelberg: Springer Vieweg, 2015.

[120] **Puente León, F.** and **Jäkel, H.** *Signale und Systeme.* 6. ed. Berlin/Boston: De Gruyter Oldenbourg, 2015.

[121] **Puente León, F.** and **Kiencke, U.** *Ereignisdiskrete Systeme: Modellierung und Steuerung verteilter Systeme.* 3. ed. München: Oldenbourg, 2013.

[122] **Rubner, Y., Tomasi, C.,** and **Guibas, L. J.** *The Earth Mover's Distance as a Metric for Image Retrieval.* In: *International Journal of Computer Vision* 40.2 (2000), pp. 99–121.

[123] **Rui, Y., Huang, T. S.,** and **Chang, S.-F.** *Image Retrieval: Current Techniques, Promising Directions, and Open Issues.* In: *Journal of Visual Communication and Image Representation* 10.1 (1999), pp. 39–62.

[124] **Sajjanhar, A.** and **Lu, G.** *A Grid-Based Shape Indexing and Retrieval Method.* In: *Australian Computer Journal* 29.4 (1997), pp. 131–140.

[125] **Sakoe, H.** and **Chiba, S.** *Dynamic Programming Algorithm Optimization for Spoken Word Recognition.* In: *IEEE Transactions on Acoustics, Speech, and Signal Processing* ASSP-26.1 (1978), pp. 43–49.

[126] **Schindler, G., Krishnamurthy, P., Lublinerman, R., Liu, Y.,** and **Dellaert, F.** *Detecting and Matching Repeated Patterns for Automatic Geotagging in Urban Environments.* In: *IEEE Conference on Computer Vision and Pattern Recognition.* 2008, pp. 1–7.

[127] **Smeulders, A. W. M., Worring, M., Santini, S., Gupta, A.,** and **Jain, R.** *Content-Based Image Retrieval at the End of the Early Years.* In: *IEEE Transactions on Pattern Analysis and Machine Intelligence* 22.12 (2000), pp. 1349–1380.

[128] **Stehling, R. O., Nascimento, M. A.,** and **Falcão, A. X.** *Cell Histograms Versus Color Histograms for Image Representation and Retrieval.* In: *Knowledge and Information Systems* 5.3 (2003), pp. 315–336.

[129] **Subrahmanyam, M., Wu, Q.M. J., Maheshwari, R.P.,** and **Balasubramanian, R.** *Modified Color Motif Co-Occurrence Matrix for Image Indexing and Retrieval*. In: *Computers and Electrical Engineering* 39.3 (2013), pp. 762–774.

[130] **Suthaharan, S.** *Machine Learning Models and Algorithms for Big Data Classification: Thinking with Examples for Effective Learning*. Vol. 36. Integrated Series in Information Systems. New York, i.a.: Springer, 2016.

[131] **Swain, M. J.** and **Ballard, D. H.** *Color Indexing*. In: *International Journal of Computer Vision* 7.1 (1991), pp. 11–32.

[132] *TinEye*. https://www.tineye.com/. Visited on 25.08.2016.

[133] *TinEye*. https://www.tineye.com/faq#how. Visited on 25.08.2016.

[134] **Tuytelaars, T.** and **Van Gool, L.** *Content-Based Image Retrieval Based on Local Affinely Invariant Regions*. In: *Visual Information and Information Systems: Third International Conference, VISUAL'99 Amsterdam, The Netherlands*. Ed. by **Huijsmans, D. P.** and **Smeulders, A. W. M.** Springer. 1999, pp. 493–500.

[135] **Tuytelaars, T.** and **Van Gool, L.** *Wide Baseline Stereo Matching Based on Local, Affinely Invariant Regions*. In: *Proceedings of the British Machine Vision Conference*. 2000.

[136] **Viola, P.** and **Jones, M.** *Rapid Object Detection Using a Boosted Cascade of Simple Features*. In: *Proceedings of the 2001 IEEE Computer Society Conference on Computer Vision and Pattern Recognition*. IEEE. 2001, pp. I-511–I-518.

[137] **Vogel, J.** and **Schiele, B.** *Semantic Modeling of Natural Scenes for Content-Based Image Retrieval*. In: *International Journal of Computer Vision* 72.2 (2007), pp. 133–157.

[138] **Vu, V. H., Huu, Q. N.,** and **Thu, H. N. T.** *Content Based Image Retrieval with Bin of Color Histogram*. In: *2012 International Conference on Audio, Language and Image Processing (ICALIP)*. IEEE. 2012, pp. 20–25.

[139] **Wang, J. Z., Li, J.,** and **Wiederhold, G.** *SIMPLIcity: Semantics-Sensitive Integrated Matching for Picture LIbraries*. In: *IEEE Transactions on Pattern Analysis and Machine Intelligence* 23.9 (2001), pp. 947–963.

[140] **Weijer, J. van de, Schmid, C.,** and **Verbeek, J.** *Learning Color Names from Real-World Images*. In: *IEEE Conference on Computer Vision and Pattern Recognition*. 2007.

[141] **West, D. B.** *Introduction to Graph Theory*. 2. ed. Upper Saddle River, NJ: Prentice Hall, 2001.

[142] *XKCD Dataset*. blog.xkcd.com/2010/05/03/color-survey-results/. Last visit on 25.10.2016.

[143] **Yang, M.**, **Kpalma, K.**, and **Ronsin, J.** *A Survey of Shape Feature Extraction Techniques*. In: *Pattern Recognition, IN-TECH* (2008. <hal-00446037>), pp. 43–90.

[144] **Yoo, H.-W.**, **Park, H.-S.**, and **Jang, D.-S.** *Expert System for Color Image Retrieval*. In: *Expert Systems with Applications* 28.2 (2005), pp. 347–357.

[145] **Zadeh, L. A.** *Fuzzy Sets*. In: *Information and Control* 8.3 (1965), pp. 338–353.

[146] **Zhang, D.** and **Lu, G.** *A Comparative Study of Fourier Descriptors for Shape Representation and Retrieval*. In: *The 5th Asian Conference on Computer Vision*. 2002.

[147] **Zhang, D.** and **Lu, G.** *Generic Fourier Descriptor for Shape-Based Image Retrieval*. In: *Proceedings. 2002 IEEE International Conference on Multimedia and Expo*. IEEE. 2002, pp. 425–428.

[148] **Zhang, D.** and **Lu, G.** *Shape-Based Image Retrieval Using Generic Fourier Descriptor*. In: *Signal Processing: Image Communication* 17.10 (2002), pp. 825–848.

[149] **Zhang, D.** and **Lu, G.** *Review of Shape Representation and Description Techniques*. In: *Pattern Recognition* 37.1 (2004), pp. 1–19.

[150] **Zhang, D.** and **Lu, G.** *Study and Evaluation of Different Fourier Methods for Image Retrieval*. In: *Image and Vision Computing* 23.1 (2005), pp. 33–49.

[151] **Zhang, D.**, **Wong, A.**, **Indrawan, M.**, and **Lu, G.** *Content-Based Image Retrieval Using Gabor Texture Features*. In: *The First IEEE Pacific-Rim Conference on Multimedia (2000 International Symposium on Multimedia Information Processing)*. 2000.

[152] **Zhang, D.**, **Monirul Islam, M.**, **Lu, G.**, and **Jahan Sumana, I.** *Rotation Invariant Curvelet Features for Region Based Image Retrieval*. In: *International Journal of Computer Vision* 98.2 (2012), pp. 187–201.

List of publications

[153] **Back, K.**, **Hernández Mesa, P.**, and **Puente León, F.** *Modellbasiertes dreidimensionales Posentracking mittels evolutionärem Algorithmus*. In: *Forum Bildverarbeitung 2012*. Ed. by **Puente León, F.** and **Heizmann, M.** Karlsruhe: KIT Scientific Publishing, 2012, pp. 267–278.

[154] **Back, K., Hernández Mesa, P., Diebold, M.,** and **Puente León, F.** *Dreidimensionales Körper-Tracking mit Hilfe eines evolutionären Algorithmus.* In: *tm - Technisches Messen* 80.10 (2013), pp. 335–342.

[155] **Hernández Mesa, P., Anastasiadis, J.,** and **Puente León, F.** *Identification and Sorting of Regular Textures According to Their Similarity.* In: *Automated Visual Inspection and Machine Vision.* Ed. by **Beyerer, J.** and **Puente León, F.** Vol. 9530. Proceedings of SPIE. Bellingham, WA: SPIE, 2015.

[156] **Hernández Mesa, P., Heiman, R.,** and **Puente León, F.** *Verdeckungs- und affin-invarianter Regionendetektor basierend auf Farb- und Frequenzinformation.* In: *Forum Bildverarbeitung 2014.* Ed. by **Puente León, F.** and **Heizmann, M.** Karlsruhe: KIT Scientific Publishing, 2014, pp. 61–72.

[157] **Hernández Mesa, P.** and **Puente León, F.** *Normalenrichtung der Kontur als Formmerkmal zur Sortierung von Objekten für die inhaltsbasierte Bildsuche.* In: *XXIX. Messtechnisches Symposium 2015.* Ed. by **Fröhlich, T.** and **Manske, E.** Berlin: De Gruyter Oldenbourg, 2015, pp. 131–138.

[158] **Hernández Mesa, P.** and **Puente León, F.** *Comparison of Fourier and Normal Angle Descriptors for the Content-Based Image Retrieval.* In: *tm - Technisches Messen* 83.4 (2016), pp. 225–233.

[159] **Hernández Mesa, P.** and **Puente León, F.** *Extraction of Regular Textures from Real Images.* In: *Forum Bildverarbeitung 2016.* Ed. by **Heizmann, M., Längle, T.,** and **Puente León, F.** Karlsruhe: KIT Scientific Publishing, 2016, pp. 87–98.

[160] **Hernández Mesa, P.** and **Puente León, F.** *Repräsentation der Farbe digitaler Bilder mit Hilfe von wahrnehmungsinspirierten Farbklassen.* In: *XXX. Messtechnisches Symposium 2016.* Ed. by **Zimmermann, S.** Berlin: De Gruyter, 2016.

[161] **Hernández Mesa, P.** and **Puente León, F.** *Detektion zusammenhängender Farbregionen in Bildern mit Hilfe wahrnehmungsrelevanter Farbklassen.* In: *tm - Technisches Messen* 84.9 (2017).

[162] **McCune, D. J., Badarinarayan, H., Hernández Mesa, P.,** and **Saikalis, G.** *Fuel Delivery System.* United States Patent 8,789,513. 2014.

[163] **McCune, D. J., Badarinarayan, H., Hernández Mesa, P.,** and **Saikalis, G.** *Fuel Delivery System.* United States Patent 9,593,655. 2017.

List of supervised theses

[164] **Anastasiadis, J.** *Indentifikation und Sortierung struktureller Texturen nach Ähnlichkeit mit Hilfe der Fourier-Transformation.* Bachelorarbeit. KIT, 2014.

[165] **Dicke, E.** *Untersuchung der Ähnlichkeit geschlossener Konturen im Orts- und Frequenzbereich.* Bachelorarbeit. KIT, 2014.

[166] **Dipika, D.** *Unsupervised Color Image Segmentation Based on K-Means Clustering and the JSEG Method.* Bachelor thesis. KIT, 2013.

[167] **Hauer, D.** *Untersuchung der menschlichen Ähnlichkeitswahrnehmung bei strukturellen grauwertigen Texturbildern.* Bachelorarbeit. KIT, 2016.

[168] **Heiman, R.** *Erkennung zusammengehörender Bildbereiche unter Ausnutzung von Farb- und Frequenzinformationen.* Masterarbeit. KIT, 2014.

[169] **Hetz, A.-M.** *Sortierung nach Ähnlichkeit von strukturell-statistischen Texturtypen extrahiert aus Bildern.* Masterarbeit. KIT, 2016.

[170] **Kohlberger, C.** *Untersuchung der Textur-Ähnlichkeit von Grauwertbildern im Ortsraum anhand von Motiven.* Bachelorarbeit. KIT, 2014.

[171] **Matthäus, R.** *Analyse und Klassifikation von Farbe basierend auf der menschlichen Wahrnehmung.* Masterarbeit. KIT, 2015.

[172] **Mitschke, N.** *Gewinnung eines Darstellungsmodells von strukturell-statistischen Texturtypen.* Bachelorarbeit. KIT, 2015.

[173] **Moser, L.** *Untersuchung histogrammbasierter Verfahren zur formbasierten Merkmalsextraktion für die Bildsortierung nach Ähnlichkeit.* Bachelorarbeit. KIT, 2015.

[174] **Nagel, C.** *Gewinnung des Darstellungsmodells von strukturell-statistischen Texturen durch Schätzung der 3D-Koordinaten.* Bachelorarbeit. KIT, 2016.

[175] **Rommel, C.** *Untersuchung von Farbklassen zur Bilddarstellung ausgehend von der menschlichen Wahrnehmung.* Masterarbeit. KIT, 2016.

[176] **Sauer, M.** *Methoden der paarweisen Angleichung von Konturen und winkelbasierten Merkmalsextraktion für die formbasierte Bildsortierung nach Ähnlichkeit.* Bachelorarbeit. KIT, 2016.

[177] **Weber, T.** *Methoden zur Erzeugung künstlicher Bilder aus deren Form- und Texturcharakteristik.* Diplomarbeit. KIT, 2014.

[178] **Weiler, J.** *Identifikation statistischer Texturen durch AR-Modelle und Sortierung nach Ähnlichkeit auf Basis der lokalen Vorzugsrichtungen.* Bachelorarbeit. KIT, 2014.

[179] **Wiegand, G.** *CRF-basiertes semantisches Labeling urbaner Szenarien.* Masterarbeit. KIT, 2015.

[180] **Zimmermann, C.** *Vergleich unterschiedlicher Verfahren zur Extraktion der Farbinformation eines Bildes.* Bachelorarbeit. KIT, 2013.

Forschungsberichte aus der Industriellen Informationstechnik (ISSN 2190-6629)

Institut für Industrielle Informationstechnik
Karlsruher Institut für Technologie (KIT)

Hrsg.: Prof. Dr.-Ing. Fernando Puente León, Prof. Dr.-Ing. habil. Klaus Dostert

Band 1 Pérez Grassi, Ana
Variable illumination and invariant features for detecting and classifying varnish defects. (2010)
ISBN 978-3-86644-537-6

Band 2 Christ, Konrad
Kalibrierung von Magnet-Injektoren für Benzin-Direkteinspritzsysteme mittels Körperschall. (2011)
ISBN 978-3-86644-718-9

Band 3 Sandmair, Andreas
Konzepte zur Trennung von Sprachsignalen in unterbestimmten Szenarien. (2011)
ISBN 978-3-86644-744-8

Band 4 Bauer, Michael
Vergleich von Mehrträger-Übertragungsverfahren und Entwurfskriterien für neuartige Powerline-Kommunikationssysteme zur Realisierung von Smart Grids. (2012)
ISBN 978-3-86644-779-0

Band 5 Kruse, Marco
Mehrobjekt-Zustandsschätzung mit verteilten Sensorträgern am Beispiel der Umfeldwahrnehmung im Straßenverkehr. (2013)
ISBN 978-3-86644-982-4

Band 6 Dudeck, Sven
Kamerabasierte In-situ-Überwachung gepulster Laserschweißprozesse. (2013)
ISBN 978-3-7315-0019-3

Band 7 Liu, Wenqing
Emulation of Narrowband Powerline Data Transmission Channels and Evaluation of PLC Systems. (2013)
ISBN 978-3-7315-0071-1

Band 8 Otto, Carola
Fusion of Data from Heterogeneous Sensors with Distributed Fields of View and Situation Evaluation for Advanced Driver Assistance Systems. (2013)
ISBN 978-3-7315-0073-5

Band 9 Wang, Limeng
Image Analysis and Evaluation of Cylinder Bore Surfaces in Micrographs. (2014)
ISBN 978-3-7315-0239-5

Band 10 Michelsburg, Matthias
Materialklassifikation in optischen Inspektionssystemen mithilfe hyperspektraler Daten. (2014)
ISBN 978-3-7315-0273-9

Band 11 Pallauf, Johannes
Objektsensitive Verfolgung und Klassifikation von Fußgängern mit verteilten Multi-Sensor-Trägern. (2016)
ISBN 978-3-7315-0529-7

Band 12 Sigle, Martin
Robuste Schmalband-Powerline-Kommunikation für Niederspannungsverteilernetze. (2016)
ISBN 978-3-7315-0539-6

Band 13 Opalko, Oliver
Powerline-Kommunikation für Batteriemanagement-Systeme in Elektro- und Hybridfahrzeugen. (2017)
ISBN 978-3-7315-0647-8

Band 14 Han, Bin
Characterization and Emulation of Low-Voltage Power Line Channels for Narrowband and Broadband Communication. (2017)
ISBN 978-3-7315-0654-6

Band 15 Alonso, Damián Ezequiel
Wireless Data Transmission for the Battery Management System of Electric and Hybrid Vehicles. (2017)
ISBN 978-3-7315-0670-6

Band 16 Hernández Mesa, Pilar
Design and analysis of a content-based image retrieval system. (2017)
ISBN 978-3-7315-0692-8